D0560491

INDIANS AND BUREAUCRATS

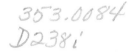
INDIANS
AND BUREAUCRATS

Administering the Reservation Policy
during the Civil War

Edmund Jefferson Danziger, Jr.

UNIVERSITY OF ILLINOIS PRESS
Urbana   Chicago   London

LIBRARY OF CONGRESS CATALOGING IN PUBLICATION DATA

Danziger, Edmund Jefferson, 1938–
  Indians and bureaucrats.

  Bibliography: p.
    1. Indians of North America—Government relations—
1789–1869. 2. United States. Bureau of Indian
Affairs. 3. Indians of North America—The West—
History. I. Title.
E93.D23   353.008'4   73-85486
ISBN 0-252-00314-4

For my parents and my wife

Contents

Preface   ix

Key to Abbreviations   xi

Introduction   1

PART I: THE NOMADIC PEOPLE

I.   The Struggle for Eastern Colorado   21

II. Problems in Montana, the Great Basin,
     and the Southwest   48

III. Mormons, Rebels, and Generals   71

     IV. Conclusion to Part I   88

PART II: THE RESERVATION PEOPLE

     V.   The Uprooted Santees   95

VI. Difficulties with Other Tribes   131

VII. Rebels, Rustlers, and Miners   165

     VIII. Conclusion   198

         Postscript   207

         Bibliography   215

         Index   231

Preface

It is hoped that United States citizens will always be interested in the American Indian, whose history sheds much light on their nation's development, particularly its treatment of minority groups. The red man's story is also part of mankind's epic struggle with the timeless problems of race and imperialism. Most Indian books which crowd library shelves across the nation deal with bizarre tribal practices, archeological finds, and frontier skirmishes between blue-coated cavalrymen and painted warriors. There is a regrettable paucity of monographs on the administration of federal Indian policy and no national study for the Civil War years. Yet the Indian's role in the expansion of the American Republic must be understood in terms of his relation to the United States government as well as to the bellicose frontiersman. To be sure, Civil War Indian affairs in the West pale in significance when compared to the clash of Blue and Gray on the Potomac, but they were important nonetheless—to the Union cause and to the drama of Indian-white relations in North America.

This study evolved from my doctoral dissertation completed at the University of Illinois in 1966. Set in the Civil War West, it is a broad analysis of the problems faced by Indian Office field officials in administering the government's reservation policy, and is based on the belief that these difficulties, and Washington's response to them, reveal the overwhelming complexity of the so-called "Indian problem" as well as the significance of Indian Office bureaucrats on the frontier. Tribal ethnologies, western political machinations, military campaigns, congressional wrangling and the varied activities of the Lincoln administration in Washington are noted only when they bear directly on the affairs of Indian agents and superintendents. Since this book is also problem oriented, I have not discussed a few peaceful tribes, such as the relatively acculturated New York Indians and the Pueblo farmers of New Mexico, which caused the Indian Office little distress.

I gratefully acknowledge the assistance given so cheerfully by many institutions and individuals during the preparation of this volume. Particularly helpful were the staffs of the University of Illinois Library, the National Archives, Bowling Green State University Library, the Beinecke Rare Book and Manuscript Library at Yale University, Harvard University Library, Wisconsin State Historical Society, Minnesota Historical Society, Kansas State Historical Society, Denver Public Library, the Bancroft Library at Berkeley, California, and the Henry E. Huntington Library and Art Gallery. My doctoral advisor, Professor Robert W. Johannsen, Miss L. Emily Grimm (formerly at the Bowling Green State University Library and now Head of Reference at the University of Cincinnati Library) and Mr. Robert M. Kvasnicka of the National Archives merit special thanks. A grant from the Faculty Leaves and Research Committee at Bowling Green and an eight-month fellowship from the National Endowment for the Humanities provided travel funds and precious time for completing my study. Robert G. Johnson, friend and one-time neighbor, made invaluable suggestions for organizing my findings. Several paragraphs in Chapters III, V, VI and VII have appeared previously in *North Dakota History*, *Southwestern Historical Quarterly*, *Kansas Historical Quarterly* and *Nebraska History*. I would like to thank the editors of these journals for permission to use this material. Mrs. Nedra B. Bradley typed the final draft of my manuscript. Above all, there was Margaret: editor, fellow devotee of the West, and kindred spirit.

Key to Abbreviations

AGO   Adjutant General's Office, Record Group 94, National Archives.

CIA   Annual Report, Commissioner of Indian Affairs.

FOR   Field Office Records.

ID   Office of the Secretary of the Interior, Indian Division, Record Group 48, National Archives.

JSC   Report of the Joint Special Committee on the Condition of the Indian Tribes, *Senate Report* No. 156, 39th Congress, 2nd Session (Serial 1279).

LR   Letters Received.

LS   Letters Sent.

OIA   Office of Indian Affairs, Record Group 75, National Archives.

OR   R. N. Scott, et al., eds., *The War of the Rebellion: A Compilation of the Official Records of the Union and Confederate Armies.* 70 volumes in 128. Washington, D.C., 1880–1901.

USAC   United States Army Commands, Record Group 98, National Archives.

INDIANS AND BUREAUCRATS

Introduction

Ominous war clouds were gathering beyond the Mississippi as well as in the East when Abraham Lincoln entered the White House in March 1861. Explosive events in the 1840s and 1850s —the Mexican cession of 1848, the discovery of gold in California, the Kansas-Nebraska Act of 1854—had sent thousands of enterprising Americans hurtling across the plains. This wrecked the government policy of assembling Indian tribes in large areas of the West and increased the threat of Indian attacks along the cutting edge of the frontier. More tragically, it uprooted tribes only recently removed from areas farther east.[1] In 1856 the commissioner of Indian affairs recommended the designation of suitable tracts of land on which the Interior Department's Office of Indian Affairs could safely colonize all red men, warlike and docile, nomad and farmer, and teach them the white man's way of life.[2] Confining tribes to more definite limits not only brought them under greater government control but opened more land to rapacious white farmers and cattlemen. The annexation of new territory in 1848, which expanded the frontier and brought more tribes under the government's jurisdiction, added to the challenge of implementing the reservation policy. Furthermore, the nation's preoccupation with the slavery question during the fifties prevented a prompt response by Congress to the new needs

1. *Sen. Report* 379, 33 Cong., 1 Sess., 2:6 (Ser. 707).
2. CIA, 1856, *Sen. Exec. Doc.* 5, 34 Cong., 3 Sess., 2:574 (Ser. 875).

of the Indian service. The year 1861 thus found the Office of Indian Affairs unable to administer efficiently the reservation policy. How were the incendiary pressures of the fifties to be eased now? Who would roll back the clouds of war? The eyes of attentive Americans looked hopefully to the new administration.

The Pandora's box that was America's Indian problem was inherited from Great Britain upon independence. After securing peace with the border tribes, Congress sought an orderly westward advance of the frontier by means of the treaty process, a practice established by England and other European countries which regarded Indian tribes as sovereign nations. England also recognized an Indian's title to the soil by virtue of occupancy, and permitted him to retain it until its surrender by treaty or conquest. The United States adhered to this precedent. Signed by its representatives as well as Indian headmen, and ratified by the Senate, the treaty was a useful and flexible document for regulating intercourse with the red man. The cession of Indian land, the fixing of boundaries, the establishment of military posts and Indian trust funds, the regulation of trade and the provision for educational services—all could be provided for by treaty.[3]

To preserve peace in the West, Congress again followed England's lead. It defined the Indian country by statute and employed commercial agents to regulate commerce and other dealings between the races.[4] These became so extensive that more machinery was needed. In 1824 the Secretary of War established an embryonic Office of Indian Affairs within his department; eight years later the president was authorized by law to appoint a commissioner to direct and manage Indian affairs under the Secretary of War. Persistent clashes between red man and white prompted Congress to act more boldly. In June 1834

3. Kenneth W. Munden and Henry Putney Beers, *Guide to Federal Archives Relating to the Civil War* (Washington, 1962), p. 534; Francis Paul Prucha, *American Indian Policy in the Formative Years: The Indian Trade and Intercourse Acts, 1790–1834* (Cambridge, Mass., 1962), p. 142.

4. For a detailed analysis of early trade and intercourse legislation, see Prucha, *American Indian Policy in the Formative Years.*

a new intercourse law modified the Licensed-Trader Act of 1790 and enlarged the power of government officers over the Indian country. An organic act passed the same day made specific provisions for Indian agents, and defined powers and responsibilities of the superintendents—thereby establishing the Indian service. Increased cooperation and effectiveness marked the efforts of Indian Office personnel after 1834, and the intercourse act remained the keystone of the Indian service for more than fifty years.[5] The Office of Indian Affairs continued as part of the War Department until 1849, when control of Indian affairs and the office was transferred to the newly created Department of the Interior. Here, it was believed, the Indian Office in conjunction with the General Land Office could more efficiently extinguish Indian title to lands west of the Mississippi.[6]

Whatever administrative unity the Indian service possessed usually resulted from the labors of the commissioner of Indian affairs, its most important functionary. To his busy Washington office came all official communications from the field. After consulting records from the proper subdivision of the central office (land, civilization, finance, and files and records), the commissioner dispatched instructions to superintendents and agents throughout the country. Treaty negotiations, the disbursement of funds for current expenses, the shipment and distribution of tribal annuities, the examination of claims arising from Indian-white relations, fostering Indian education and auditing field accounts fell under his purview. The commissioner corresponded with an endless number of powerful Indian chiefs, pious missionaries, traders, and ambitious politicians. In addition he was expected to seek the secretary's counsel on important matters of policy and finance, and to keep the Interior Depart-

5. *United States Statutes at Large* 4:564, 729-37; Edward Everett Dale, *The Indians of the Southwest: A Century of Development under the United States* (Norman, Okla., 1949), pp. 5-6; Prucha, *American Indian Policy in the Formative Years*, pp. 250-51.

6. William Errol Unrau, "The Role of the Indian Agent in the Settlement of the South-Central Plains, 1861-1868," doctoral dissertation, University of Colorado, 1963, p. 25.

ment sufficiently advised about Indian affairs so that it could coordinate its efforts with other executive departments.[7]

In the field the chief representatives of the Indian Office were the superintendents. Like the commissioner, the superintendent of Indian affairs directed the work of subordinates—the agents and their staffs—and apprised his superiors by means of periodic financial reports and detailed descriptions of affairs within his district (usually a territory but sometimes a larger area). The superintendent occasionally shared with the agent such duties as the negotiation of treaties and the licensing of traders. Normally he limited his function to supervisor. This included the communication of departmental directives from Washington and the periodic inspection of local conditions. Because the superintendent was not in intimate contact with any tribe, his opinions on local affairs evinced more objectivity than those of the agents.[8] Territorial governors sometimes served as ex officio superintendents, but more often a man who could devote full time to the office filled the position.

The Indian Office hierarchy existed primarily to coordinate and supervise the activities of the Indian agents, who, scattered across the vast frontier, were ultimately responsible for implementing decisions made in Washington. Their management of Indian relations often decided questions of war and peace. Agents disbursed annuity payments to the tribes and advised them of policy decisions. If possible they also settled potentially explosive tribal disputes. During the 1850s, when treaties established Indian reservations with definite boundaries in the trans-Mississippi West, the agent was charged with protecting these sanctuaries from unlicensed traders and other intruders. Washington further hoped that each agent, assisted by a small staff of physicians, teachers, blacksmiths, farmers, clerks and interpreters,

7. Edward E. Hill, comp., *Preliminary Inventory of the Records of the Bureau of Indian Affairs* (2 vols., Washington, 1965) 1:3; Alban W. Hoopes, *Indian Affairs and Their Administration, with Special Reference to the Far West, 1849–1860* (Philadelphia, 1932), p. 18; Munden and Beers, *Guide to Federal Archives Relating to the Civil War*, pp. 529–30.

8. Hoopes, *Indian Affairs*, pp. 21–22; Munden and Beers, *Guide to Federal Archives Relating to the Civil War*, pp. 545–46.

could transform his "uncivilized" charges into acculturated frontier farmers, so that the rapid disappearance of game would not precipitate famine and war. To his superintendent or directly to the commissioner, the agent sent frequent and detailed reports about such activities as well as Indian attitudes on particular issues. Yet these field officials were more than informants and executors of government programs. In times of local crises when primitive communication facilities prevented consultation with superiors, the isolated agent might create and execute his own policy.[9]

When Congress reorganized the Office of Indian Affairs in the 1830s, the War Department was removing most woodland and prairie Indians to lands beyond the Mississippi. This policy resulted from the pressure of westward expansion, the weakened position of the enveloped red man, the desires of some high-minded humanitarians to safeguard the Indians from harmful white influences, and the dwindling threat of foreign intervention after the War of 1812, which previously caused the government to be conciliatory toward the tribes.[10] West of Arkansas, Missouri, and the Territory of Iowa, from the Red River to Canada, the Indians occupied an area known as the "Great American Desert," which was to be theirs forever. In less than a decade streams of canvas-topped wagons bound for Texas, Santa Fe, California, and Oregon surged into the Indian country. Gone was the myth of a permanent Indian frontier. Federal bureaucrats had no choice but to negotiate treaties to open a corridor through the central plains. Land-hungry settlers thereupon swept into the Kansas and Nebraska Territories and onto former Indian lands before the survey crews completed their work, and before the uprooted red men could pack up and scurry off to their new homes. "They have been personally maltreated," the commissioner wrote of the Kansas tribes in 1856, "their property stolen, their timber destroyed, their possession en-

9. Dale, *Indians of the Southwest*, pp. 8–9; Hoopes, *Indian Affairs*, pp. 28–29; Munden and Beers, *Guide to Federal Archives Relating to the Civil War*, p. 546.

10. William T. Hagan, *American Indians* (Chicago, 1961), p. 66, and Prucha, *American Indian Policy in the Formative Years*, pp. 224–25.

croached upon, and divers other wrongs and injuries done them.
. . . In the din and strife between the anti-slavery and pro-slavery
parties . . . the rights and interests of the red man have been completely overlooked and disregarded. . . ."[11]

The plight of the Kansas refugees was but one of the many
problems that frustrated the Indian Office in the 1850s. The
dynamic frontier doubled the prodigious responsibilities of the
commissioner of Indian affairs and his staff between 1852 and
1856. Fifty-two treaties negotiated during the three years following March 1853 extended the province of the office over an
additional four to six thousand square miles. It staffed thirteen
new agencies and nine subagencies during the same time period.[12]
Even these proved inadequate to deal with the increased scope
of operations, and soon there followed the inevitable frontier
skirmishes and exploitations of the red man.

Deterioration of the understaffed Office of Indian Affairs was
most obvious on the local level, where the forces of change bore
down the heaviest. Knowledgeable agents and men of good will
were needed to preserve the tenuous peace. Instead there came
underpaid political appointees, often ignorant of Indian ways.[13]
Into their hands the government placed the considerable annuity
monies it periodically paid to the tribes for lands they had ceded.

11. CIA, 1856, p. 572.
12. CIA, 1856, 571–72.
13. Commenting on the problem of low wages in the Indian service, the governor of Arizona Territory, an ex officio superintendent of Indian affairs, wrote
to the commissioner in September 1864:

"It is impossible to secure the services of a faithful and competent superintendent for the sum of two thousand dollars per annum in currency; that
amount will not support a superintendent in any respectable manner in the
Territory, and he must needs resort to some other means of support, to
the derogation of the government service. The Indian service ought either
to be maintained in respectability or turned over to the military authorities.

"Mining superintendents on the Pacific coast receive as high as twenty-
five thousand dollars per annum in gold or silver for their services. Five
thousand dollars per annum does not secure very brilliant ability. I therefore recommend that the salary of superintendent of Indian affairs be fixed
at five thousand dollars per annum."

Charles D. Poston to William P. Dole, September 30, 1864, CIA, *House Exec.
Doc.* I, 38 Cong., 2 Sess., 5:302 (Ser. 1220).

A more perfect seedbed for corruption would be difficult to find.

One clever swindle for obtaining the Indians' annuity payment was the so-called "Indian Ring." Three interdependent elements usually composed the group: the politician, the agent, and the contractor or trader. The politician helped to secure the agent's appointment; the agent issued the indispensable license to the trader; and the wily trader defrauded the red man of his annuity. The stakes ran high in such an operation, for the profit on trade goods ranged from 100 to 400 percent.[14] A traveler acquainted with the Great Nemaha Agency near Highland, Kansas, described one procedure these crafty profiteers used to plunder the Iowa tribe. As soon as Washington notified the Iowa agent that the yearly payment (often in cash) would soon be sent, the agent informed the trader, who then extended large amounts of credit to the luxury-starved Indians. When the shipment arrived a few weeks later, the Indians had already spent the entire amount, if not more, and received nothing for the ensuing year.[15]

The Indians' fondness for alcohol, which avaricious traders had capitalized on since colonial days, contributed to their degradation. Honest agents fought an unending battle to prevent whiskey peddlers from slaking this thirst. Congress's numerous attempts to combat the whiskey problem with legislation fizzled. At first, fines for intruding on Indian reservations were too lenient; when penalties increased, as in 1852 and 1862, juries balked at convicting the culprits.[16] Whiskey, wrote the commissioner in 1855, "has been the greatest barrier to his [the Indian's] improvement in the past, and will continue to be in the future, if some means cannot be adopted to inhibit its use."[17] Money wasted on liquor was a minor detriment to an Indian's well-being

14. CIA, 1865, *House Exec. Doc.* 1, 39 Cong., 1 Sess., 2:170 (Ser. 1248); William Watts Folwell, *A History of Minnesota* (4 vols., St. Paul, 1924) 2:214–15; Henry E. Fritz, *The Movement for Indian Assimilation, 1860–1890* (Philadelphia, 1963), p. 27.

15. Lewis Henry Morgan, "Journal of an Expedition to the Rocky Mountains by the Missouri River in May, June, and July, 1862," *The Indian Journals, 1859–62*, edited by Leslie A. White (Ann Arbor, 1959), pp. 138–39. Of course the agent and politician received their shares from the trader.

16. *United States Statutes at Large* 12:339; Fritz, *Assimilation*, pp. 20, 141.

17. CIA, 1855, *Sen. Exec. Doc.* 1, 34 Cong., 1 Sess., 1:340 (Ser. 810).

when compared to whiskey's effect on his behavior. A drunken native, desperate for more alcohol, would barter horses, clothing, weapons, even children, to quench his burning thirst.[18] On Sunday, August 17, 1862, four Sioux Indians, either intoxicated or in search of whiskey, murdered five innocent whites near the town of Acton, Minnesota, and within a few days the whole frontier was ablaze. Whiskey kindled the flames of war which brought about the removal of the Sioux from Minnesota.

The extent of such illegal activities by the "Indian Ring" and the whiskey peddler remained largely unknown to the outside world. Isolation of the agencies was one reason for this, but there were others. After talking with the Cheyennes near Rulo, Nebraska, Lewis Henry Morgan confided to his journal:

> The Indians on this reserve complain of their agent. They say he is a mere speculator out of their affairs. . . . When I tell them that they make too much of a man of the agent, who has really no power over them, by inviting him to interfere with and decide upon their affairs, they say they cannot help this. That if any of them denounce the agent, they in turn are denounced by him, and as their payments come through his hands, they are afraid to come into collision with him.[19]

Another reason why fraud went unnoticed, or at least was unprovable, was the falsification of records, such as those of the number of Indians who received annuity payments. Sometimes insidious agents bribed Indian accomplices to swindle their own tribe. Statistics other than those provided by agents were rarely available to Washington officials and the district superintendent. Since agents often absconded with records when they left the reservation, proving fraud was doubly difficult. Lack of records also made it impossible for a new agent to work smoothly into his new post. So disruptive was the violation to an efficient working of the Indian service that in 1865 the commissioner issued a

18. Louis H. Roddis, *The Indian Wars of Minnesota* (Cedar Rapids, Iowa, 1956), p. 53.

19. Morgan, "Journal of a Visit to Kansas and Nebraska in May and June, 1859," *Indian Journals*, p. 97.

circular to all agents emphasizing that public records of any type should not be removed from their agencies.[20]

Conflict with the War Department impeded the work of the Office of Indian Affairs both in the field and on the national level. With its transfer in 1849, responsibility for Indian matters rested with the Interior Department. No serious revision in Indian policy or machinery took place; in effect the act divided the field work between military and civilian authorities. The United States Army exercised authority over warring tribes and provided logistic aid and protection for reservations in more settled areas. The two departments of government should have cooperated more in their duties. Instead, their bickering lasted thirty years. The arbitrary transfer of the Indian Office outraged many military men who were reluctant to take orders from civilian officials. When the expansive burst of the 1850s precipitated bloody Indian outbreaks, such officers, who preferred the sword to the peace pipe in dealing with the hostiles, were quick to censure the Interior Department. With the support of many frontier editors and politicians who likewise considered the renegades a military problem, they agitated for the return of the Office of Indian Affairs to the War Department.[21]

Besides the accelerated expansion of the fifties, another obstacle to peace was the cultural conflict between red man and white. Since colonial times in America, European attitudes of cultural superiority and forceful attempts to uplift the "primitive" Indian prevented understanding between the races. Nurtured in a competitive world in which the acquisition of property was the goal, the European viewed the communal and essentially cooperative world of the Indian as curious. Seldom noted by historians was the great diversity of Indian cultures—estimated to number as many as six hundred—that frustrated peaceful whites who tried to understand their way of life. Both races, it

20. CIA, 1865, p. 169.
21. Hoopes, *Indian Affairs*, p. 17; Henry George Waltman, "The Interior Department, War Department, and Indian Policy, 1865–1887," doctoral dissertation, University of Nebraska, 1962, pp. 17–18, 370–71, 376.

is true, clung to the habits of the past, but the Indian often favored coexistence as a suitable compromise. Believing themselves more highly civilized, Europeans saw no reason to compromise with "savages." Furthermore, they could not understand why it took Indians so long to abandon their cultures.[22] The European's belief that he possessed a superior right to the land also boded ill for peace between the races. Although the friendly Nez Percés accommodated themselves to the whites, for example, they were still dispossessed.[23] Such reluctance by the Europeans either to compromise or coexist doomed relations from the start. They could adapt to the environment of the New World, "but not to America's people."[24]

Race hatred, bred from this sort of misunderstanding, fanned the flames of frontier war and compounded the managerial difficulties of the Office of Indian Affairs. The education of pioneer children in the metaphysics of Indian hating began early, according to Herman Melville:

> As the child born to a backwoodsman must in turn lead his father's life . . . it is thought best not to mince matters, out of delicacy; but to tell the boy pretty plainly what an Indian is, and what he must expect from him. . . . Accordingly, if in youth the backwoodsman incline to knowledge, as is generally the case, he hears little from his schoolmasters, the old chroniclers of the forest, but histories of Indian lying, Indian theft, Indian double-dealing, Indian fraud and perfidy, Indian want of conscience, Indian blood-thirstiness, Indian diabolism—histories which, though of wild woods, are almost as full of things unangelic as the Newgate Calendar or the Annals of Europe. In these Indian narratives and traditions the lad is thoroughly grounded. "As the twig is bent the tree's inclined." The instinct of antipathy against an

22. Hagan, *American Indians*, p. 3; Loring Benson Priest, *Uncle Sam's Stepchildren: The Reformation of United States Indian Policy, 1865–1887* (New Brunswick, N.J., 1942), pp. 3, 132; S. Lyman Tyler, *Indian Affairs: A Study of the Changes in Policy of the United States toward Indians* (Provo, Utah, 1964), p. 2.

23. See Chapter VII.

24. Jack D. Forbes, ed., *The Indian in America's Past* (Englewood Cliffs, N.J., 1964), p. 39.

Indian grows in the backwoodsman with the sense of good and bad, right and wrong. In one breath he learns that a brother is to be loved, and an Indian to be hated.[25]

America's democratic system of government often undermined the work of the Indian Office. Episcopal Bishop Henry B. Whipple, a fervent champion of the Indian cause, visited Washington in 1862 to present the administration with his views on the recent uprising in Minnesota. Whipple wrote: "After pleading in vain and finding no redress, Secretary Stanton said to a friend, 'What does the Bishop want? If he came here to tell us that our Indian system is a sink of iniquity, tell him we all know it. Tell him the United States never cures a wrong until the people demand it; and when the hearts of the people are reached the Indian will be saved.' "[26] During most of the nineteenth century white Americans, East and West, failed to demand the needed reforms. Separated by time and distance from frontier conditions, the easterner expressed pity for the Indian only after a tragic occurrence such as the Sand Creek "Massacre."[27] In 1868 the Indian Peace Commission observed that members of Congress, though conversant with the many ramifications of the Negro problem and learned in matters of high finance, showed little concern for the Indian except how best to get his lands. Missionary and benevolent societies were so preoccupied with promoting civilization in Asia and Africa that they neglected American natives.[28] Not until the 1880s did the publication of reform tracts by Helen Hunt Jackson and others partially dispel the easterner's sense of separation from the West. That the pioneer's avarice for land and hatred of the red man thwarted reformers such as Bishop Whipple was due not

25. Herman Melville, *The Confidence-Man: His Masquerade* (New York, 1963), pp. 194–95.

26. Henry B. Whipple, Preface to Helen Hunt Jackson, *A Century of Dishonor: A Sketch of the United States Government's Dealings with Some of the Indian Tribes* (New York, 1881), pp. viii–ix.

27. See Chapter I.

28. Report to the President by the Indian Peace Commission, January 7, 1868, *House Exec. Doc.* 97, 40 Cong., 2 Sess., 11:16 (Ser. 1337).

only to eastern apathy but to the West's influence on local federal bureaucrats and its strength in Congress. Frontier representatives dominated the committees on Indian affairs in both houses and succeeded in nominating men of their choice to Indian Office field positions. In matters of patronage, the White House was usually receptive to western demands. Sectional interests, not party politics, influenced the voting on Indian bills. Thus it is easy to understand why the West for so many years dictated the fate of the Indian.[29]

These administrative problems of the 1850s—accelerated territorial expansion, the nation's preoccupation with the slavery question, the "Indian ring," whiskey hucksters, fraudulent records, disagreements with the War Department, cultural clash, race hatreds and the political power of frontiersmen in Indian matters—created insurmountable problems for the understaffed Office of Indian Affairs. Because events moved so rapidly, even the establishment of reservations could not insulate the aborigines from westward tramping pioneers. Consequently, justice was not rendered, Indian good will vanished, and with it the hope of peace.

The pulsating frontier paused in eastern Kansas on the eve of Fort Sumter. From this point the unbroken line of settlement swung back on both flanks as far as the young state of Minnesota to the northeast and the Ozarks in the South. Bending around the unorganized Indian country that is today the state of Oklahoma, it extended westward again to about the ninety-ninth meridian, before turning south through east Texas. Pioneer farmers thrust fingers of settlement beyond this jagged border, along the valleys of the Platte and Missouri on the central plains and the Upper Rio Grande in New Mexico Territory. Also, isolated nuclei of settlements flourished just east of Great Salt Lake and in the mining region around Denver. Along the California coast there were concentrations of population, as well as in the rich central valleys of that state, Oregon, and the Territory of Washington. As yet, no gleaming steel rails linked these outposts with the

29. Fritz, *Assimilation*, p. 168; Tyler, *Indian Affairs*, p. 5.

Mississippi Valley. The overland trails were still rugged, treacherous, slow, seasonal and subject to Indian attacks.[30]

Tribesmen roamed freely across the plains and mountains of the trans-Mississippi West in 1861. Colorful Teton Sioux, Arapaho, Cheyenne, Kiowa and Comanche warriors rode with the wind as they chased giant herds of shaggy buffalo from Texas to Canada. The less nomadic Civilized Nations farmed and herded cattle in the Indian country south of Kansas. Pasturing sheep, raising a few crops, and warring against the whites provided a livelihood for the Navajos of the parched Southwest. Their treacherous Apache neighbors, on the other hand, lived entirely on native products and plunder from nearby farms and ranches. The warlike Utes roamed the central Rockies. They practiced no agriculture, sustaining themselves by the fruit of the chase and their trade with the Navajos. Low on the scale of civilization, the destitute Diggers of Utah, western New Mexico Territory, and California used roots extensively for food and did a little hunting and fishing. In the Pacific Northwest the selective breeding of the Nez Percés won fame for them as horsemen. Besides their trading business, they raised cattle, farmed, fished, and hunted the buffalo. Across the plains in western Minnesota, some Santee Sioux had forsaken the warrior's life and taken up agriculture under government tutelage.

To hold hostile Indians in check, the army stationed most of its sixteen thousand regulars at scattered posts throughout the West. The attack on Fort Sumter drew almost all of them to eastern battlefields, leaving volunteers in their places.[31]

Since most western tribes were not at war with the United States when Lincoln took the presidential oath beneath the unfinished Capitol dome in March 1861, they came under the jurisdiction of the civilian Office of Indian Affairs and its far-flung field officials. The New York, Michigan, and Green Bay agencies reported directly to the commissioner, whereas more

30. Randall D. Sale and Edwin D. Karn, *American Expansion: A Book of Maps* (Homewood, Ill., 1962), p. 17.

31. Munden and Beers, *Guide to Federal Archives Relating to the Civil War*, p. 242.

than forty-five agents were responsible to the eleven superintendents stationed in western territories and states.

During the Civil War years the problems of concentrating the
red men on reservations multiplied. The conflict itself directly
affected Indian relations only in Kansas, the Indian country just
west of Arkansas, and the Southwest. An indirect consequence
was the preoccupation of Congress and the president with the
war effort; neither had much time for events beyond the Mississippi, particularly since Union military strategists viewed this
theater as of secondary importance in comparison to the Eastern
front. Such inattention produced decreased and frequently
delayed Indian Office appropriations and the postponement of
needed reforms.

Congress enacted some significant legislation to facilitate the
administration of the reservation policy. For example, in February 1862 it amended the intercourse act of 1834, making it a
crime to sell spirituous liquors to aborigines under the charge of
an Indian Office official, whether or not the red men were on
their reservation. The intention was to thwart hucksters who set
up grog shops on the borders of Indian reserves.[32] In March 1864
Congress granted Indian Office and military officers the right to
search the property of any person whom they suspected was
"about to introduce or has introduced any spirituous liquor or
wine into the Indian country" and to seize all the liquor that was
found.[33] However, not until March 1865 did the legislative
branch, in response to a public outcry after the Sand Creek incident of November 1864, pass a resolution for a joint special
committee to inquire into the condition of the Indian tribes and
their treatment by civil and military officials.[34] Even then, two
years elapsed before the commission filed its report.

President Lincoln exerted minimal influence on Indian affairs
during his presidency. When he did intervene, as in the case of
the Minnesota Sioux condemned to be hanged for their outrages
during the uprising of 1862, he demonstrated wisdom and fore-

32. *United States Statutes at Large* 12:339.
33. *Ibid.*, 13:29.
34. *Ibid.*, pp. 572–73.

sight. Generally the president deferred questions of Indian policy and administration to appropriate congressional committees or to the Office of Indian Affairs. The federal official most responsible for directing Indian matters between 1861 and 1865 was the energetic commissioner of Indian affairs, William P. Dole, a personal friend of the president's from the days when Lincoln rode the Eighth Judicial Circuit in Illinois. Dole skillfully handled numerous policy decisions as well as administrative chores, such as claims questions and the mounting paper work which choked his overcrowded office. Throughout the war he retained the confidence of Secretaries of the Interior Caleb B. Smith and John P. Usher, the president, and many leaders.[35]

If Dole's appointment was an exceptionally astute one, the men selected by the administration to be superintendents and agents for the western tribes seemed no better than their predecessors. Wartime pressures prevented Lincoln from carefully assessing the qualifications of each nominee. Also, he adhered to the custom of appointing men nominated for Indian Office positions by frontier congressional delegations, which sought to reward some aging politician or ambitious young man for party work. Beyond this, the administration apparently had but four criteria for an Indian Office bureaucrat: could he give the proper bond, was he well liked in his community, might his past military or financial activities embarrass the president and, finally, was Commissioner Dole inclined to favor his candidacy. Not all appointees were unqualified, but the Indian service had a reputation for inefficiency and corruption. Low salaries—$2,000 a year for superintendents and $1,500 for agents—encouraged fraud and speculation with Indian monies.[36] "To tempt any really capable person to leave home and civilized resorts for a life among savages," wrote one critic, "something more was

35. Elmo R. Richardson and Alan W. Farley, *John Palmer Usher, Lincoln's Secretary of the Interior* (Lawrence, Kans., 1960), p. 34.

36. Howard Lamar, *Dakota Territory, 1861–1889: A Study of Frontier Politics* (New Haven, 1956), p. 67; Thomas A. Marshall to John P. Usher, October 9, 1862, John P. Usher Papers, Kansas State Historical Society, Topeka; Laurence F. Schmeckebier, *The Office of Indian Affairs: Its History, Activities, and Organization* (Baltimore, 1927), p. 47.

required than a salary less than is paid to a first-class clerk in a dry goods store."[37] Lincoln had scant time for civil service reform, however, and without strong executive leadership, little could be done to upgrade the quality of Indian Office employees.

The North-South struggle, Washington's absorption with military matters, and the personnel problem were not the sources of the Indian Office's most serious administrative troubles between 1861 and 1865. Rather it was the persistent encroachment of frontiersmen on Indian land throughout the trans-Mississippi West. The Civil War slowed but did not halt the process. This grasping for the red man's territory fanned into flames the smoldering unsolved problems of the 1850s and created a variety of difficulties—some new, some old. When white intruders violated reservation boundaries, the resident agent was duty-bound to expel them. Sometimes this was possible; more often, as in the case of the miners who invaded the Nez Percé reservation in the Pacific Northwest, the whites could not be dislodged. If pioneers pushed into regions set aside for nomadic tribes, such as eastern Colorado, the Indian Office tried to gather the tribes on small reservations remote from the advancing Americans. In either case, whether the Indian Office sought to keep whites off a reservation or to collect the Indians on one, it faced a myriad of difficulties and became entangled in frustrating relationships—not only with the red man but with the United States Army and the rugged men on the cutting edge of the frontier.

If, in 1861, the Indian Office's most serious administrative problems originated in the field, then it was incumbent on the Indian agents and superintendents to solve them. Should the means be lacking on the local level to meet these challenges, then the Indian service could not successfully carry out the reservation policy, and the stage was set for a tragedy in the West as well as in the East. Confederate cannon overlooking Charleston harbor signaled the opening of the drama when their shells shattered the quiet dawn on April 12.

A chapter-by-chapter analysis of the administrative problems

37. "Our Indian Policy." *The Nation* 2 (January 25, 1866): 103.

in each superintendency would be too repetitive and would bog down the text in detail, obscuring the main interpretations of this study. Instead I shall discuss rather thoroughly Indian Office relations with the two most representative Indian groups. The Cheyennes, for example, were more than just a typically nomadic people. Their geographic location on the central plains, athwart the overland trails, made government dealings with them crucial to the well-being of Colorado and points west. Furthermore, after tallying the types of field problems the Indian Office faced, it was apparent that of the nomadic tribes which shunned reservation life, the Cheyennes posed the widest variety of administrative difficulties. For similar reasons the Santee Sioux best exemplified the reservation tribes. A powerful people, they occupied an important frontier position, and many of their hunters and warriors likewise resisted government plans for their future. Particularly challenging was the enforced removal of the Santees following the uprising of 1862 and their relocation on the Dakota plains. To call the Cheyennes and the Santees the most representative nomadic and reservation people is not the same as proving it. Therefore, to give national scope to this analysis, chapters are included which compare and contrast field problems within other superintendencies.

PART I

The Nomadic People

CHAPTER I

The Struggle for Eastern Colorado

Iroquois! Sioux! Apaches! Cheyennes! Once such words alarmed countless American pioneer families. More important, they were once powerful Indian tribes which helped to shape America's destiny and whose ways few white men understood or lived to tell about. Of these four tribes none was more noble than the Cheyennes: tall, proud, indomitable lords of the central plains.

It was not always so. In the late seventeenth century the Cheyennes, then residing on the Minnesota River, were driven from their land onto the Dakota Plains, no doubt by the Sioux or Crees and Assiniboins. A century passed during which this new environment wrought a major change in their culture.[1] In his classic study of the Great Plains, Walter Prescott Webb explained that if human beings would live in this inhospitable land, they must adapt to its semi-arid climate and endlessly flat surfaces. Nature had equipped the wolf, coyote, jackrabbit, and antelope for survival with an inborn shyness, speed, and cunning.[2] The Cheyennes were on their own, and the quick modification of a woodland-prairie culture assured their survival. The acquisition of horses from southern tribes gave Cheyenne hunters the necessary speed to chase the swift grassland animals. Garden patches were abandoned as mounted bands turned to the vast

1. Donald J. Berthrong, *The Southern Cheyennes* (Norman, 1963), p. 6.
2. Walter Prescott Webb, *The Great Plains* (Boston, 1931), p. 41.

buffalo herds for subsistence. Meanwhile, relentless pressure from the Teton Sioux to the east kept Cheyenne villagers hustling westward, first to the Black Hills and finally south to the Platte and the Arkansas. Until the 1830s Cheyenne warriors bartered with Missouri River fur traders; then, with the construction of two trading posts in their own country, Bent's Fort and Fort St. Vrain, they broke this link with the past. Henceforth the northern Cheyenne bands dwelt on the Tongue and the North Platte Rivers, the southern ones mostly on the Arkansas.[3] This constituted the Cheyennes' world in the mid-nineteenth century.

Life for the Cheyenne brave centered about his hunt for the shaggy buffalo. So important was the quest that chiefs carefully planned communal hunts to be executed under the close supervision of soldier societies. Slain bison provided for most of life's necessities. Buffalo meat, for example, supplemented with wild fruits made up the entire family diet; cured hides, stitched together and stretched around conically arranged lodge poles, created a functional, year-round dwelling. As much a part of the plains culture as the buffalo and the mobile tepee was the sure-footed Indian pony. His strength and speed made possible a successful hunt. Furthermore, a warrior could trade his mustang herd for whatever else he might need, such as the white man's rifle, which later replaced the Indian lance, bow, and arrows.[4]

The Cheyennes indulged in their share of wars. Already possessed of a fighting spirit, their choice of a new homeland accentuated this quality by placing them between two powerful adversaries: to the north the Teton Sioux, and south of the Arkansas the Comanches, Kiowas, and Kiowa-Apaches, whom the Cheyennes had driven from southeast Wyoming. As part of their struggle for supremacy on the Arkansas, the Cheyennes raided wealthy Kiowa and Comanche villages for horses, which the

3. Berthrong, *Southern Cheyennes*, pp. 6ff; George Bent to George Hyde, January 23, 1905, George Bent Papers, Yale University Library Western Americana Collection, New Haven, Conn. (referred to hereafter as Bent Papers).

4. Berthrong, *Southern Cheyennes*, pp. 31–32; Clark Wissler, "The North American Indians of the Plains," *Popular Science Monthly* 82 (January–June, 1913): 438ff; David Sievert Lavender, *Bent's Fort* (Garden City, N.Y., 1954), pp. 110–11.

latter had stolen from Spanish settlements. Warfare on neighbors north and south ceased in 1840 and was replaced by mutually protective alliances against such non-plains tribes as the Pawnees, Utes, and Shoshonis.[5]

Bravery, the goal of the warrior, was rewarded with wealth in captured ponies and political influence. In his quest for glory the Cheyenne brave became highly skilled in the art of war. The thrill of personal combat he had savored from childhood. Likewise he had been made to understand the importance of endurance and wisdom in the face of danger. The wise Cheyennes found few if any causes worth dying for and exhibited none of your charge-of-the-Light-Brigade foolishness. A successful raiding party stealthily played the odds; against a well-fortified foe or one which could not be taken by surprise, it withdrew in order to fight another day.[6]

While men monopolized the excitement and glory of the chase, the deerskin-clad squaw was responsible for the well-being of home and family. Besides the preparation of meals she spent most of her days drying meat and dressing buffalo hides. So all-providing was the wooly buffalo that a woman apparently had little need for such expressive arts as weaving, basketry, or pottery. The village's constant search for buffalo and fresh grazing land for its pony herds meant that much of her time was consumed striking or setting up the lodge, packing and unpacking the family's possessions, herding children as well as her husband's ponies, and fixing trail-side meals. A final note on the importance of the woman's role is that a clever Cheyenne woman, though barred from tribal councils, could decisively affect village policies by means of her influence on her husband's economic and political affairs.[7]

The sexual division of labor was but one way in which the Cheyennes' world influenced their culture. The fierce plains at

5. Berthrong, *Southern Cheyennes*, pp. 23, 26; Frederick Webb Hodge, ed., *Handbook of American Indians North of Mexico* (2 vols., Washington, D.C., 1907–10), 1:72.

6. Berthrong, *Southern Cheyennes*, p. 43; Lavender, *Bent's Fort*, pp. 116–19.

7. George Bent to George Hyde, October 15, 1905, Bent Papers; Berthrong, *Southern Cheyennes*, pp. 34–36.

once drove bands apart and bound them together. Because the semi-arid land could not support large villages for long, the band became the basic social and political unit. Nevertheless, enough tribal cohesiveness persisted that band chiefs could council together to consummate treaties with foreign powers or to plan for war. Common religious beliefs and practices likewise integrated the tribe. The Cheyennes' religion, complete with a sun dance and buffalo worship, had its genesis in their attempts to understand and to cope with such plains phenomena as wind storms, blinding blizzards, drought, and animal migrations.[8]

The Cheyennes' modest numbers (2,500 to 3,000 in the early 1860s)[9] together with their exposed geographic location led to a mutually profitable alliance with the Arapahos. An Algonquin people, they too were once farmers in Minnesota before being driven onto the plains long before the Cheyennes. Little of the early association of these tribes is known except that the Cheyennes acted both as allies in their common wars and prior to the 1830s as middlemen with Missouri River traders. Their relationship became more than one of mere convenience; Southern Arapahos and Southern Cheyennes camped in the same places, intermarriage occurred between the tribes and the easygoing Arapahos apparently exercised a sobering influence on their hotheaded allies.[10]

Close association also led to the mixing of Cheyenne blood with that of Arkansas River traders such as William Bent. In the early 1850s Bent sent his half-breed sons, Charles and George, to school in Missouri. About their return to the Upper Arkansas in 1862 George Bent wrote years later:

8. Berthrong, *Southern Cheyennes*, pp. 50ff.

9. Testimony of John S. Smith, March 8, 1865, JSC, p. 41; Agent John Loree's 1862 census for the Upper Platte Agency, enclosed in Harrison B. Branch to Charles E. Mix, September 10, 1862, OIA, LR, Upper Platte Agency.

10. E. B. Renaud, "The Indians of Colorado," in Junius Henderson et al., *Colorado: Short Studies of Its Past and Present* (Boulder, 1927), pp. 25–26; Virginia Cole Trenholm, *The Arapahoes, Our People* (Norman, 1970), p. 10; Berthrong, *Southern Cheyennes*, p. 26; George Bird Grinnell, *The Fighting Cheyennes* (Norman, 1956), p. 5; William H. Leckie, *The Military Conquest of the Southern Plains* (Norman, 1963), p. 12.

I found everything in the Upper Country greatly changed, since I had left in 1853. At that time there had been very few whites in all that region. . . . The country did not even have a name in those days. . . . Now, in 1862, it was Colorado Territory and had an organized government and some thirty thousand whites, mostly men, were within its borders. . . . Now there were two stage lines running up the Arkansas, stage stations, and ranches every few miles; Fort Larned (old Camp Alert) had been built near the site of the present Larned, Kansas, and my father's fort had been purchased by the War Department and garrisoned with troops. Denver was a city; Pueblo, Colorado Springs, Booneville, and a score of other towns had been founded, and hundreds of farms and ranches had been started around Denver and in the upper valleys of the Arkansas and the South Platte.[11]

The overland migration to the Pacific had alarmed Indians of the central plains as early as the 1840s, for they realized their way of life was threatened by the white man's indiscriminate slaughter of buffalo. To obtain a right-of-way through the Indian country for the emigrants and to insure peaceful relations, the United States in 1851 negotiated the Treaty of Fort Laramie with several plains tribes. By its terms the grasslands of the central plains between the North Platte and the Arkansas Rivers were jointly assigned to the Cheyennes and Arapahos. Two years later a similar treaty of peace was concluded at Fort Atkinson with the lords of the Staked Plains south of the Arkansas: the Comanches, Kiowas, and Kiowa-Apaches.[12]

Though the Cheyennes and their Arapaho allies clashed with federal military forces in the mid-1850s, the Fort Laramie settlement generally pleased the two tribes. Then came the fateful discovery of gold on the South Platte in 1858, which ignited the rush to Pike's Peak. Thousands of miners crossed the plains and squatted boldly on lands pledged to the Indians. By November

11. George E. Hyde, *The Life of George Bent, Written from His Letters,* ed. Savoie Lottinville (Norman, 1968), pp. 110–11.

12. Charles J. Kappler, ed., *Indian Affairs: Laws and Treaties* (2 vols., 2d ed., Washington, D.C., 1904) 2:594–96, 600–602.

of the following year the commissioner of Indian affairs recorded that "we have substantially taken possession of the country and deprived them of their accustomed means of support."[13] This stampeding, land-grabbing, gold-seeking, town-building society numbered 34,277 whites in 1860, many of whom wanted immediate statehood.[14] Government officials, cognizant of the new forces at work in Colorado, sought a further reduction of the Indians' domain. In February 1861 they concluded the Treaty of Fort Wise with ten chiefs and delegates "representing the confederated tribes of Arapaho and Cheyenne Indians of the Upper Arkansas river," who were induced by bribery (so they later claimed) to accept a greatly diminished triangular reserve between the Big Sandy and the Arkansas. There, a hundred miles southeast of Denver, they would settle, and with the help of the government become self-supporting farmers.[15]

After the South's withdrawal from the Union, Congress created the Territory of Colorado and established within it a new Indian superintendency. The Upper Arkansas Agency, which embraced the Southern Cheyennes, Southern Arapahos, Kiowas, Comanches, and Kiowa-Apaches, was shifted from the Central Superintendency. Northern Cheyennes, Northern Arapahos, and Teton Sioux ranging north of the South Platte remained under the jurisdiction of the Upper Platte Agency of the Central Superintendency. The Sioux, especially the Smoke People Oglalas and some of the Miniconjous and Sans Arcs, roamed as far north as the headwaters of the Tongue and Powder Rivers in present-day Wyoming. Other Teton divisions were the responsibility of the Upper Missouri Agency. In 1861 the Indian Office also transferred the Ute Agency at Conejos from the New Mexico to the

13. CIA, 1859, *Sen. Exec. Doc.* 2, 36 Cong., 1 Sess., 1:384–85 (Ser. 1023).

14. United States Superintendent of the Census, *Population of the United States in 1860 . . .* (Washington, D.C., 1864), p. iv; Ray Allen Billington, *Westward Expansion: A History of the American Frontier* (3rd ed., New York, 1967), p. 625.

15. Kappler, *Indian Affairs* 2:807–10. In 1865 Arapaho chief Little Raven claimed that he and his fellow headmen did not understand what they were signing at Fort Wise in February 1861, Grinnell, *The Fighting Cheyennes*, p. 126n.

new Colorado Superintendency. The Utes—numerous and unremittingly hostile toward their traditional enemies on the plains—occupied the canyons, semi-arid plateaus, and snowy ranges of western and central Colorado.[16]

The territory's first governor as well as ex officio superintendent of Indian affairs was William Gilpin, an explorer and organizer of Missouri's Republican party. He realized that the Cheyennes and Arapahos must be isolated on their Arkansas reservation as soon as possible in order to avoid serious skirmishes with whites scattered throughout the Indians' old hunting grounds.[17] John Evans replaced Gilpin as governor in May 1862 and pursued the same policy. He hoped not only to reduce the number of encounters between red and white but to render the Cheyennes and Arapahos less financially burdensome in the future by promoting stock raising on the reservation.[18]

These guidelines of Indian policy in Colorado during the Civil War era were in no way unique. From the Atlantic Coast to Kansas, the predecessors of Gilpin and Evans had dislodged the Indian for his own protection and to make way for the settler. Set against the reservation plan in Colorado was the Indians' nomadism. To abandon their plains culture and settle on a limited tract of land was repugnant to the Cheyennes and other tribesmen of the superintendency. It was a gloomy picture indeed, for if they would not give up the hunt and could not be driven further west due to the mountain barrier, fighting between the Indians and Colorado's burgeoning white population was inevitable. To the Indian Office was assigned the task of preserving a peace already doomed.

Because all the Cheyennes and Arapahos did not accept the

16. John Evans to Dole, October 30, 1862, CIA, *House Exec. Doc.* 1, 37 Cong., 3 Sess., 2:373–74 (Ser. 1157); George E. Hyde, *Red Cloud's Folk: A History of the Oglala Sioux Indians* (Norman, 1937), p. 115.

17. Gilpin to Dole, June 8, 1861, OIA, LR, Colorado Supty.

18. Berthrong, *Southern Cheyennes*, pp. 158–59. Gilpin was removed from office when the Secretary of the Treasury refused to honor his drafts on the government for outfitting a cavalry regiment in 1861 to defend Colorado from a threatened Indian massacre, Vincent G. Tegeder, "Lincoln and the Territorial Patronage: The Ascendency of the Radicals in the West," *Mississippi Valley Historical Review* 35 (June, 1948): 81–82.

Treaty of Fort Wise, they frustrated Governor Evans's early efforts to separate red men from white in Colorado. The treaty was signed by the Arkansas bands of Southern Cheyennes and Southern Arapahos, who were recognized after 1851 as distinct from the North Platte bands.[19] The sixth article of the Fort Wise agreement provided for the future inclusion of the northerners; nevertheless, the southern bands ceded to the government all Cheyenne and Arapaho lands between the North Platte and the Arkansas, except the triangular reserve on the Arkansas.[20] The North Platt tribesmen refused to be cooped up on this tract, arguing that all bands must consent before territory could be alienated.[21] Governor Evans tried unsuccessfully to obtain their endorsement of the Fort Wise treaty. During the winter of 1862–63, after smallpox had raged along the Platte, he instructed the Northern Cheyennes and Arapahos to come down to the Arkansas reservation to receive their annuities, but this lure also failed. One Arapaho band which went south later returned to the Platte country as obdurate as ever.[22]

As Colorado's population moved into the region ceded in 1861, another serious problem confronted the governor and the Indian Office. Federal officers in Colorado were charged with enforcing the trade and intercourse acts in the Indian country, which included the triangular Arkansas reservation and the area north of the Fort Wise cession line.[23] In December 1862 and again in February 1863, the United States Attorney in Denver, Sam E. Brown, asked the Interior Department and the Office of Indian Affairs for a clarification of the line. Brown recommended acknowledging the South Platte as the northern limit of the cession; north of the river roamed the Upper Platte bands who obviously

19. Hodge, *Handbook of American Indians* 1:72, 252.

20. Kappler, *Indian Affairs* 2:809–10.

21. Raymond G. Carey, "The Puzzle of Sand Creek," *Colorado Magazine* 41 (Fall, 1964): 283.

22. James Mooney, "The Cheyenne Indians," *Memoirs of the American Anthropological Association* (Lancaster, Pa., 1905), 1:283–84; Berthrong, *Southern Cheyennes*, pp. 159–60.

23. William E. Unrau, "A Prelude to War," *Colorado Magazine* 41 (Fall, 1964): 305–7.

would not become signatories to the 1861 treaty.[24] Dole concurred with Brown's decision after consulting the records of the Indian Office. Federal jurisdiction could now be extended into the Indian country between the forks of the Platte and, in theory, squatters might be removed.[25]

Dole's decree infuriated Coloradans. The South Fork diagonally bisected the most populous sector of Colorado, including the Denver area; north and west of the fork sprawled the richest mines and most productive farms in the territory. The counties of Laramie, Boulder, Jefferson, Gilpin, Clear Creek, and a part of Arapaho also lay in Indian country, according to the commissioner's decision.[26] Hiram Pitt Bennet, Colorado's delegate to Congress, and Governor Evans spearheaded the attack against the Indian Office's ruling. Evans predicted a bloody Indian war should the government relinquish the disputed area to the red man; moreover, after examining numerous documents he could find no mention of the South Fork ever having been a tribal boundary. If it were, the Fort Wise treaty, intended to win title to the settled portions of the country, was an utter failure and a new agreement must be negotiated at once.[27]

The protests forced Dole to recant his previous declaration, which, he explained, was based on false information given by agent William W. Bent in 1859. No division existed, whether at the South Fork or elsewhere, between the northern and southern bands of the Cheyennes and Arapahos. The treaty of 1861 ceded all Indian lands between the North Platte and the Arkansas. The large annuities which the government pledged proved that its terms embraced all the Cheyennes and Arapahos, not just the southern divisions. Having found in Agent Bent a scapegoat for the current disharmony in Colorado, the commissioner consigned to John Evans the onerous responsibility for future developments. In May 1863 he directed the governor to convene

24. Brown to Dole, February 4, 1863, OIA, LR, Upper Arkansas Agency; Unrau, "A Prelude to War," pp. 309–10.
25. Dole to Brown, February 27, 1863, OIA, LR, Upper Arkansas Agency.
26. Bennet to John P. Usher, April 14, 1863, *ibid*.
27. Evans to Dole, April 10, 1863, OIA, LR, Colorado Supty.

a general council of the bands not party to the treaty of 1861, to arrange for their concentration on the reservation.[28]

Dole's expedient manipulation of the Fort Wise cession line revealed that the Indian Office, when faced with the incongruity of upholding the South Fork terminus, could create a new rationale as easily as a new boundary. United States Attorney Brown protested Dole's retraction, but to no avail.[29] The land dispute also made manifest the distressing ambiguity of the Fort Wise treaty. Dole's movement of the boundary to the North Platte solved the question of the cession's limits to Colorado's satisfaction, but the Northern Cheyenne and Arapaho bands still had to be appeased and relocated.

In June 1863 Evans met with some Arapaho representatives of the Upper Platte bands who agreed to treat with the superintendent.[30] Thus encouraged, he planned a general council of all the Cheyenne and Arapaho chiefs in September on the Arikaree Fork of the Republican River. Runners carried the news to widely scattered camps. The governor's commission included, besides himself, Samuel G. Colley of the Upper Arkansas Agency (a cousin of Commissioner Dole) and John Loree, agent on the Upper Platte.[31]

By the end of August, Evans was already pessimistic about the success of the conference. Colley reported that the southern bands probably would not attend.[32] Also, the general inability of the tribes to unite and stay united boded ill for the governor's efforts. George E. Hyde, a noted historian of the plains Indians, wrote of this disunity: "The men of each small camp talked, then they either disagreed hopelessly and took no action, or else they agreed and their chief accepted their views. Then the chief met chiefs of other bands and found they held other views, so he was

28. Dole to Evans, May 18, 1863, OIA, LS 70:457; Unrau, "A Prelude to War," pp. 310–12.
29. Brown to Dole, June 6, 1863, OIA, LR, Upper Arkansas Agency.
30. Evans to Dole, June 24, 1863, OIA, LR, Colorado Supty.
31. Evans to Dole, July 13, 1863, *ibid.*; Testimony of John Evans, JSC, pp. 45–46; Harry Kelsey, "Background to Sand Creek," *Colorado Magazine* 45 (Fall, 1968): 281.
32. Evans to Dole, August 26, 1863, OIA, LR, Upper Arkansas Agency.

talked around by them; and when he got back to his own camp, his headmen disapproved and forced him to go back on any pledges he had made."[33]

As the governor's commission and the escort company of Colorado cavalry approached the council grounds in mid-September 1863, they expected to see a throng of Indians and to hear grunts of pleasure when the treaty presents were spread out before them: a dozen silver-mounted rifles, ten pieces of calico, twelve blue cloth suits, soft hats, one-half box of plug tobacco, two dozen red flannel or plaid shirts and two dozen pairs of blankets. Instead, the solitary figure of Eldridge Gerry, one of the governor's runners, greeted the cavalcade. Evans sent Gerry out again to search for the bands, hoping to lure them with the promise of presents. He met a large band of Cheyennes forty miles east of the council ground. Despite several conferences with the headmen and the enticement of gifts, he could not persuade them to attend the council or to accept reservation life. Chief Bull Bear was particularly inflexible:

"Does the Great Father want us to live like white men? . . ."

"Yes," said Gerry. "That is what he wants."

"You tell white chief," was the scornful answer, "Indian maybe not so low yet."[34]

Those leaders tempted by Gerry's promises hesitated to accompany him to the rendezvous, and negotiations collapsed. The governor returned to Denver with his escort.[35] George Bent later claimed that the Cheyennes, inclined toward peace that fall, did not attend the governor's conference because their small bands had already scattered to prepare for winter. This Gerry knew but failed to tell Evans.[36]

More overtures were made to the Platte bands. While the governor negotiated with the Utes in late September, Agent Loree

33. George E. Hyde, *Spotted Tail's Folk: A History of the Brulé Sioux* (Norman, 1961), p. 85.

34. Edgar C. McMechen, *Life of John Evans, Second Territorial Governor of Colorado* (Denver, 1924), pp. 117–19.

35. *Ibid.*

36. Bent to Hyde, April 30, 1906, Bent Papers.

counciled with the northern nomads. That he accomplished little
was blamed this time on the traders and whiskey dealers who
told the Indians to wait until next spring when they could demand more horses and a better treaty.[37] After Evans's return to
Denver he met with a band of Northern Arapahos who had
recently stolen several horses during a raid near the territorial
capital. The headmen agreed to return the stock but would not
listen to treaty talk unless their people could get a reservation on
the Cache La Poudre River, a tributary of the South Platte,
rather than on the Arkansas. The governor promised to consult
his superiors in Washington.[38]

    John Evans's abortive parleys with the Cheyennes and Arap-
ahos during the summer and fall of 1863 illustrated some of the
problems of treating with them. Perhaps a less nomadic and self-
sufficient people would have recognized the white menace by
the close of 1863 and realized their their ultimate welfare required
an immediate separation from Colorado pioneers and settlement
on a protected reservation. Certainly the Cheyennes and Arapahos, particularly the northern bands, did not grasp these realities.
Consequently, Governor Evans as ex officio superintendent of
Indian affairs could do little; he had only the treaty process with
which to exert leverage on the red man. Until the Indians submitted to reservation life, they would continue to clash with
whites and be the target of military reprisals.

    Cheyenne and Arapaho bands had skirmished with army pa-
trols several times since the outbreak of the Civil War. The
reason for Indian unrest was the conspicuous presence of the
white man, who overran their lands, slaughtered the buffalo
herds and sold whiskey to young braves. In the early sixties the
Overland Stage shifted north to the Platte, and stage stations
were built every twenty miles or so. Concord coaches also clat-
tered along the Arkansas, bound for Denver and Santa Fe. An
even more direct route linked the Colorado capital with Leaven-

    37. Loree to Evans, October 24, 1863, enclosed in Evans to Dole, November
4, 1863, OIA, LR, Colorado Supty.
    38. Evans to Dole, November 11, 1863, *ibid.*; Testimony of John Evans, JSC,,
pp. 45–46.

worth and Atchison, Kansas.[39] Indian resentment could have caused serious military problems during the early sixties, since the North-South struggle drew off regular army troops as well as Colorado volunteer regiments. Until 1864, however, hostilities consisted only of minor depredations and skirmishes.[40]

The most active pillagers, the Kiowas, Comanches, and Kiowa-Apaches, operated along the Santa Fe Trail. Driven by disease, starvation, and the Indian Office's neglect of their desire for a treaty in 1861, they waited like hungry spiders for emigrant wagons and freight trains to enter their web.[41] To establish peace and to allay the fears of westerners, the Interior Department brought a delegation of plains chiefs to Washington. On March 27, 1863, they met with President Lincoln and on April 6 signed a treaty in which they agreed to stay away from the Santa Fe road. In return the government promised to supply them with staples and other merchandise. For indeterminate reasons the Senate refused to ratify the document, and attacks along the Arkansas continued.[42]

By the spring of 1864 Agent Colley's scattered Cheyennes and Arapahos demanded so much attention that the Interior Department detached the Kiowas, Kiowa-Apaches, and Comanches from the Upper Arkansas Agency and assigned them to Special Agent Jesse H. Leavenworth, whose task was to prevent the tribes from molesting emigrants on the Santa Fe Trail. Also, the Indian Office had been informed that hostile Sioux from the northern plains were counciling with Leavenworth's charges and arousing them with the war dance. These influences he must counteract.[43]

39. Hyde, *Red Cloud's Folk*, p. 105.

40. For detailed accounts of the numerous clashes, see Berthrong, *Southern Cheyennes*, and Stan Hoig, *The Sand Creek Massacre* (Norman, 1961).

41. Albert G. Boone to Dole, March 1, 1862, OIA, LR, Upper Arkansas Agency; Colley to Evans, September 30, 1862, OIA, LR, Colorado Supty.

42. Dole to Evans, November 21, 1862, OIA, LS, 69:359–60; Lincoln's Speech to the Indians, March 27, 1863, Abraham Lincoln, *The Collected Works of Abraham Lincoln*, ed. Roy P. Basler et al. (9 vols., New Brunswick, N.J., 1953), 6:152; Ernest Wallace and E. Adamson Hoebel, *The Comanches, Lords of the South Plains* (Norman, 1952), pp. 305–6.

43. Dole to Leavenworth, May 16, 1864, OIA, LS, 74:132.

The apprehension of a conspiracy among all the plains tribes further hindered the smooth administration of Indian affairs in Colorado. The first serious reference to the plot came from Governor Evans in November 1863. United States interpreter John Smith reported the presence of two large Sioux bands, one on the Arkansas and the other on the Smokey Hill, which reputedly were "offering the war pipe" to their southern brethren.[44] Robert North, an Indian trader and squaw man, claimed to have seen the chiefs of the Comanches, Apaches, Kiowas, Northern Arapahos, Cheyennes, and Sioux pledge to go to war against the whites as soon as they could get guns and ammunition.[45]

North's talk of conspiracy so convinced the governor that on November 7 he ordered Agent Colley to cease issuing arms and ammunition to the tribes. A month later Evans called Secretary of War Stanton's attention to the Indian alliance and emphasized that no more troops should be withdrawn from Colorado. Regulars should be posted along the Platte and Arkansas to ward off hostiles in the spring, carbines issued to the First Colorado Cavalry and the District Commander given authority to call out the militia if needed to repel an Indian assault. The militia got its carbines, but Evans's other proposals went unheeded until the following fall.[46]

Minor clashes occurred between Union troops and plains tribes in the spring of 1864, but none approaching a coordinated attack.[47] Still afraid that Colorado would be left unprotected before

44. Smith to Colley, November 9, 1863, enclosed in Evans to Dole, November 9, 1863, OIA, LR, Colorado Supty.

45. Evans to Dole, November 10, 1863, *ibid.* George Bent later said that he had been in the Cheyenne camps at this time and that North's story was fallacious; both the Cheyennes and Arapahos refused to smoke the Sioux war pipe. He conceded, however, that Governor Evans believed North spoke the truth, Hyde, *Life of George Bent*, pp. 119–21.

46. Evans to Colley, November 7, 1863, enclosed in Evans to Dole, November 9, 1863, OIA, LR, Colorado Supty.; Evans to Stanton, December 14, 1863, Abraham Lincoln Papers, Library of Congress, Washington, D.C.; Dolores C. Renze, Preface, Indian Affairs Letterpress Book, 1863–1864, Colorado State Archives and Records Service, Denver. A letterpress book consisted of bound copies of letters made by pressing onionskin paper on the undried ink of the originals.

47. Hoig, *Sand Creek*, p. 36.

a red onslaught, Evans requested support from General Samuel R. Curtis, commander of the Department of Kansas.[48] In June the massacre of the Hungate family on a ranch thirty miles southeast of Denver alarmed every settlement in eastern Colorado. The Denver militia drilled while the women gathered in public shelters. Evans again asked for military help and permission to call out the militia.[49]

Through most of the summer Indian attacks persisted along the emigrant trails, but Colorado settlements remained undisturbed.[50] What accounted for the governor's exaggerated reports of an Indian plot? Perhaps he hoped for some political advantage by galvanizing the public behind him and forcing the Cheyennes and Arapahos to the Arkansas reservation.[51] The answer is not clear.

In addition to the fear of Indian attacks, John Evans was troubled by the reluctance of the more friendly southern bands of Arapahos and Cheyennes to remain on the reservation. Their nomadic nature was partly to blame, yet the government hardly encouraged them to settle down. Shortly after arriving in Colorado, Evans journeyed south to inspect the lands assigned to the two tribes. Conspicuously absent from the Arkansas reserve were both water and timber, though Evans could see it was fine grazing country. If the Indians could so adeptly raise ponies, he reasoned, it would be easy enough for them to herd cattle and sheep as well. Until these red men learned to make a living other than by the chase, Indian Office school plans would have to wait. Evans's distribution of thousands of cattle and sheep pleased the

48. Evans to Curtis, May 28, 1864, OR, Ser. 1, 34, Pt. 4, p. 99. General Curtis had previously written to Evans: "I am obliged to draw every man who can be spared from the Indian frontier to operate against rebels who have devastated this State of Kansas and should be kept south of the Arkansas," Curtis to Evans, March 26, 1864, *ibid.*, Pt. 2, p. 743.

49. LeRoy Reuben and Ann W. Hafen, *Colorado, A Story of the State and Its People* (Denver, 1945), pp. 210–11; Evans to Dole, June 14, 1864 (telegram), OIA, LR, Colorado Supty.

50. Berthrong, *Southern Cheyennes*, p. 194.

51. Berthrong in his *Southern Cheyennes* (pp. 169–71, 211) follows this interpretation of Evans's motives, whereas other scholars find this viewpoint "unnecessarily restrictive," Carey, "Puzzle of Sand Creek," p. 286.

nomads, but for reasons that are not clear Commissioner Dole rejected the innovation.[52] It was more traditional and perhaps less expensive for the Indian Office to establish small farms on the Arkansas reserve. If watered the land could indeed be farmed, but little progress was made on the irrigation ditch during the Civil War years. Likewise delayed were the other provisions of the treaty of 1861 which promised the Indians money, a blacksmith, a grist mill, and farming instructions.[53] Headmen complained that whites at nearby Fort Lyon (formerly Fort Wise) stole Indian ponies, debauched their women, peddled whiskey, and spread pestilence. The testimonies of Colonel William W. Bent and former Indian agent Kit Carson before a postwar congressional committee suggest still another reason for the unpopularity of the Arkansas reserve: Agent Colley, his son Dexter, and John Smith had robbed the Indians of their annuity payments. Bent believed that the latter two traders had sold the Cheyennes and Arapahos a portion of their own treaty goods. If this were true—and Carson's corroboration suggests that Bent did not speak merely as a jealous trader—such a swindle could only discourage the tribes from walking in the white man's way.[54] Clearly, the roving treaty bands had little incentive, except at annuity time, to live on their Arkansas reservation. Instead they followed the buffalo herds, loitered outside army posts or, when disease or starvation made them desperate, robbed emigrant trains on the Santa Fe road.[55]

With the treaty bands and North Platte bands commingled, military and Indian Office officials had difficulty detecting those

52. John Evans, Autobiographical Statement of [1888?], Hubert Howe Bancroft Collection, Bancroft Library, University of California, Berkeley; Harry E. Kelsey, Jr., *Frontier Capitalist: The Life of John Evans* (Denver, 1969), p. 138.

53. Jackson, *A Century of Dishonor*, pp. 86–87; Janet Lecompte, "Charles Autobees," *Colorado Magazine* 35 (July, 1958): 221–23.

54. Testimony of Bent, JSC, pp. 93–95; Testimony of Carson, JSC, p. 96. In later years Bent's son George claimed that the Colleys also sold Indian annuity goods to soldiers and teamsters, Bent to Hyde, February 4, 1915, Bent Papers.

55. Denver *Colorado Republican and Rocky Mountain Herald*, February 13, 1862; Colley to Gilpin, April 2, 1862, OIA, LR, Colorado Supty.; Evans to Dole, June 24, 1862, *ibid.*; Evans to Chivington, September 21, 1863, *ibid.*

guilty of depredations. To separate the friendlies from the others, Governor Evans requested permission to select additional reservation sites on which the peaceful bands would willingly congregate.[56] In mid-June he instructed Colley to group his friendly Cheyennes and Arapahos at Fort Lyon and the Comanches and Kiowas at Fort Larned, Kansas, and to support them there with the aid of the military. After fighting the hostiles these families would form a nucleus for peace. In extending Evans's policy to northern Colorado, Washington permitted settlement of the Arapahos on the Cache La Poudre. Headmen were directed to avoid the hostile Cheyennes and to move without delay to the refuge, where the government would feed and protect them.[57] Evans sent Agent Simeon Whitely to Camp Collins on the Cache La Poudre to look after the bands which came in. Special Agent W. M. Curtis had orders to communicate the superintendent's instructions to other Platte bands. Late in June the governor issued a proclamation to all friendlies directing them to congregate at designated places of safety and to stay away from the hostiles.[58]

Agent Whitely notified Evans late in August that he and the commanding officer at Camp Collins were providing subsistence for 170 Arapahos camped nearby. Both men believed these tribesmen wished peace. Less encouraging messages came from Agent Colley in the south, who believed that the young Cheyenne dog soldiers wished a fight and that their chiefs feared to challenge them. The Kiowas were also openly hostile.[59] Having learned from District Commander Colonel John Chivington about killings near Fort Larned which involved all the tribes,

56. Evans to Dole, October 14, 1863, CIA, *House Exec. Doc.* 1, 38 Cong., 1 Sess., 3:239 (Ser. 1182); Evans to Dole, December 20, 1863, OIA, LR, Colorado Supty.

57. Evans to Colley, June 16, 1864, and Evans to Roman Nose, June 17, 1864, enclosed in Evans to Dole, June 30, 1864, OIA, LR, Colorado Supty.

58. Evans to Whitely, June 25, 1864 and Evans to Curtis, June 28, 1864, enclosed in Evans to Dole, June 30, 1864, *ibid.*; Evans to Dole, October 15, 1864, CIA, pp. 362–63.

59. Whitely to Evans, August 30, 1864, enclosed in Evans to Dole, October 15, 1864, CIA, pp. 380–81; Colley to Evans, June 21, 1864, enclosed in Evans to Dole, June 30, 1864, OIA, LR, Colorado Supty.

Colley conceded the failure of the governor's strategy. "There is no dependence to be placed in any of them," he wrote. "I have done everything in my power to keep peace. I now think a little powder and lead is the best for them."[60]

Well-planned, coordinated Indian raids so threatened Colorado in August that Evans too lost whatever sympathy he had for his Indian charges. He again requested that the War Department intervene on behalf of Colorado, which desperately needed troops. The governor wanted permission as well to raise a regiment of hundred-day militia.[61] Still without authority to call out the militia, Evans on August 11 authorized each citizen,

> ... either individually or in such parties as they may organize, to go in pursuit of all hostile Indians on the plains, scrupulously avoiding those who have responded to my call to rendezvous at the points indicated; also to kill and destroy as enemies of the country wherever they may be found, all such hostile Indians; and further, as the only reward I am authorized to offer for such services, I hereby empower such citizens, or parties of citizens, to take captive, and hold to their own private use and benefit, all the property of said hostile Indians that they may capture, and to receive for all stolen property recovered from said Indians such reward as may be deemed proper and just therefore....[62]

Three days later the War Department empowered Evans to call out a regiment of hundred-day militia.[63]

The governor's message greatly disturbed the Indian commissioner, who feared that the proclamation was couched in such indefinite terms that the vigilante hordes would make no distinction between friendly and hostile bands. Dole asked if the Kiowa and Comanche agent might induce Evans to modify his orders lest a general Indian war result.[64]

The raids continued. During the month and a half following

60. Colley to Evans, July 26, 1864, enclosed in Evans to Dole, August 9, 1864, OIA, LR, Colorado Supty.

61. Evans to Dole, August 9, 1864, CIA, p. 395.

62. Proclamation of Governor Evans, CIA, 1864, pp. 374–75.

63. Carey, "Puzzle of Sand Creek," pp. 287–88.

64. Leavenworth to Dole, August 24, 1864, OIA, LR, Colorado Supty.; Dole to Leavenworth, September 2, 1864, OIA, LS, 75:171–72.

the governor's August proclamation, Indian warriors repeatedly interrupted direct communication between Colorado and the East, severing telegraph lines and forcing the Post Office Department to send westward-bound mail by sea to California. Shrinking inventories in Denver pushed the price of a hundred pounds of flour from nine dollars to sixteen, then up to twenty-five dollars.[65] A *New York Times* correspondent described conditions east of the capital:

> Upon the overland route, devastation, terror, murder, has held a perfect carnival. From Denver and Fort Larimee to the Little Blue in Kansas, and to the Big Sandy in Nebraska, both within 150 miles of the Missouri, the Rebel Indians have swept like a hurricane. In a distance of four hundred miles along this great route they have captured at least 50 trains of merchandise or Government freight, driving stock, plundering and destroying to the value at least of a quarter million dollars. They have murdered two hundred white persons, among them many women and children. The stark bodies lie stripped and mutilated in the glaring sunlight, festering and rotting for want of burial, or half charred, are seen mouldering amid the ruins of ranches, cabins, and stage-stations.[66]

Such a volatile atmosphere made it as difficult for Indian service officers to keep their sense of proportion as it was to keep the peace. John Evans found himself in the middle of the Indian-white struggle. As ex efficio superintendent he was expected to promote the Indians' welfare; as governor he assumed responsibility for the development and safety of the territory as well as the maturation of Colorado's fledgling Republican party. As a prominent Chicago doctor and friend of Abraham Lincoln, it soon became personally important to Evans that the territory grow rapidly. Like most territorial executives, Evans had political ambitions. A minor figure in Illinois politics, he was nevertheless an ardent Republican and hoped to become one of Colorado's first senators.[67] Whenever the Indian threatened,

---

65. Hyde, *Life of George Bent*, p. 141.
66. Letter of August 30, 1864, *New York Times*, September 8, 1864.
67. Kelsey, *John Evans*, p. xii; Tegeder, "Lincoln and the Territorial Patron-

Evans was thus tempted to do the popular thing and be heavy-handed with the tribes. In a dynamic situation such as existed in Colorado in the 1860s, with the duties of territorial governor and Indian superintendent often antithetical, it was impossible to strike the balance which Evans's position required. Congress finally recognized this and terminated the last such combination in 1871, seven years after Sand Creek.[68]

Commissioner Dole alluded to still another administrative difficulty in his annual report for 1864, compiled two weeks before Sand Creek: sufficient military strength early in the spring could have dissuaded some tribes from joining the hostiles.[69] Military weakness had been an important part of the Colorado Indian problem since the outbreak of the Civil War, when the army withdrew Colorado troops needed to protect Colorado settlements and major routes to the territory which crisscrossed tribal hunting grounds. Denver, the business and supply center for the entire area, had become a good sized city of between five and six thousand by 1863, yet neither it nor the nearby mining towns and ranches were economically self-sufficient. Supplies had to be shipped from the East.[70] Plains outfitters in eastern Kansas also feared being cut off from the West. With Washington's eyes fixed on the Potomac, the drain of military power from Colorado left the solution to the red menace in the hands of the politically sensitive governor. General Curtis persistently neglected Evans's talk of an Indian conspiracy and his requests for more military aid. To Coloradans the Indian danger was real enough. Indeed, because of their frequent isolation from the East, public opinion soon became a dominant factor in determining Indian and military policy.

Another factor which raised public concern to fever pitch was

age," p. 82; Janet Lecompte, "Sand Creek," *Colorado Magazine* 41 (Fall, 1964): 317–18.

68. Earl S. Pomeroy, *The Territories and the United States, 1861–1890: Studies in Colonial Administration* (Philadelphia, 1947), p. 17.

69. CIA, 1864, pp. 166–67.

70. John S. Nicolay to Dole, November 10, 1863, CIA, pp. 262–63; Howard Roberts Lamar, *The Far Southwest, 1849–1912: A Territorial History* (New Haven, 1966), p. 243.

the widespread belief that the plains tribes, aroused by Southern emissaries, intended to launch a coordinated attack against all whites in the territory. Within a few months after the outbreak of civil war, Colorado officials reported rebel intrigue among the Kiowas and Comanches who hunted south of the Arkansas. When one party arrived at Fort Wise in August 1861 to sue for peace, commanding officer Captain Elmer Otis reported that Texans had urged them to fight the Union and in return Texas would help them drive whites off their land. Agent Albert G. Boone, Colley's predecessor at the Upper Arkansas Agency, also took note of rebel plotting.[71] Though Boone and Otis doubted that the Kiowas and Comanches would align with the South, Governor Gilpin insisted that an outbreak of agency Indians was imminent.[72] The frontier press magnified the war fever. At any moment, it was claimed, thousands of screaming savages could fill the military void on the plains.[73]

Such fears proved unfounded. True, Confederate Commissioner Albert Pike of Arkansas sought an alliance with the southern plains tribes in order to sever communications between the Union and its western states and territories, but only a few Comanche chiefs attended his grand council at Fort Cobb during the summer of 1861. The Indians wished to avoid the white man's battles, and their indiscriminate raids on southern as well as northern frontier settlements testified to their impartiality. Union and Confederate officials nevertheless continued to accuse each other of inciting the depredations.[74]

Prior to June 1864, Colorado newspaper editorials were concerned with recalling Colorado troops to foil the Indian conspiracy. In the wake of the Hungate murders, they emphasized

71. Otis to Dole, August 17, 1861, OIA, LR, Upper Arkansas Agency; Boone to Dole, September 7, 1861, *ibid.*

72. Gilpin to Dole, October 8, 1861, CIA, *Sen. Exec. Doc.* 1, 37 Cong., 2 Sess., 1:713–14 (Ser. 1117).

73. Denver *Commonwealth and Republican*, May 14, 1863; Marvin H. Garfield, "Defense of the Kansas Frontier, 1864–'65," *Kansas Historical Quarterly*, 1 (February, 1932): 140.

74. Garfield, *ibid.*; George E. Hyde, *Rangers and Regulars* (Columbus, Ohio, 1952), pp. 97–100.

chastisement of the renegades. The political aspirations of Evans
and congressional candidate John Chivington, former missionary,
Methodist elder and hero of the Battle of Glorietta Pass, made
each more susceptible to these pressures.[75] For example, the Colorado hundred-day militia, composed of frontiersmen whose
families and friends had suffered from Indian depredations, exerted such personal and political power that Colonel Chivington
apparently disliked sending them home without a fight. Perhaps
Sand Creek offered an easy victory.[76] Governor Evans, though
responsible for Indian rights as well as the public safety, likewise
had difficulty ignoring the desire of Coloradans to give the tribes
a good whipping.

Evans's surrender occurred in September 1864, when he had
another opportunity to further the cause of peace. With the
coming of winter, Black Kettle and certain other Cheyenne
chiefs proposed a treaty of friendship with the government and
the exchange of some prisoners. After surrendering their captives, Major Edward Wynkoop, commander at Fort Lyon, escorted the headmen to Camp Weld, outside Denver, to meet with
the governor.[77] Though the seven Arapaho and Cheyenne chiefs
expressed a willingness to lay down their arms, Evans doubted
their sincerity and admonished them for failing to come in to the
agencies in June. No longer could the Indian Office receive peace
overtures. Evans advised that they detach themselves from the
hostile bands and apply to the military for peace terms. If they
did not, all the Indians would be regarded as enemies. Colonel
Chivington, also present at the conference, suggested that when
the chiefs were ready to surrender they go to Major Wynkoop

75. Berthrong, *Southern Cheyennes*, pp. 211–12; Raymond G. Carey, "Colonel
Chivington, Brigadier General Connor and Sand Creek," *The 1960 Brand Book;
Being Volume Sixteen of the Denver Posse of Westerners* (Denver, 1961), p.
112.

76. Carey, "The Puzzle of Sand Creek," pp. 287ff.; Lecompte, "Sand Creek,"
p. 316.

77. Black Kettle et al. to Colley, August 29, 1864, enclosed in Colley to Evans,
September 4, 1864, in Report of the Secretary of War, *Sen. Exec. Doc.* 26, 39
Cong., 2 Sess., 2 (Ser. 1277); Wynkoop to Evans, September 18, 1864, enclosed
in Testimony of Wynkoop, *ibid.*

at Fort Lyon. The council then adjourned.[78] The next day Governor Evans instructed Colley to reemphasize to the now-penitent chiefs that no promises had been made at the Camp Weld meeting. They must deal with the military authorities.[79]

Dole's reaction to Evans's latest effort at reconciliation was not unlike the office's response to the governor's August proclamation. Each was expedient under the circumstances but unlikely to promote peace. The commissioner wrote in October that although civil authorities were in abeyance during hostilities, they must be ready to encourage and receive Indian peace overtures.[80]

Commissioner Dole justifiably concluded that Governor Evans, as a representative of the Indian Office, should have been more accommodating when the Indians offered the pipe of peace. Yet a stern approach to these nomads was hardly responsible for the war on the plains. Moreover, as governor of Colorado, Evans had every right to be skeptical of the overtures of Black Kettle and the other chiefs, for theirs was a typical plains Indian tactic: live off the government during the winter when game was scarce and then resume hostilities in the spring. "The time when you can make war best is in the summer-time; when I can make war best is in the winter," Evans remarked to the assembled chiefs at Camp Weld. "You, so far, have had the advantage; my time is just coming."[81] Though Colorado volunteers would have applauded such remarks, Evans's vengeful tone would not do for an Indian superintendent. By September 1864 his unwillingness to play the two roles which his governorship required crippled the Indian Office in Colorado. Had there been a superintendent separate and independent of the governor's office, it is still doubtful that a lasting peace could have been won at Camp Weld.

78. "Report of council with Cheyenne and Arapaho chiefs and warriors, brought to [Camp Weld,] Denver by Major Wynkoop," September 1864, JSC, pp. 87–90.
79. Evans to Colley, September 29, 1864, OR, Ser. 1, 41, Pt. 3, p. 495.
80. Dole to Evans, October 15, 1864, CIA, p. 100.
81. "Report of council with Cheyenne and Arapaho chiefs and warriors," JSC, pp. 87–90.

Nevertheless, such an individual might have prevented the tragedy two months later. For his part, Dole failed to appreciate the seriousness of the hostile threat. He not only expected too much of the isolated and unaided governor but failed to give adequate financial support in June 1864 when Evans tried to gather and care for the friendly bands at newly established sanctuaries.[82]

After the September council Major Wynkoop took the chiefs back to Fort Lyon. During October, 113 lodges of Arapahos congregated nearby and received provisions from the army. Early in November a new post commander ordered the headmen to take their bands to Sand Creek, in the ridge country about forty miles to the northeast. There they encamped and were joined by some Cheyennes under Chief Black Kettle. Apparently the Indians believed themselves safe from attack.[83] Events proved otherwise.

Following a day of bloody fighting at Sand Creek, Colonel Chivington, commander of a force of 750 troops, reported triumphantly on November 29, 1864:

> After a march of forty miles last night, I, at daylight this morning, attacked a Cheyenne village of one hundred anc [sic] thirty lodges, from nine hundred to one thousand warriors strong. We killed chiefs Black Kettle, White Antelope, and Little Robe, and between four and five hundred other Indians; captured between four and five hundred ponies and mules. Our loss is nine killed and thirty-eight wounded. All did nobly.[84]

Since that November day, controversy has raged over whether the incident at Sand Creek was a "battle" or a "massacre." Chivington's defenders claimed that the Indians at Sand Creek were unmistakably hostile. As evidence they cited the discovery

82. Kelsey, *John Evans*, pp. 142–43.

83. Major Scott J. Anthony to Assistant Adjutant General, District of the Upper Arkansas, Fort Riley, Kansas, November 6, 1864, *Sen. Report* 142, Pt. 3, 38 Cong., 2 Sess., pp. 70–71 (Ser. 1214); Hafen and Hafen, *Colorado*, pp. 212ff.

84. Chivington to Curtis, November 29, 1864, enclosed in C. Wheeler to the editors of the Denver *Rocky Mountain News*, December 7, 1864, JSC, p. 91. Chief Black Kettle was not killed at Sand Creek, as Chivington reported.

of a white man's scalp in a chief's lodge, taken less than three days before the attack.[85] The colonel's opponents argue that he "surprised and murdered, in cold blood, the unsuspecting men, women and children on Sand Creek, who had every reason to believe they were under the protection of the United States authorities."[86] A fact-finding military commission conducted hearings from February to May 1865, but drew no conclusions from the testimony. Also, Colonel Chivington, his term of enlistment having expired, was beyond the reach of the military.[87] Two congressional committees inquired into the affair as well. Though critical of Chivington's conduct, they took no action against him.[88] Those still seeking to settle the dispute of "battle" or "massacre" are confronted with a labyrinth of personal ambitions and animosities as well as intertwined private and public interests. Since several historians have culled through the testimony of traders, military men and Indian service personnel, the tedious process need not be repeated here.[89] Besides, the hearings were conducted

85. *Ibid.*

86. *Sen. Report* 142, Pt. 3, 38 Cong., 2 Sess., p. iv.

87. Garfield, "Defense of Kansas," p. 145; Hoig, *Sand Creek*, p. 173.

88. In regard to Chivington's conduct the Joint Committee on the Conduct of the War concluded: "As to Colonel Chivington, your committee can hardly find fitting terms to describe his conduct. Wearing the uniform of the United States, which should be the emblem of justice and humanity; holding the important position of commander of a military district, and therefore having the honor of the government to that extent in his keeping, he deliberately planned and executed a foul and dastardly massacre which would have disgraced the veriest savage among those who were the victims of his cruelty." *Sen. Report* 142, Pt. 3, 38 Cong., 2 Sess., p. v. The Joint Special Committee on the Condition of the Indian Tribes considered Chivington's attack equally villainous. "But the fact which gives such terrible force to the condemnation of the wholesale massacre of the Arapahoes and Cheyennes, by the Colorado troops under Colonel Chivington, near Fort Lyon, was, that those Indians were there encamped under the direction of our own officers, and believed themselves to be under the protection of our flag." JSC, pp. 5–6.

89. Accounts of the trial may be found in Carey, "The Puzzle of Sand Creek," pp. 279–98; Hoig, *Sand Creek*, pp. 165–73; and William J. Mellor, "The Military Investigation of Colonel John M. Chivington Following the Sand Creek Massacre," *Chronicles of Oklahoma* 16 (December, 1938): 444–64. Subsequent historical controversies about the attack are thoughtfully analyzed in Michael A. Sievers, "Sands of Sand Creek Historiography," *Colorado Magazine* 49 (Spring, 1972): 116–42.

with such a neglect of legal procedure that serious doubts have been cast upon the usefulness of the information gathered.[90] So, the puzzle of "battle" versus "massacre" still defies solution.

Though it was not the primary purpose of this chapter to add to the burden of Sand Creek historiography, the incident exhibits so many problems of Indian administration generally neglected by military-oriented chroniclers that an analysis of them should make more understandable the prelude to Chivington's attack on the Cheyennes and Arapahos.

Sand Creek was not an end but a beginning of serious problems on the plains. As word of Chivington's deed spread across the land it became a rallying cry for warriors from Canada to the Red River, who one by one took up weapons against the white man. Acting Governor Samuel H. Elbert informed the people of Colorado in mid-January 1865 that mails and supplies from the East were again cut off, and called for six companies of volunteers to open the road to Julesburg on the South Platte. Three weeks later Colonel Thomas Moonlight, Chivington's successor as commander of the District of Colorado, declared martial law.[91] In addition to the Sand Creek incident, Teton Sioux, Northern Cheyennes, and Northern Arapahos resented the proposed Bozeman Trail, and their protests merged into Red Cloud's War. Peace did not come to the northern plains until 1868. Military operations in the south ceased by the close of 1865 and a council convened at the mouth of the Little Arkansas with the Southern Cheyennes, Southern Arapahos, Comanches, Kiowas, and Kiowa-Apaches. The outcome no doubt pleased Coloradans, for the Cheyennes and Arapahos accepted lands south of the Arkansas. The agreement in effect reiterated the Fort Wise cession, except

90. Raymond Carey remarks concerning the jungle of half-truths and exaggerations collected by the investigators: "As one reads the statements made in the various hearings and in the affidavits and depositions collected by the committees and published in their reports, he leans in despair toward one of two conclusions: either one-quarter of the people present at Sand Creek were blind, another quarter nearsighted, and the other half were seeing double; or, more congenital liars participated in the Sand Creek affair than in any other battle, ancient or modern." Carey, "The Puzzle of Sand Creek," p. 297.

91. Ray C. Colton, *The Civil War in the Western Territories: Arizona, Colorado, New Mexico, and Utah* (Norman, 1959), pp. 159–60.

that the tribesmen did not retain the Sand Creek reserve. The Kiowas, Comanches, and Kiowa-Apaches were confined to a narrower reservation in northern Texas and the western part of present-day Oklahoma.[92] As usual the treaties proved ephemeral, for the Cheyennes and other plainsmen refused to relinquish the land of their ancestors.

92. Kappler, *Indian Affairs* 2:887–95; Charles C. Royce, "Indian Land Cessions in the United States," *Eighteenth Annual Report of the Bureau of American Ethnology* (Washington, D.C., 1896–97), p. 839.

CHAPTER II

Problems in Montana, the Great Basin, and the Southwest

The progression of events which led to the tragedy at Sand Creek recurred with variations in Montana, Nevada, Utah, Arizona, New Mexico, and on the Colorado–New Mexico border. Here the rapid movement of miners and farmers onto the hunting grounds of nomadic tribes and the resultant racial hostilities demanded concentration of the Indians on reservations for their own protection and for the welfare of nearby white communities. Here, too, the Indian Office failed to meet the challenge of change and preserve the peace. The spectacular rush to Montana set the pace for the Civil War years.

Shoshoni and Sioux bands occasionally invaded Montana, but the Crows and Blackfeet dominated the region prior to 1870. The Blackfoot nations, members of the Algonquin language family, consisted of three independent divisions—the Blackfoot proper, Piegan, and Blood—which in turn were subdivided into bands. These disciplined, wisely led nomads lived in tepees, followed the buffalo herds, and cultivated tobacco. James Mooney of the Bureau of American Ethnology termed them "a restless, aggressive, and predatory people," constantly at war with the Crees, Assiniboins, Sioux, Crows, Flatheads, and Kutenais.[1] Though the Blackfeet never fought formal wars with stalwart white pioneers, interracial contact was less than uplifting for these tribesmen. For example, in the mid-1830s when they reached the

1. Hodge, *Handbook of American Indians* 2:570.

peak of their power and numbered perhaps ten thousand, the smallpox swept through Blackfoot villages, carrying away about half the population. Again in 1845 and in 1857 the dread disease struck, and reduced their former strength to about one-third.[2] The Crows numbered about 460 lodges in 1862. Though part of the Siouan language family and as much a plains people as the Teton Sioux, the Crows had to defend their Yellowstone Valley hunting grounds against attacks from neighboring Blackfeet, Shoshonis, and Sioux. One frontiersman characterized the Crows as the "most treacherous and insolent of all the native tribes." And well he might, for they justified their reputation as skillful thieves. A dependence on the white man's trade goods induced affirmations of Crow friendship for the Great Father in Washington but did not rule out intermittent raids on immigrant trains.[3]

Intertribal warfare among the Montana bands abounded prior to 1851, despite the intercessions of fur traders and missionaries. Only when overland emigrants were thoroughly terrorized did the federal government assume the role of peacemaker.[4] Fruitful negotiations in the 1850s secured an apportionment of the Montana country as follows. Land west of the Continental Divide, with the exception of the Flathead reserve and part of the Bitterroot Valley, became public domain. Southwestern Montana was a common hunting ground as far north as the Musselshell, beyond which lay the Blackfoot reserve. The Assiniboin lands embraced much of northeastern Montana between the Missouri and Yellowstone Rivers. Crow country extended east of the common hunting ground as far as the Powder River, the western limit of the Arikara, Gros Ventres of the Missouri, and Mandan lands.[5]

2. Kenneth Ross Toole, *Montana: An Uncommon Land* (Norman, 1959), p. 120.

3. Hodge, *Handbook of American Indians* 1:368; Robert Edwin Albright, "The Relations of Montana with the Federal Government: 1864–1889," doctoral dissertation, Stanford University, 1933, p. 103; Granville Stuart, *Forty Years on the Frontier As Seen in the Journals and Reminiscences of Granville Stuart...*, ed. Paul C. Phillips (Glendale, Calif., 1957), p. 59.

4. Albright, "Relations of Montana with the Federal Government," p. 106.

5. Merrill G. Burlingame, "The Military-Indian Frontier in Montana, 1860–1890," doctoral dissertation, University of Iowa, 1936, p. 138A.

Indian problems in Montana during the Civil War years resulted from the rapid influx of whites after the July 1862 gold
strike on Grasshopper Creek. The town of Bannack was born
and by October boasted a population of 400. Virginia City,
Helena, and Diamond City sprang up in rapid succession during
the next two years as frenzied prospectors struck it rich in Alder,
Last Chance, and Confederate gulches.⁶ Westerners heady with
optimism flocked to the Montana mines from several directions.
James L. Fish pioneered a northern overland route from Minnesota in 1862. Though seasonal and not as direct, the Missouri
River was navigable by steamboat as far as Fort Benton. Farther
south miners trudged westward on the Oregon Trail to Fort
Hall, Idaho, then turned north to Montana. In the spring of 1863,
the Bozeman cutoff shortened the latter route considerably; laid
out by John Bozeman and John M. Jacobs, it branched northwest
from Fort Laramie, veered east of the Big Horn Mountains and
terminated at Bannack. The Mullan road, completed in 1863,
provided access to the gold fields from the Pacific Northwest.
Servicing Montana's mining population promised such handsome
profits that A. J. Oliver and Company opened a stage line from
Virginia City to Bannack and Salt Lake City in 1863. The following year shrewd Ben Holladay won a mail contract between
Fort Hall and Virginia City.⁷

In September 1864, Blackfoot Agent Gad E. Upson surveyed
the important changes which had taken place during the past
two years. Weekly discoveries of placer deposits lured at least
thirty thousand farmers and miners to the territory, who seized
control of valley after valley. Consequently, there was a pressing
need to modify federal Indian policy in newly organized Montana Territory.⁸

Though miners were more interested in finding gold than
molesting the natives, contacts between the races degraded the

6. Merrill G. Burlingame and K. Ross Toole, *A History of Montana* (3 vols.,
New York, 1957) 1:124–26.
7. William S. Greever, *The Bonanza West: The Story of the Western Mining
Rushes, 1848–1900* (Norman, 1963), pp. 223–25.
8. Upson to Dole, September 1, 1864, CIA, p. 442.

Montana tribes in several ways. In April 1864 the Sacramento (California) *Daily Union* printed the report of a gentleman recently returned from the Crow and Blackfoot country. What most impressed him was the rapid decline in the number of Indians and his failure to find a completely healthy red man in the mountains or on the plains. The culprits, white pioneers, overran the West and spread misery and pestilence among the aborigines. Doubtless these findings were exaggerated. Nevertheless, in 1865 Upson confirmed the decimating effects of communicable diseases. During the previous winter an epidemic of measles struck down approximately 280 Piegans, 150 Gros Ventres, and 1,500 Bloods and Blackfeet. The Bloods lost 50 tribal leaders, whose lodges remained as standing memorials when the tribe broke camp that spring. Ignorant of how a contagious virus could spread and refusing to believe that an angered Great Spirit willed their suffering, the Blackfoot confederacy accused whites of poisoning their annuity goods.[9] Nor were the Blackfeet alone in their suffering. Unhappy days had befallen their cousins in the Great Basin.

At noon on May 3, 1862, Joe Triplett left Carson City, Nevada, "bound for the sink of the Carson River, for the Truckee and Humboldt rivers, and for such other portions of this ill-begotten, God-forsaken, sage-brush, alkali, sand, lice and mosquito country, that used to be set down on the map when I was a boy, as Unexplored regions."[10] The Territory of Nevada, organized by Congress on March 2, 1861, evoked similar reactions from other travelers. The discovery of rich ore deposits on the eastern slope of the Sierras in 1859 touched off the rush to what was then western Utah. Home for nearly one-fourth of the 6,857 residents a year later was Carson City, soon to become Nevada's territorial capital. Sixteen miles east of Virginia City and the Comstock Lode, Carson City could boast of its newspaper, the *Territorial Enterprise*, its hotels, saloons, stores, telegraph office, school

9. Sacramento *Daily Union*, April 10, 1864; Upson to Dennis N. Cooley, October 2, 1864, CIA (1865), pp. 695–96.

10. Joe F. Triplett, "The Diary of Joe F. Triplett," transcribed by Edna B. Patterson, *Nevada Historical Society Quarterly* 2 (January–March, 1959): 3.

house, and water company.[11] James Warren Nye of New York City, a friend of Secretary of State Seward, was Lincoln's choice for Nevada's first territorial governor.[12]

In 1861 the Department of the Interior created a Nevada Superintendency, which embraced three Indian tribes. The Washos dwelt along the headwaters of the Carson, Walker, and Truckee Rivers and in the Long and Sierra Valleys, having been driven there by their eastern enemies, the Paiutes. When white Americans first encountered them, the degraded and docile Washos possessed no property of value. Estimated at about five hundred in the summer of 1861, their number had diminished rapidly due to disease and harsh treatment by whites. More than ten times as numerous and considerably more wealthy, the Paiutes likewise lived mainly in western Nevada. The tribe's political and social organization was neither complex nor cohesive, since its principal food sources of pine nuts, roots, seeds, and small game had to be gathered seasonally by small, scattered bands.[13] Along the Utah border to the east roamed three peaceful Shoshoni bands which the Nevada superintendent neglected during the war years, in part because of imprecise jurisdictional lines. Well-armed Bannock warriors, not under the province of the Nevada Indian Office, frequently ranged north of the forty-first parallel, terrorizing the Nevada tribesmen.[14]

The Indian Office was typically ill-prepared to solve the problems triggered by the rapid influx of whites into Nevada. The Carson Valley Agency had neither reservations nor Indian schools for the Paiutes and Washos in the early sixties. The Secretary of the Interior had set aside the Walker River reserve in

11. *Population of the United States in 1860*, p. iv; J. Ross Browne, "A Peep at Washoe," *Harper's New Monthly Magazine* 22 (January, 1861): 150; Hubert Howe Bancroft, *History of Nevada, Colorado, and Wyoming 1540–1888* (San Francisco, 1890), pp. 169–71.

12. Tegeder, "Lincoln and the Territorial Patronage," pp. 85–86.

13. Hodge, *Handbook of American Indians* 2:187–88, 920; Warren Wasson to Nye, July 13, 1861, enclosed in Nye to Caleb Smith, July 19, 1861, CIA, pp. 723–24.

14. Nye to Dole, October 27, 1863, CIA, p. 536; John C. Burche to Nye, August 1, 1864, CIA, p. 292.

November 1859, but Eugene Monroe's survey would not be made until December 1864.[15]

The mercurial movements of white miners and their camp followers left the red men of western Nevada destitute by 1861. A case in point was the Washos. Fish, a major food source, vanished from streams diverted, dammed, and polluted by miners, and could no longer be taken from Lake Bigler (Lake Tahoe), which came under the control of vacationing Californians. The simultaneous exodus of game reduced the Indians to gathering large bugs and a weed called tulé. By 1862 white encroachment had also undermined the Paiutes' economy, making them restless and irritable. Cattlemen bribed one chief to permit the grazing of stock on Indian land, but Nye revoked the agreement lest the federal government and the Paiutes be held responsible for lost or stolen animals.[16] Gold discoveries near Big Meadows triggered more trespassing and such harassment by the Indians that the governor stationed John C. Burche there for the winter to forestall bloodshed. White penetration of Indian lands intensified in 1864, when large numbers of immigrants bound for Idaho mining districts traversed two hundred miles of the Humboldt region claimed by the Paiutes and Bannocks. Yet northern Nevada was more than a highway to Idaho. Attracted by mineral deposits and the fecundity of the soil along the Humboldt and its tributaries, many pioneers stopped to settle. The resultant destruction of game, seed-bearing grass and pine nut trees impaired the Indian economy as it had in the Sierra foothills.[17]

Such were the major thrusts of Nevada's white population in the early 1860s and their economic effects on the red man. The Indian Office was left to deal with vengeful native outbreaks and the pressing need to concentrate the red men on reserves away from immigrant trails.

15. Wasson to Nye, August 13, 1861, CIA, p. 720; Royce, "Indian Land Cessions in the United States," p. 873.

16. Lieutenant E. M. Baker to Adjutant, Fort Churchill, October 20, 1861, OR, Ser. 1, 50, Pt. 1, p. 667; Nye to Caleb Smith, July 19, 1861, CIA, pp. 721–22; Nye to Dole, February 3, 1862, CIA, p. 359.

17. Nye to Dole, February 3, 1862, CIA, p. 366; Burche to Nye, August 1, 1864, CIA, pp. 288–89.

The Indian Office faced a similar set of circumstances with four Southern Ute bands on the New Mexico–Colorado border. The Tabeguaches roamed the Los Pinos Valley, and with the organization of Colorado Territory in 1861 an agency was established for them at Conejos under Lafayette Head.[18] The Indian Office assigned three other bands to agencies in New Mexico. The Moache Utes and Jicarilla Apaches, together numbering about 1,500, reported to a field office of rented buildings at Lucien B. Maxwell's ranch on the beautiful Cimarron River, fifty miles east of Taos. Though the tribes received annuities, they continued to roam where they pleased, raiding Navajo camps and selling captives to Mexicans.[19] At the Abiquiu Agency, about forty miles southwest of Taos, Agent José Antonio Mausinares distributed presents to 2,500 Capote and Wiminuche Utes, who ranged forty thousand square miles in eastern Utah, western Colorado and northwest New Mexico.[20]

Several parties of Ute chiefs journeyed to Santa Fe during the early months of 1861 to protest the invasion of the Rio San Juan by miners, who had erected buildings, planted crops and obviously sought possession of the land. Superintendent James L. Collins sent an Office official to the mines to preserve peace, if possible, and promised the Indians he would write to Washington on their behalf. Yet it seemed inevitable that the Utes would lose their homeland. Even if the mines proved disappointing, the whites would stay to farm. Collins urged that the Utes at least be compensated for the loss of their hunting grounds,[21] but the United States Senate, disgusted with the capriciousness of New Mexico's Navajos and Apaches, refused ratification of any cession treaties. Dole told his superintendent to assure the Indians that the government knew of their complaints and that until Congress took action they should maintain friendly relations

18. Hodge, *Handbook of American Indians* 2:664; Dole to Collins, April 15, 1861, OIA, FOR, New Mexico Supty., LR.

19. William F. M. Arny to Dole, January 6, 1862, OIA, LR, New Mexico Supty.

20. Mausinares to Collins, September 3, 1862, CIA, p. 391.

21. Collins to Alfred B. Greenwood, January 13, 1861, and Collins to Dole, April 7, 1861, OIA, LR, New Mexico Supty.

with the United States. Though Collins was instructed to prevent further encroachments by settlers, this was impossible without government intervention.[22]

Destruction of game by miners forced the Utes to visit their agencies or to steal cattle and grain from white ranches and farms. Peace thus became somewhat contingent on the Indian Office's regular issuance of supplies. In the fall of 1862, when the New Mexico Superintendency could furnish only half the goods needed for the winter, Moache and Jicarilla chiefs warned that there would be more thefts unless the Indians received enough supplies. Being too late for a congressional appropriation, acting governor William F. M. Arny appealed to the district military commander, General James H. Carleton, for beef cattle. Carleton delivered sixty head to Superintendent Collins at Fort Union, which temporarily staved off raids.[23] But the Utes pillaged again that winter and during the spring of 1863.

Whether due to the rapid advance of miners, farmers, stage lines or the like, racial conflicts blazed in many western areas besides the land of the Cheyennes. Fought between Americans of differing views, these too were civil wars.

When the United States acquired Mexico's northern provinces in 1848 by the Treaty of Guadalupe Hidalgo, the victorious Americans fell heir to the native peoples of the Southwest. The Navajos, numbering between twelve and fifteen thousand, inhabited an extensive area in what is now northwestern New Mexico and adjoining portions of northern Arizona, southern Utah, and southern Colorado. This arid, canyon-cut tableland provided excellent pasturage for cattle, sheep, and goats, the Indians' principal sources of wealth, while in the Canyon de Chelly, an inner bastion, they raised crops and tended orchards. Also a predatory people, the Navajos raided Pueblo and Mexican settlements, enabling restless young warriors to seize captives and to amass horse and sheep herds of their own. The tribe's political

22. Dole to Collins, May 9, 1861, OIA, FOR, New Mexico Supty., LR.

23. Arny to Carleton, October 25, 1862, and Carleton to Amos F. Garrison, October 29, 1862, both enclosed in Arny to Dole, November 3, 1862, CIA, pp. 393–94.

structure was nominal, like that of other nomadic peoples. Each local band was autonomous and there was no tribal council.[24] More troublesome to the white man were the Apaches: fierce, speedy, shrewd, and nearly as numerous as the Navajos. These warriors neither grew crops nor tended flocks, but lived off the game and native products of their domain and the plunder seized during marauding excursions against isolated ranches. Apacheria, their rugged stronghold, extended from the Pecos to the Colorado River, and from southern Colorado and Utah to northern Mexico. Loosely knit Jicarilla and Mescalero bands lived in New Mexico; the Gilas (Mimbreños, Mogollon, Arivaipa and Chiricahua) were scattered about the headwaters of the Gila River in southwestern New Mexico and southeastern Arizona; the Western Apaches roamed the Arizona country.[25] John Cremony, a captain in the California Volunteers during the Civil War, wrote of the self-reliant Apaches in 1868:

> In point of intellect, in cunning and duplicity, in warlike skill and untiring energy, in tenacity of purpose and wondrous powers of endurance, the Apaches have no equals among the existing Indians of North America. . . .
>
> Cautious, suspicious, treacherous and crafty, the Apache meets all other races on the ground of distrust and doubt. . . . he is a viper, an untamable, ferocious, sanguinary monster, bent upon the destruction of all with whom he comes in contact, and only restrained by fear.[26]

The Apaches and Navajos professed peaceful intentions toward their new American sovereigns, yet hostilities continued in the Southwest throughout the 1850s due to white encroachment, the Indians' traditional hostility to Europeans, their warlike cultures, and their predatory economies. Despite the recommendations of James S. Calhoun and other Indian agents that the New Mexican nomads be forced onto reservations, Congress did

24. Dale, *Indians of the Southwest*, p. 21; Alvin M. Josephy, Jr., *The Indian Heritage of America* (New York, 1968), p. 173.

25. Hodge, *Handbook of American Indians* 1:66.

26. John C. Cremony, "The Apache Race," *The Overland Monthly* 1 (September, 1868): 203, 205.

not appropriate adequate funds or authorize the creation of reserves. Military impotence was another problem. The army constructed a chain of forts along the Rio Grande and across southern New Mexico prior to the Civil War, but it garrisoned them with poorly trained and equipped infantry rather than cavalry.[27]

During the early 1860s the Indian Office operated under wartime conditions, as hostile tribes pillaged and whites retaliated. In 1862 the Navajos alone stole a hundred thousand sheep and a thousand head of cattle. Other statistics were more alarming: 62 New Mexicans killed, 134 wounded. No part of the land over which the marauders roamed remained safe for unescorted travel.[28] The capture and enslavement of Indian children by Mexican vigilantes, bitter enemies of the Navajos and Apaches since the days when Sante Fe was a distant outpost of the Spanish Empire, intensified hostilities and incited retaliatory raids, often against innocent frontier ranchers. Kidnapped children sold for $200 to $300 throughout the territory. Estimates of their number at the beginning of the decade ranged from six hundred to two thousand.[29]

Far to the north, in Montana, Blackfoot antagonism toward invading miners and farmers who enveloped their hunting grounds also eroded hopes for peace. Red belligerence first took the form of horse stealing, but after the measles epidemic during the winter of 1864–65 and the murder of five Indians in May 1865, they retaliated by slaughtering ten white woodcutters at the mouth of the Marias. Agent Upson insisted the tribesmen had

27. Warren A. Beck, *New Mexico: A History of Four Centuries* (Norman, 1962), pp. 178ff; A. B. Bender, "Frontier Defense in the Territory of New Mexico," *New Mexico Historical Review* 9 (October, 1934): 372–73.

28. Lorenzo Labadi to Collins, September 25, 1862, CIA, pp. 391–92; Memorial of the Legislative Assembly of the Territory of New Mexico to the President of the United States and the Secretary of War, January 26, 1863, OIA, Records of the Civilization Division.

29. William Need (for Don Manuel Garcia, Alcalde of Cubero, New Mexico) to Collins, May 16, 1862, OIA, FOR, New Mexico Supty., 1862 (Misc.); Memorial of the Legislative Assembly of the Territory of New Mexico to the United States Senate and House of Representatives, January 24, 1863, OIA, Records of the Civilization Division; Michael Steck to Dole, January 13, 1864, OIA, LR, New Mexico Supty.

no desire for a war to the death; many had fled to Canada and those left behind behaved themselves.[30] Nevertheless, in this atmosphere of horse stealing, frontier greed, pestilence, intertribal warfare, and broken treaties, the prospect for peace in the territory was indeed remote. The same was true for Utah and Nevada.

In the course of a summer stagecoach journey across the trans-Mississippi West in 1865, Massachusetts journalist Samuel Bowles was struck by the virtuousness of the Mormans. Small wonder they deemed themselves a chosen people, he felt. Their leaders were wise, the Saints hard working and thrifty, their homeland "the richest region . . . between the Mississippi valley and the Pacific shore. . . ."[31]

Utah was indeed a magnificent land. The Wasatch Range, its most conspicuous feature, ran majestically from the northern to the central portion of the territory, while the Uintah Mountains stretched east and west along the northeastern border. Marching off to the south was the rugged and immense Colorado Plateau. The western third of the territory formed part of the semi-arid Great Basin, within whose confines lay Great Salt Lake and the salt flats of the Great Salt Lake Desert.

Estimated to number twenty-thousand in June 1861, the Indians of Utah belonged to the Shoshonean language family. Three bands of Northern Utes—Uintah, White River, and Uncompahgre (Tabeguache)—inhabited the eastern portion of the territory. The introduction of horses intensified their warlike culture and by the mid-nineteenth century they were entirely nomadic, deriving their living from trade with the Navajos, hunting buffalo, and gathering roots, nuts, and berries.[32] From the Snake River country of Idaho, Shoshoni bands pushed into

30. Upson to Cooley, October 2, 1865, CIA, pp. 694-95; John C. Ewers, *The Blackfeet: Raiders on the Northwestern Plains* (Norman, 1958), p. 238.

31. Samuel Bowles, *Across the Continent: A Summer's Journey to the Rocky Mountains, the Mormons, and the Pacific States, with Speaker Colfax* (Springfield, Mass., 1865), p. 79.

32. Benjamin Davies to Dole, June 30, 1861, CIA, p. 742; Dale, *Indians of the Southwest*, p. 23; Hodge, *Handbook of American Indians* 2:874.

northern Utah in pursuit of bison. Their friendliness toward the Bannocks and Utes did not extend to such plainsmen as the Sioux, Arapahos, and Crows.[33] Whites classified as "Diggers" the poorer, unmounted Western Shoshoni and Northern Ute bands which roamed the bleak Great Basin. This derogatory epithet soon applied to any Far Western desert tribe dependent upon roots for food and which, because of its subsistence-level economy and elementary technology, appeared to be low on the scale of civilization.[34] Other Utah Diggers included the Paiutes and Gosiutes. The latter, numbering about eight hundred in the mid-sixties, wandered west of Great Salt Lake and Utah Lake, subsisting on roots, fish, and pine nuts, since they possessed no horses or guns. Seven or eight times as numerous and considerably more hostile, the Paiutes roamed southern Utah. Though equally as destitute as the Gosiutes, the Paiutes cultivated small grain fields along meandering streams.[35]

No full-scale Indian war was in progress when the Lincoln administration took office, but minor depredations occurred in Utah—emigrants robbed, mail carriers waylaid, white settlers attacked. Superintendent Benjamin Davies blamed these outrages on the Indians' loss of confidence in the federal government.[36] Whatever their cause, the tenuous overland route had to be protected, and in mid-November General George Wright, head of the military Department of the Pacific, received orders to send two or three regiments of California Volunteers to police the trail as far east as Salt Lake City. Mountain passes, choked with snow, prevented the immediate consignment of troops; Wright therefore authorized the Overland Mail agent to issue at government expense a limited amount of supplies to starving Indians along its Great Basin route.[37]

33. Luther Mann to Orasmus H. Irish, September 28, 1865, CIA, p. 327.

34. Bernard DeVoto, *The Year of Decision: 1846* (Boston, 1943), p. 337.

35. Irish to Cooley, September 9, 1865, CIA, pp. 312–14.

36. Davies to Dole, June 30, 1861, CIA, p. 739.

37. Aurora Hunt, *The Army of the Pacific: Its Operations in California, Texas, Arizona, New Mexico, Utah, Nevada, Oregon, Washington, Plains Region, Mexico, etc. 1860–1866* (Glendale, Calif., 1958), p. 186; Wright to Louis McLane, December 16, 1861, OR, Ser. 1, 50, Pt. 1, p. 766.

Problems with the hostiles worsened in 1862. Since the previous spring many Eastern Shoshonis had rejected the leadership of Chief Washakie, noted for his friendship toward whites; they turned instead to Chief Pash-e-co to lead them in resisting the emigrant influx. Fighting commenced in March when Pash-e-co's warriors simultaneously swept down on overland way stations between the North Platte and Salt Lake City. That summer the Bannocks helped hostile Shoshonis to carry death and destruction to much of northern Utah.[38] Washington took steps to protect the vital stage and telegraph lines. At Lincoln's request a Mormon volunteer company guarded the six hundred miles of trail east of Salt Lake City; to patrol the western segment the army sent the Third California Infantry and the Second California Cavalry under Colonel (later General) Patrick E. Connor, who established Camp Douglas at the mouth of Red Butte Canyon, three miles east of Salt Lake City.[39] Congress appropriated $20,000 during the summer of 1862 to secure a treaty of friendship with the Shoshonis and to compensate them for game driven away by travelers, but due to the lateness of the season and the difficulty of gathering the hostiles for peace talks, no negotiations took place.[40] As winter descended on the Utah country, the danger of a general outbreak persisted.

The climax came early the following year. Provoked by Shoshoni and Bannock winter raids, particularly those of a large band under chiefs Bear Hunter, Pocatello, and Sagwitch camped near Bear River in what is today southern Idaho, Connor marched northward in January and snapped the hostiles' power in the bloody battle of Bear River. Bluecoats killed more than 200 Indians, including Bear Hunter; they destroyed provisions and lodges, rounded up 175 ponies, and took 160 prisoners. In the April battle of Spanish Fork Canyon, 200 cavalrymen commanded by Lieutenant Colonel George S. Evans gave the Utes a similar

38. Virginia Cole Trenholm and Maurine Carley, *The Shoshonis: Sentinels of the Rockies* (Norman, 1964), pp. 188–91; CIA, 1862, p. 185.

39. Margaret M. Fisher, comp. and ed., *Utah and the Civil War ...* (Salt Lake City, 1929), p. 27; Colton, *Civil War in the Western Territories*, p. 163.

40. *United States Statutes at Large* 12:529; CIA, 1862, pp. 185–86.

object lesson. Throughout the summer and fall Connor sent soldiers from Fort Bridger, Camp Douglas, and Camp Connor (at Soda Springs) to search for other obstinate hostiles.[41] Such relentlessness together with Connor's skillful deployment of troops demonstrated for the first time United States mastery of the western portions of the Oregon and California trails.

As for Nevada, peace prevailed in July 1861 when a party of Indian Office employees with Governor Nye, ex officio superintendent of Indian affairs, distributed presents among the territory's western tribesmen. An escort of dragoons from Fort Churchill accompanied the party to Walker Lake, where they counciled with a dozen leaders who pledged to keep the peace with white Nevadans and immigrants passing through the territory. After parceling out gifts, Nye's party returned to the garrison on August 1. The next morning an army detachment accompanied them to Pyramid Lake for another parley, with the same encouraging results. Only the Shoshonis marred a placid picture that summer. Encouraged by the death of Chief Shokup, intractable headman Buck sought to restore Indian primacy in the territory by driving out the whites. Nye sent provisions to Ruby Valley in hopes of halting the raids on overland stations, but the forays continued.[42]

To curtail depredations along Nevada's overland trail during the winter of 1861–62, General Wright transferred to Governor Nye large quantities of flour and meat to feed starving Indians. The Owens River War, which erupted in southern California in March 1862, threatened to involve the skittish and impoverished Paiutes of Nevada until Agent Jacob T. Lockhart sent Warren Wasson to pacify them. That fall serious Shoshonis and Gosiutes attacks necessitated stationing troops in Ruby Valley to patrol the overland route between the Utah line and Austin, Nevada.[43]

41. Colton, *Civil War in the Western Territories*, pp. 164–65; Robert M. Utley, *Frontiersmen in Blue: The United States Army and the Indian, 1848–1865* (New York, 1967), pp. 224–25.

42. Nye to Caleb Smith, August 14, 1861, CIA, pp. 717–18; Nye to Seward, July 20, 1861, General Records of the Department of State, Nevada Territorial Papers, National Archives.

43. Wright to Nye, December 2, 1861, enclosed in Nye to Dole, February

General Connor's chastisement of Utah hostiles inhibited poten-
tial Nevada troublemakers in 1863. Except for occasional attacks
in March and May on prospecting parties in the Humboldt
Mountains, Nevada Indians remained peaceful during most of
1864. In his fall report Nye credited this to his stationing of
agents in the areas most frequented by the Indians. Yet race relations took a turn for the worse that December, when marauding
Indians stepped up their raids in eastern Nevada.[44]

With hostiles temporarily cowed in Utah but still ravaging in
Montana, the Southwest, and Nevada, Indian Office field officials
turned to their stock procedure to promote peace and protect
Indian rights: separation of the races and assemblage of the red
men on isolated reservations.

Lincoln's 1861 executive order setting aside Uintah Valley for
the Indians laid the foundation for concentration in Utah Territory. Well watered by the Uintah River and its tributaries, well
timbered, surrounded by mountain ranges, and isolated from the
major commercial routes, these two million acres provided an
ideal site for a reservation.[45] Yet years passed before it became an
important Indian sanctuary. Not that official support was lacking. During the early sixties when the hostiles were on the ram-
page, Superintendent James Duane Doty emphasized that only
by keeping the races apart could the Indian be brought under
government control and the peace maintained. To collect the
Utes in the Uintah Valley would also preserve reservation improvements and encourage Indian agriculture. In January 1864
the Utah Assembly urged Lincoln to do away with existing small,
scattered reserves. Two months later Dole recommended that
they be opened to white farmers. In May Congress authorized

3, 1862, OIA, LR, Nevada Supty.; Agent Jacob T. Lockhart to Nye, June 15,
1862, enclosed in Nye to Dole, June 17, 1862, CIA, p. 372; Trenholm and Carley,
The Shoshonis, p. 186.

44. Myron Angel, ed., *History of Nevada* ... (Oakland, Calif., 1881; reproduced in Berkeley, 1958), p. 169; Nye to Usher, September 20, 1864, CIA, p. 283.

45. Royce, "Indian Land Cessions," p. 824; Amos Reed to Doty, September
12, 1862, enclosed in Doty to Dole, September 12, 1862, CIA, pp. 344, 346;
Hubert Howe Bancroft, *History of Utah, 1540–1886* (San Francisco, 1889), p.
635.

the sale of all Utah reservations except the Uintah Valley and appropriated $30,000 for relocation costs and making the tribesmen self-supporting farmers.[46]

Great was the need for concentration and instruction in agricultural techniques. With game driven away or destroyed, with former hunting grounds in the hands of emigrant farmers, the government had to provide a new livelihood for the Indians; otherwise it would risk another rash of Indian attacks or the permanent support of scattered and impoverished native families.

Establishing sanctuaries for their red men was also the goal of the Indian Office in Nevada. As early as July 1861 Governor Nye advocated agriculture and cattle raising for red men whose traditional food sources were no longer adequate. In February 1862 he advocated settling the nomadic Shoshonis on a reserve in their own country as the best way to control them. The commissioner concurred and directed the governor to select tracts for Nevada Indians which had natural boundaries and sufficient arable soil, grazing land, water, and timber for the natives' present and future wants.[47] Nye reoccupied the Ruby Valley reservation and placed an agent there following the October 1863 Shoshonis treaty. By confining its activities to the vicinity, the tribe signified its approval. In the belief that the Paiutes would not be able to keep their lands on both the Walker and Truckee Rivers, Nye and Agent Lockhart focused their efforts during 1863 and 1864 on the fertile Truckee. If it could support all the western Nevada Indians, perhaps the aborigines might be permitted to keep the Truckee, and only the Walker Valley would be opened to whites. Fortunately for the Nevada Indians, the Interior Department instructed Lockhart in February 1864 to survey the boundaries for two reservations. When Eugene Monroe marked off the Walker River reserve in December,[48] the sixty-by-twelve-

46. Doty to Dole, June 20, 1863, CIA, p. 539; Dole to William Windom, Chairman of the House Committee on Indian Affairs, March 2, 1864, OIA, Report Books, 13:322.

47. Nye to Caleb Smith, July 19, 1861, CIA, p. 722; Nye to Dole, February 3, 1862, CIA, p. 365; Dole to Nye, April 5, 1862, OIA, LS, 68:40.

48. Nye to Usher, September 20, 1864, CIA, p. 284; Nye to Dole, October 27, 1863, CIA, p. 537; Royce, "Indian Land Cessions," p. 873.

mile sanctuary encompassed the lower sections of the Walker River and all of Walker Lake—a hundred square miles of sparkling blue water. Cutthroat trout taken from the lake by Paiute fishermen remained their principal food source.[49] In January Monroe delineated the Pyramid Lake reserve, which embraced the lower Truckee River and Pyramid Lake, the largest body of water entirely within the state. Though established for the Washos as well as the Paiutes, intertribal hostility and the Paiutes' superior numbers deprived the Washos of this haven.[50]

Early in 1865 Agent Upson felt it a propitious time to gather up Montana's troublesome tribesmen. Whites had penetrated many of the western valleys, the Blackfoot treaty of 1855 would soon expire and the Crows wanted a new treaty. At the urgent request of Montana civil authorities as well as the Interior Department, Congress appropriated $15,000 that March for a new agreement with the Blackfoot confederation and the Gros Ventres, in order to open gold-rich territory south of the Missouri.[51]

At Fort Benton in mid-November 1865, Upson met with the principal Piegan and Gros Ventres chiefs, a few Blood headmen, and one Blackfoot. With a promise of generous annuities and the added inducement of personal cash gifts, tribal chiefs ceded much of western Montana. The hollowness of Upson's diplomatic triumph became apparent less than two months later, when Piegan and Blood raiders slew several white prospectors and traders, and the commissioner of Indian affairs refused to recommend ratification of the treaty.[52]

The wisdom of gathering the Utes on reservations was not lost to Colorado and New Mexican officials. There could be no devel-

49. Statement of Agent Franklin Campbell, September 11, 1865, JSC, pp. 514–15.

50. Royce, "Indian Land Cessions," p. 873; Nye to Caleb Smith, August 14, 1861, CIA, p. 719.

51. Upson to Dole, January 17, 1865, enclosed in Mix to Usher, January 21, 1865, ID, LR; Usher to Thaddeus Stevens, January 27, 1865, Records of the Legislative Branch, House Committee on Indian Affairs, Wartime Records, 38 Cong., National Archives; *United States Statutes at Large* 13:559.

52. Ewers, *The Blackfeet*, pp. 239–40.

opment of mineral regions or improvement of the Indians' condition until each Ute band was restricted to a remote reservation with fixed limits and trained to be self-sufficient. Dole recommended such a program and in July 1863 instructed Governor Evans of Colorado to meet with the Utes in conjunction with representatives of the New Mexico Superintendency. Dole suggested the San Juan Valley as a suitable place to settle the bands, though he gave the commissioners discretion to select other locations.[53]

The council at Conejos, Colorado Territory, in October 1863 was partly successful. No New Mexican Utes and only one Colorado band attended the parley, probably because of their unwillingness to give up the chase and to be attached to the Colorado Superintendency. Nonetheless, the government concluded an important treaty with the Tabeguaches in which the band accepted a restricted hunting ground (not a reservation) in the Gunnison Valley and relinquished about half its lands in return for annuities.[54] Governor Evans described the region as "one of the most extensive and perhaps the most valuable cessions ever secured in a single treaty from any tribe of Indians in the country. It included all of the settled portions of the mountains and of the San Louis valley, and also most of the valuable mines yet discovered in the Territory, as well as secured the privilege of mining on any part of their lands reserved from the cession."[55]

That the reservation system was the only way to solve New Mexico's Indian problem became obvious to northern field officials following the Confederate invasion in 1862. General Carleton approved the policy, as did long-time New Mexico resident Governor Henry Connelly, Secretary Arny (a former Indian agent) and Superintendent Collins. There was really no alternative to concentrating the Navajos, Apaches, and Utes on reserves;

53. CIA, 1862, p. 187; Dole to Evans, July 22, 1863, OIA, FOR, New Mexico Supty., LR.
54. Steck to Dole, October 10, 1863, OIA, FOR, New Mexico Supty., LR; John G. Nicolay to Dole, November 10, 1863, CIA, p. 267; Kappler, *Indian Affairs* 2:856–59.
55. Evans to Dole, October 14, 1863, CIA, p. 244.

they could neither be permitted to wander about perpetrating depredations nor be ruthlessly exterminated.[56]

Such a policy offered many advantages. For New Mexico's more than 86,000 non-Indians it promised safety in addition to the peaceful and speedy development of their territory's agricultural and mineral resources. Also the system would cost the government far less than the three million dollars annually spent on half-hearted, fruitless military campaigns.[57] Theoretically the Indians could benefit from this plan as well. In exchange for the bulk of their lands and acceptance of a sedentary life, they would be protected from slavehunters, guaranteed an annuity of clothing and other provisions, and receive farming equipment, blacksmith and carpentry services, industrial schools for the children, and instruction in farming techniques.[58]

Once the reservation plan was agreed upon in various superintendencies, there arose the problem of implementing it. This formed the crux of the Indian Office's administrative difficulties in Colorado and elsewhere, and the record shows that its agents and superintendents found very few answers. The reasons were several. First, the task of rounding up the Indians became difficult when the military lacked strength to aid the Interior Department. Twice in 1865 Montana Agent Upson recommended the establishment of needed military posts in the Blackfoot country, preferably near Fort Benton and the mouths of the Musselshell, Powder, and Yellowstone Rivers. Such a show of force would curtail Blackfoot raids, protect Montana miners, and open up to whites the valleys of the Big Horn, Powder, Tongue, and Rosebud, which hostile Sioux previously made impassable. Upson had advanced proposals of this sort for the previous two years, and maintained that if they had been heeded there would have been less bloodshed in 1865.[59] Such military weakness in dealing with nomadic tribesmen prevailed throughout much of the West.

56. Collins to Dole, October 8, 1861, CIA, p. 735.

57. *Population of the United States in 1860*, p. iv; Arny to Collins, September 24, 1861, CIA, p. 738; Beck, *New Mexico*, p. 188.

58. Arny to Dole, January 6, 1862, OIA, LR, New Mexico Supty.

59. Upson to Dole, January 17, 1865, enclosed in Mix to Usher, January 21, 1865, ID, LR; Upson to Cooley, October 2, 1865, CIA, p. 696.

The most impotent agency of all was the Indian Office. Its staff lacked a police force under its own command and grew frustrated by the futility of negotiation. In New Mexico, for example, when public dissatisfaction mounted early in 1862 regarding the government's handling of the Indian problem, Superintendent Collins responded in the press. What was the Indian Office to do? How could it procure the arrest and trial of young bucks guilty of committing crimes in the territory when the superintendency had but five agents and a subagent on its staff, each of whom resided in a different part of the territory and must inevitably be far from the scene of a crime? By the time an official learned of such an incident, the Indian had already escaped into the mountains. Agents had no authorization to raise a posse of citizens. Furthermore, the Office rarely knew which tribe committed a particular attack, much less the individual warriors involved. The entire system seemed designed to embarrass the Indian Office.[60]

The futility of negotiation compounded the dilemma in New Mexico. Because the Indian felt superior to the white, he regarded peace offers as signs of weakness, motivated by fear. The red man used treaties, when he signed them, simply to win time to build up his forces or to placate the whites. In either case, the covenant was no more than a ruse.[61] In addition, wrote John Cremony of the Apaches,

> If a hundred or more of them were gathered together to sign a treaty, that instrument would be binding upon none but the absolute signers. Every other individual present, although consenting by such presence, would hold himself entirely free from its conditions. What follows? Those who have not bound themselves continued their original course of depredations and massacres; we accuse them of want of faith and treachery, and forthwith proceed to punish the offenders. Hostilities are again urged on either side, and those who did sign claim that we have violated our contract.[62]

60. Santa Fe *Weekly Gazette*, January 18, 1862.
61. Beck, *New Mexico*, pp. 177–78; Ruth M. Underhill, *The Navajos* (Norman, 1956), pp. 112–13.
62. Cremony, "The Apache Race," p. 206.

By 1862 the Navajos had broken six treaties with the United States before the Senate could act upon them. Therefore, officials of the New Mexico Superintendency agreed to turn the hostiles over to the military for chastisement.[63]

Indian Office impotence in Montana stemmed partially from inattentiveness. No agent had set foot in the Blackfoot country for a year and a half when Upson began his tenure in December 1863. Affairs in central Montana mirrored this neglect. Not only was Upson compelled to use rooms at Fort Benton for storage and office space, but communications were inordinately long and tenuous. For at least six months each year no correspondence whatever could be carried on with Washington. In light of Indian attitudes that winter, such isolation also proved dangerous for Upson and other whites. Some Indians had already become hostiles. Many others grumbled about the Great Father's inability or unwillingness to fulfill treaty obligations.[64]

Blackfoot complaints about annuities were legitimate. Due to the Missouri's unusually low waters, the 1863 payment in goods could not be shipped to Fort Benton until the fall of 1864, when that year's supplies also arrived. The following year the military commander of Fort Union (at the mouth of the Yellowstone) seized Blackfoot annuities thinking the tribe hostile—a false assumption according to Upson. When the army released the goods, the Missouri waters had fallen and Upson had to haul them overland to Fort Benton.[65]

Similar supply problems occurred in southern Colorado following the Conejos treaty of October 1863. Governor Evans tried to restrict the Tabeguache Utes to the Gunnison Valley but they continued to wander through the settlements in their old hunting grounds. The band grew particularly restless during the winter of 1864–65 when plains warfare and deep mountain snows prevented supplies from reaching Conejos. By spring the starv-

63. Steck to Dole, September 19, 1863, CIA, pp. 225–26; Collins to Dole, October 10, 1862, CIA, p. 385.

64. Upson to Dole, September 1, 1864, CIA, pp. 437, 441.

65. Upson to Dole, *ibid.*, pp. 437, 439–40; Upson to Cooley, October 2, 1865, CIA, p. 697.

ing Tabegauches, angered by unfulfilled promises, bivouacked around Colorado City and stole food. Special funds for the band were unavailable to Evans until June.[66] The New Mexican Utes also became troublesome. The Wiminuches and Capotes, for example, raided ranches because of the scarcity of game and the failure of government supplies to arrive during the winter of 1864–65.[67] Transferred by fiat to the Colorado Superintendency in February 1864, the Moaches refused to leave New Mexico and settle among the Tabeguaches, though Colorado was their original home. The agent informed them that supplies would only be issued at Conejos. Still they refused to move and continued to commit minor offenses, such as stealing stock. By September 1864 many had drifted north into Colorado.[68]

In Utah, gathering up the Indians was also painfully slow. The Indian Commissioner attributed the delay to the Interior Department's insufficient knowledge about the resources of the Uintah Valley and the military's determination to punish certain hostiles beforehand. Also noted in superintendency correspondence was the Paiutes' fear of the Utes and consequent unwillingness to share the Uintah Valley.[69] After additional prodding by Congress to extinguish Indian title to good farming and mining lands, ex-governor Brigham Young, Superintendent Orasmus H. Irish, and other federal officials counciled with the Utes early in June 1865. The tribe pledged to move to the Uintah Valley and to abandon claims to all other lands in return for more than a million dollars in annuities.[70] Because the treaty failed ratification, the concentration plan was postponed until March 1868, when the Indian Office established a reserve in western Colorado for all the Utes

66. John Evans, Interview with H. H. Bancroft, 1884, Hubert Howe Bancroft Collection, Bancroft Library, pp. 13–14; Lafayette Head to Dole, April 25, 1865, and Evans to Dole, June 3, 1865, OIA, LR, Colorado Supty.

67. Frank D. Reeve, "The Federal Indian Policy in New Mexico, 1858–1880," *New Mexico Historical Review* 13 (April, 1938): 146.

68. Ferdinand Maxwell to Dole, August 25, 1864, CIA, pp. 345–46; Steck to Dole, October 10, 1864, CIA, pp. 325–26.

69. CIA, 1864, pp. 160–61; Special Agent Thomas Sale to Irish, May 4, 1865, enclosed in Irish to Dole, May 15, 1865, CIA, p. 323.

70. Dole to Irish, March 28, 1865, CIA, p. 316; OIA, Documents Relating to Ratified and Unratified Treaties, Unratified.

of that territory and Utah north of the Rio San Juan and east of the Colorado and Green Rivers. The Uintah Valley was held for other Utah tribes. In the 1880s Ute chiefs ceded lands in the Silver State and their people returned to reserves in Mormon country.[71]

71. Kappler, *Indian Affairs* 2:990–96; Hodge, *Handbook of American Indians* 2:875.

CHAPTER III

Mormons, Rebels, and Generals

Varied and challenging as the Indian Office's administrative problems were in Colorado, ex officio Superintendent Evans evaded certain thorny issues which hampered his counterparts in other western territories. These included fiscal troubles, whiskey traders, intertribal warfare, disunion within the white community, and jurisdictional bouts with the War Department.

All told, the Indian Office in Utah administered three reserves and two farms which had reservation status. At Fort Bridger Agency in present-day southwest Wyoming, Luther Mann supervised the affairs of neighboring Shoshonis and Bannocks. Spanish Fork covered about fifteen thousand acres along the southern shore of Utah Lake, and during most of the Civil War years Frederick W. Hatch served as agent for its six Ute bands and some Shoshonis, Gosiutes, and Paiutes. Only Kibe's band of Utes lived permanently at Spanish Fork; the others hunted and fished primarily in Uintah Valley and on the Green River. Because his predecessor sold most movable agency property in order to feed his charges, Hatch found much to be done. The farm needed to be restocked, fences repaired, the dam on Spanish Fork reinforced.[1] Established in 1859 for the Gosiutes and western Sho-

1. A Humphreys to Dole, September 30, 1861, CIA, p. 750; Hatch to Doty, September 16, 1862, CIA, pp. 350–51; Henry Martin to Dole, October 1, 1861, CIA, p. 746.

71

shonis, Deep Creek reserve in Juab County contained some arable soil. The government had neglected Deep Creek since the turn of the decade, but those Indians who stayed on seemed peaceful and anxious to farm when Hatch visited them in February 1862 to issue provisions.[2] Corn Creek and San Pete Indian farms lay in Millard County, in central Utah. They too had largely gone to ruin because of government abandonment. The remaining Indians seemed peaceful, and field officials estimated that a $1,000 appropriation would restore San Pete farm to working order.[3]

The new administration could not immediately ameliorate this plight. May 1861 found the superintendent of Indian affairs, destitute of funds, directing the Spanish Fork agent to sell certain government property in order to feed his Indians and preserve order. Yet, when their reservations were divested of such minimal improvements as farm animals and implements and agency furniture, more residents dispersed in a futile search for food, only to fall victim to hunger and exposure.[4] The following year the territory's farms and reservations remained unproductive. The expense of subduing hostiles along the overland trail contributed in part to the slash in congressional appropriations, which in the past ranged from $40,000 to $60,000 annually, but were reduced to $10,500 for the 1862–63 fiscal year. Left without funds to care for his needy charges, Agent Hatch could not pay his employees and had to buy supplies with his own salary or on credit.[5] In December 1862 Superintendent Doty sent his clerk, Amos Reed, to Washington for additional funds to feed reservation Indians during the winter and coming spring. Congress approved a special $20,000 appropriation for Utah early in March 1863, and for the 1863–64 year increased the superintendency allocation to

2. Royce, "Indian Land Cessions," p. 831; Hatch to Doty, September 16, 1862, CIA, p. 351.

3. Dyman S. Wood to Superintendent Henry Martin, October 1, 1861, enclosed in Martin to Dole, October 1, 1861, CIA, p. 747.

4. Benjamin Davies to Humphreys, May 6, 1861, CIA, p. 749; Davies to Dole, June 30, 1861, CIA, p. 741; *ibid.*, p. 638.

5. *United States Statutes at Large* 12:629; CIA, 1862, p. 186; Hatch to Doty, September 16, 1862, CIA, p. 349.

$26,500.[6] Nevertheless, superintendency correspondence reveals continued problems with inadequate congressional funding.

In Nevada, white encroachment was not the sole source of administrative difficulties. Due to the enormous distances between mining settlements, the Indian Office contended with a high cost of living, high-priced labor, and slow movement of supplies.[7] Official correspondence took particular note of the currency problem. Proximity to California compelled Nevada businessmen to keep their territory on the gold standard. The consequent prejudice against greenbacks, which circulated at between sixty and sixty-eight cents on the dollar, meant that federal employees paid in paper currency would be justifiably unhappy. Under such conditions Nye could only get agency personnel by hiring poorly qualified men. Commissioner Dole at first refused to accept the fact that United States Treasury notes circulated at less than par value; when finally he did in July 1864, the commissioner suggested that Agent Lockhart reduce his staff or cut their salaries, since payments in gold or increased superintendency appropriations would not be forthcoming.[8]

Good technical training and productive Indian farms bulked large in the government's economic plans for most agencies, yet in Montana progress along these lines was painfully slow during the Civil War years. In 1864 Upson's efforts to pacify the restless Blackfeet left little time for their edification. Moreover, plans for a hundred-acre agency farm were ruined by the proximity of gold mines, which increased the price of white laborers 200 percent and depreciated Treasury notes by one-third. The gush of spring rains that year administered the coup de grace by laying waste the potato crop and damaging others.[9]

Agency reports show that the sale of alcohol to Indians was

6. Amos Reed to Dole, December 30, 1862, enclosed in Dole to Usher, January 5, 1863, ID, LR; *United States Statutes at Large* 12:791–92.

7. Rodman Wilson Paul, *Mining Frontiers of the Far West: 1848–1880* (New York, 1963), pp. 96–97.

8. Nye to Dole, October 27, 1863, CIA, p. 358; Dole to Lockhart, August 3, 1863, OIA, LS, 71:220–21; Dole to Lockhart, July 27, 1864, OIA, LS, 74:532.

9. Upson to Dole, September 1, 1864, CIA, pp. 439, 441.

more widespread in Montana than in Nevada, Utah, Colorado, or the Southwest. Upson postulated that all Blackfoot raids resulted from the activities of whiskey hucksters who still evaded legal punishment. Flathead Agent Charles Hutchins spoke of similar problems west of the Divide, and recommended the establishment of nearby courts to enforce federal laws or the posting of soldiers on his reservation.[10]

Intertribal warfare further limited Indian Office accomplishments in Montana. When Upson assumed his duties in December 1863, skirmishes occurred at least once a week, particularly between the Piegans and Gros Ventres. By mid-February persistent efforts at reconciliation bore fruit, and both tribes concluded a peace at Fort Benton. Mutual distrust within the confederation lingered, nevertheless, with the Bloods and Blackfeet openly antagonistic toward the Gros Ventres. What kept them from each others' throats was the fear of white aggression.[11]

Schism within the white community proved equally detrimental to Indian Office operations in the Southwest and Utah because it diverted federal resources. The rebel invasion of New Mexico and Arizona was a good example. Confederate General Henry Hopkins Sibley, with a force of nearly three thousand Texans, marched up the Rio Grande Valley and by March 1862 had seized Albuquerque and Santa Fe, the territory's capital and principal city. At the high point of its success, the South held sway over half of New Mexico and most of present-day Arizona. By conquering this area the Southerners hoped to obtain mineral wealth, provisions, men for her armies, a quick route to California, and English recognition of the Confederacy.[12]

Rebel inroads disrupted the work of Superintendent Collins. Texans captured annuity goods stored in Santa Fe and hounded his employees from their agencies. The retreat of federal troops

10. Upson to Cooley, October 2, 1865, CIA, p. 698; Hutchins to Governor Sidney Edgerton, June 30, 1865, CIA, p. 429.

11. Upson to Dole, September 1, 1864, CIA, pp. 437–38.

12. Charles S. Walker, "Causes of the Confederate Invasion of New Mexico," *New Mexico Historical Review* 8 (April, 1933): 97. Confederate General Henry Hopkins Sibley should not be confused with Henry Hastings Sibley, brigadier general of volunteers in the Union Army during the Civil War (see p. 106).

from much of the Southwest also emboldened the intractable Apaches and Navajos to strike at unprotected mining camps and settlements which dotted the territory. Only the Pueblos, Utes, and Jicarilla Apaches did not use the turmoil to their advantage.[13]

Colonel Edward R. S. Canby, gallant commander of the United States army in New Mexico, raised volunteer regiments and pleaded for reinforcements to save the Southwest for the Union. From north and west came columns of California and Colorado volunteers, driving the rebels before them. By the fall of 1862 the Texans found themselves back on their own soil, their dreams of conquest shattered.[14]

Unlike her neighbors to the south, Utah Territory experienced no Confederate invasion, and few among the more than forty thousand settlers championed the rebel cause. In fact, patriotic Mormons used the completion of the Pacific telegraph line in October 1861 as an opportunity to proclaim their loyalty to Lincoln.[15] Nevertheless, distrust existed in Washington and Salt Lake City, due in part to the Mormons' suspicion of Republicans, who in 1856 had labeled polygamy and slavery "twin relics of barbarism." The Latter-Day Saints also disliked carpetbag political appointees. Brigham Young instructed Utah Territorial Delegate W. H. Hooper to inform President Lincoln that if Mormons could not have their officials selected "from actual residents among us, which is but right, we had much rather have none."[16]

13. Collins to Dole, April 26, 1862, OIA, LR, New Mexico Supty.; Collins to Dole, October 10, 1862, CIA, p. 382; Carleton to Adjutant General Lorenzo Thomas, September 30, 1863, JSC, p. 98; Arny to Dole, March 28, 1862, OIA, LR, New Mexico Supty.

14. L. R. Bailey, *The Long Walk: A History of the Navajo Wars, 1846–1868* (Los Angeles, 1964), pp. 141–42.

15. Colton, *Civil War in the Western Territories*, p. 180; Vincent G. Tegeder, "The Territories and the Lincoln Administration: Northern Ascendency and Radical Experiments in the West," doctoral dissertation, University of Wisconsin, 1949, p. 224.

16. Rupert N. Richardson and Carl C. Rister, *The Greater Southwest: The Economic, Social, and Cultural Development of Kansas, Oklahoma, Texas, Utah, Colorado, Nevada, New Mexico, Arizona, and California from the Spanish Conquest to the Twentieth Century* (Glendale, Calif., 1935), pp. 254–55; Young to Hooper, March 28, 1861, Brigham Young Papers, Yale University Library Western Americana Collection, New Haven, Conn.

Quarrels in the early sixties between the Saints and Gentile civil officials provoked the removal of John W. Dawson and Stephen S. Harding, Lincoln's first two gubernatorial appointees, and the departure of two federal judges after less than a year in the territory. James Duane Doty's appointment to the governorship in June 1863 reduced these tensions somewhat. A former Midwest politician, land speculator, and superintendent of Indian affairs in Utah since 1861, Doty was known to the Mormons as a capable and tolerant civil servant.[17]

Mistrust manifested itself in still another way. After Connor's chastisement of Indian hostiles in 1863, the army and the Mormons turned on one another rather than working for the red man's welfare. Connor had orders to keep the Mormons as well as the Indians under surveillance. Personally he believed the Saints were guilty of treason and were awaiting an opportunity to rise up against the Union. Meanwhile, the proximity of Camp Douglas to Salt Lake City startled and insulted Brigham Young, who appealed to the courts to relocate this public nuisance. A verbal war waged by the pro-Mormon *Deseret News* and the *Union Vedette*, owned by Connor and other Union officers, precipitated a physical attack on the *Vedette* editorial staff.[18] Mineral discoveries at Brigham Canyon in the fall of 1863 offered Connor a chance to neutralize Mormon political power, if only he could attract a large population of Gentile miners to the territory. Despite costly publicity the mining bonanza never materialized; richer strikes and lower transportation costs in neighboring territories proved more appealing.[19]

Meanwhile, a feud far more detrimental to the administration of federal Indian policy was developing in New Mexico. On September 16, 1862, General Carleton arrived in Santa Fe to in-

17. Tegeder, "Lincoln and the Territorial Patronage," pp. 86–89.

18. Lamar, *The Far Southwest*, pp. 360–61; Fred B. Rogers, *Soldiers of the Overland: Being Some Account of the Services of General Patrick Edward Connor and His Volunteers in the Old West* (San Francisco, 1938), pp. 78–79; Herbert M. Hart, *Old Forts of the Northwest* (Seattle, 1963), p. 23.

19. Paul, *Mining Frontiers of the Far West*, p. 150; Robert E. Riegal and Robert G. Athearn, *America Moves West* (4th ed., New York, 1964), pp. 460–61.

augurate a new military approach to the Indian problem which frustrated Indian Office officials had surrendered to him. Stern, unbending, arbitrary, aggressive, "Gentleman Jimmy" eschewed Indian peace overtures and tracked down the hostiles with unshakable determination. The Mescalero campaign was practically over in March 1863. More than four hundred men, women, and children surrendered unconditionally to Carleton's field commander, Colonel Kit Carson, and were sent to Fort Sumner on the Pecos River in east-central New Mexico, where Carleton planned to colonize and make farmers of them. Scarcely more than a year later, with most Navajos captives also located on the Pecos, Governor Connelly announced the Indian war ended.[20]

To Carleton, Fort Sumner seemed a fine place to settle the bothersome Mescaleros, for the barren plains provided no hiding places. Near the river a small, round cluster of cottonwoods, which the Spanish called Bosque Redondo, was the only visible greenery. Adobe quarters for four hundred men, a hospital, store houses, stables, a guard house, a bake house, and parade grounds composed the military complex. The general expected that the fort's strategic location would also block Comanche and Kiowa raids against the Rio Grande Valley and seal off the Pecos plunder trail to Mexico.[21]

At first Carleton intended to send only Apache contingents to Bosque Redondo, but by September 1863 he determined to colonize the Navajos there as well, despite the fact that he had not worked out the details nor won the approval of civilian authorities. Neither he nor the Indian Office in New Mexico had adequate funds to feed and clothe the additional prisoners.[22]

Carleton's plans for civilizing the Indians were too optimistic. During the spring and summer of 1864 he directed that irrigation trenches be dug, and arranged the planting of over 1,500 acres in corn, beans, wheat, melons, and pumpkins. Most of the crop went

20. Carleton to Lorenzo Thomas, March 19, 1863, JSC, p. 106; Proclamation of Connelly, May 4, 1864, *ibid.*, p. 333.
21. Bailey, *The Long Walk*, pp. 146–48, 174; Carleton to Thomas, November 9, 1862, JSC, p. 101.
22. Carleton to Thomas, September 6, 1863, CIA, p. 230; Bailey, *The Long Walk*, pp. 174–75.

unharvested that season and the next because army worms, grass-hoppers, and severe storms devastated the fields. Poor soil, lack of water, and inadequate farm implements were additional handi-caps.[23] Although forced to reduce rations for soldiers as well as Indians at Fort Sumner and to order that no more Navajos be sent to the Pecos, Carleton insisted on settling the tribe at Bosque Redondo. To the Adjutant General in Washington he explained that "The future of not only New Mexico but of Arizona, de-pends on the determination and the ability of the General Gov-ernment to hold this formidable tribe [Navajos], now that it has been subdued and gotten in hand, until it can support itself. Noth-ing should arise or conspire to let them go again."[24] Congress and the War Department allotted more money to the military Depart-ment of New Mexico, but Carleton never had sufficient funds adequately to feed and clothe the nine thousand Mescaleros and Navajos gathered at Fort Sumner, much less to educate their children in the white man's ways.

The low morale of the Navajos was also a problem. Most were herders rather than farmers, and bleak Bosque Redondo lacked ample pasturage for their cattle. Also, the Navajos frequently clashed with their Mescalero cohabitants on the reserve. Disease and the ever present whiskey scourge further undermined the red man's desire to wrench subsistence from the soil.[25]

The Indian Office gave Carleton token assistance. When the first Navajo captives arrived at Bosque Redondo in September 1863, the new superintendent, Michael Steck, a Pennsylvania physician who had come to the Southwest in the early fifties as an Apache agent, ordered Mescalero Agent Lorenzo Labadi to re-ject any suggestion that the office care for them; as prisoners of

23. Superintendent Felipe Delgado to Dole, September 10, 1865, CIA, p. 345; Reeve, "Federal Indian Policy in New Mexico," pp. 24–28.

24. Carlton to Commanding Officer, Fort Wingate, October 27, 1864, JSC, p. 203; Carleton to Thomas, October 30, 1864, USAC, Department of New Mexico, LS, 15:256–57.

25. Hubert Howe Bancroft, *History of Arizona and New Mexico, 1530–1888* (San Francisco, 1889), p. 732; Beck, *New Mexico*, pp. 190–91; Major Henry D. Wallen to Editor, February 18, 1864, Santa Fe *Weekly Gazette*, March 5, 1864.

war they were the responsibility of the army. Moreover, the superintendency was at the time financially unable to support the tribe. Secretary of War Edwin M. Stanton had little choice but to continue caring for the captives.[26]

Though expedient, Steck's decision left unanswered the question of which service had ultimate responsibility for the captive Navajos and Apaches. The military, as reluctant foster parents, fed their wards at Bosque Redondo and exercised general control over them, while the Indian Office, which received its appropriation for the New Mexico Superintendency after June 1864, provided the Indians with limited quantities of clothing and farm equipment.[27] Yet the relationship between General Carleton and Superintendent Steck grew increasingly hostile. Their full cooperation, so essential to the success of the Bosque Redondo experiment, was never realized.

Before the Navajos' arrival at Fort Sumner, Labadi cleared strips of land along the Pecos and planted crops to feed his four hundred Apaches. When the army allotted many of these fields to Navajo prisoners, Labadi complained that the apportionment violated his wishes and the Mescaleros' right to the full fruits of their labor.[28] According to the military, more serious issues were involved. In March 1864 it accused Labadi of fomenting unrest among the Navajos by suggesting they leave the reservation. That fall, after the harvesting of Apaches' grain, Carleton charged that he refused to give the produce to the army's disbursing officials, the implication being that Labadi kept the crop for his own benefit. Carleton told Labadi that the reservation was temporarily under the exclusive control of the army and all residents subject to military authority.[29]

26. William Aloysius Keleher, *Turmoil in New Mexico, 1846–68* (Santa Fe, 1952), pp. 409–10; Steck to Carleton, September 6, 1863, enclosed in Steck to Dole, January 23, 1864, OIA, LR, New Mexico Supty.; Stanton to John P. Usher, March 31, 1861, enclosed in Usher to Hannibal Hamlin, April 5, 1864, *Sen. Misc. Doc.* 97, 38 Cong., 1 Sess., I (Ser. 1177).

27. Reeve, "Federal Indian Policy in New Mexico," pp. 14–15.

28. Labadi to Dole, June 30, 1863, and Steck to Dole, May 20, 1864, OIA, LR, New Mexico Supty.

29. Carleton to Wallen, March 20, 1864, JSC, p. 173; Carleton to Steck, USAC, Department of New Mexico, LS, 15:179–80.

The army evicted Labadi from the reservation in March 1865, because of his alleged private purchase of government cattle designated for Indian subsistence.[30] No doubt any agent assigned to the Navajo or Apache captives would have felt the general's wrath because of the difficulty of a dual administration of Indian policy when jurisdictional lines were unclear. Even the Indian Office's concession to the military of overall control on the Pecos was unsatisfactory to Carleton, who would not tolerate any independence by Indian service personnel. Labadi's supposed nefarious dealings merely crystallized Carleton's thinking on the subject.

Steck's disbursement of Indian goods at Bosque Redondo, purchased with the $100,000 congressional appropriation of June 30, 1864, was another source of friction. The War and Interior Departments had recommended the allocation in April as the best way to relieve the subsistence problem at Fort Sumner.[31] The Secretary of the Interior appointed Jesse H. Leavenworth and William B. Baker to buy Indian supplies with these funds and to deliver them to Steck at Fort Union. Steck oversaw the distribution of goods during a five-day stay at Bosque Redondo in late December.[32]

Two of Carleton's officers at Fort Sumner as well as the post sutler inspected the provisions and concluded that the Indians had been defrauded. Dr. George Gwyther, a witness to the inspection, noted in later years that most articles were substandard: "rusty, old-fashioned, unserviceable, and unsalable plows, soft-iron spades, rakes and hoes, knives and hatchets, coarse, gaudy calicoes and muslin, and thin, flimsy, shoddy cloths and blankets." Gwyther weighed the blankets and found each to be a full pound less than army issue and more than twice as expensive. The sutler

30. Carleton to Thomas, March 22, 1865, JSC, p. 223.

31. *United States Statutes at Large* 13:333; Usher to Hamblin, April 5, 1864, *Congressional Globe*, 38 Cong., 1 Sess., p. 2172.

32. Mix to Steck, August 12, 1864, Michael Steck Papers, Zimmerman Library, University of New Mexico, Albuquerque, N.M.; Steck to Dole, January 1, 1865, OIA, LR, New Mexico Supty.

reckoned the entire shipment to be worth about $30,000, which meant a $70,000 profit for somebody. Upon learning that the military implicated his office in the fraud, Steck attributed the allegations to a "low and malicious spirit."[33]

As in the Labadi affair, the verity of the army's charges, which would be difficult to prove, is not as important for this study as its obvious distrust of the Indian Office. In fact, each department believed the other to be a conspirator. Carleton's incapacity to support the Indians at Bosque Redondo meant that any challenge to his authority or attempt to prevent the maximum amount of goods from being supplied to the Navajos and Apaches infuriated him. On the other hand, the Indian service believed the army was undermining its prerogatives in New Mexico. To be accused of subverting Carleton's Pecos project was doubly odious to Steck, since a special investigator had arrived in the territory to evaluate his suggestion that the Navajos be removed from Bosque Redondo to another reservation. In this atmosphere of mutual distrust and name-calling, the execution of the reservation policy was encumbered by its own administrators.

Carleton's quarrel with Steck over the army's campaign against the Kiowas and Comanches was another cause of contention. These roving Indians occasionally made forays against the Bosque Redondo reservation and so harassed the Santa Fe trail as to threaten Carleton's lines of communication. The sharp increase in attacks during the summer of 1864 prompted the mobilization of a force to punish the Indians before winter.[34]

Steck objected to the proposed Comanche campaign; he had concrete evidence that the tribe was at peace and had not participated in the recent plains outrages, whereas the Kiowas admitted their involvement. The superintendent suggested an investigation by his office before engulfing eastern New Mexico in a war. Carleton's disregard for Indian Office authority, especially his

33. Gwyther, "An Indian Reservation," *The Overland Monthly* 10 (February, 1873): 129; Steck to Dole, February 4, 1865, OIA, FOR, New Mexico Supty., LR.

34. Underhill, *The Navajos*, pp. 138–39; Steck to Carleton, October 26, 1864, Steck Papers.

use of Ute and Jicarilla scouts who were under Steck's direct control, seemed but another blatant attempt by the army to dominate Indian affairs.[35]

Carleton responded that his information about Comanche culpability differed from Steck's. Furthermore, he was unaware of the military's obligation to permit civil investigations before it took action against hostiles. Concerning the Ute and Jicarilla scouts, Carleton believed that with so many plains tribes warring against the whites, the mountain Indians must be allied with the government.[36]

Confident in Steck's judgment, Commissioner Dole recommended early in January 1865 that hostilities not be pursued against the Comanches while the least doubt of their guilt existed. By then, Kit Carson's force had already defeated a Comanche and Kiowa party at the Battle of Adobe Walls.[37]

Carleton next accused Steck of issuing licenses to New Mexican traders who bartered guns and ammunition with the Kiowas and Comanches in exchange for livestock stolen during the summer. Though the superintendent denied the charge,[38] Carleton's suspicions strengthened his determination to follow his own Indian plan.

The most bitter dispute between Carleton and the Indian Office concerned the propriety of colonizing the Navajos at the forty-mile square Bosque Redondo reserve. Though settlement of the Apaches on the Pecos seemed wise, Steck believed it impossible to manage two tribes, age-old enemies, on the same reservation. Nor was there sufficient arable land along the river to support twelve to fifteen thousand Navajos. With only his superinten-

35. Steck to Carleton, Steck Papers; Steck to Carleton, November 5, 1864, enclosed in Steck to Dole, November 16, 1864, OIA, LR, New Mexico Supty.

36. Carleton to Steck, October 29, 1864, enclosed in Steck to Dole, November 16, 1864, OIA, LR, New Mexico Supty.; Carleton to Steck, November 8, 1864, USAC, Department of New Mexico, LS, 15:271-72.

37. Dole to Usher, January 7, 1865, OIA, Report Books, 14:82-83. See Robert M. Utley, "Kit Carson and the Adobe Falls Campaign," *The American West*, 2 (Winter, 1965): 4-11, 73-75 for a description of this engagement.

38. Carleton to Thomas, January 29, 1865, JSC, p. 217.

dent's statements before him, Dole agreed that the Navajos should be located on a special tract in their own country.[39]

When Carleton learned of Steck's objection to his Navajo scheme, he informed Adjutant General Thomas that the governor, the Territorial Assembly of New Mexico, Colonel Carson, and former superintendent Collins endorsed the project, as had Steck at one time. That Steck should now oppose the plan when "every intelligent man in the country approves it" was baffling. If Steck's proposal were accepted, the resumption of Navajo raids and consequent severing of trails to the new gold fields would ruin New Mexico and Arizona.[40]

During these polemics the superintendent's views became so distorted that he was even accused of opposing the colonization scheme, though he had backed it for ten years as the only hope for racial peace. Steck merely objected to grouping both tribes on the same reserve. As an alternative to Bosque Redondo he suggested the Colorado Chiquito (Little Colorado), which in 1862 Colonel Canby considered an excellent place to settle the wily Navajos. In Carleton's view, neither the Colorado Chiquito nor any other place in the Navajo country had as much tillable land or would be as militarily practical as Bosque Redondo.[41]

In April 1864, after consulting various sources in the territory, Dole ceased looking for a more suitable home for the Navajos. Apparently most of the tribe was already on the Pecos and could become self-supporting. Perhaps because of Carleton's insistent communications, Dole merely bowed to the military's superior position in New Mexican Indian matters.[42] In either case, the imbroglio in the field had not ended.

Until his resignation in March 1865, Michael Steck opposed

39. Steck to Dole, December 10, 1863, CIA (1864), pp. 351–52; Dole to Usher, December 16, 1863, OIA, Report Books, 13:266–67.

40. Carleton to Thomas and Carleton to Francisco Perea, January 12, 1864, JSC, p. 155.

41. Steck to Dole, February 16, 1864, Steck Papers; Carleton to Thomas, March 19, 1864, JSC, pp. 168–69.

42. Dole to Usher, April 4, 1864, OIA, Report Books, 13:361; Keleher, *Turmoil in New Mexico*, p. 418.

Navajo colonization at Bosque Redondo. Not only would military restraint always be needed to keep them at Fort Sumner, but
the reserve was financially impractical. Local farmers advised him
that the salty Pecos waters would impregnate the irrigated reservation fields, making them worthless for agriculture. According
to Steck a military board of inquiry disclosed that the army spent
about $510,000 on the captives during the four-month period
beginning March 1, 1864. Had this included transportation costs
and those of the quartermaster, who employed sixty men and
twenty teams, the total would be closer to $700,000.[43]

After consulting Agents John Ward, Ramon Luna, and José
Mausinares, as well as army officers lately engaged in the Navajo
war, Steck reckoned that half the Indians still lived in the mountains and that those at Bosque Redondo longed to return. Given
the Navajos' ability to sustain themselves in their own country,
would not a reservation on the Colorado Chiquito be effective
and more economical? As a precaution against future incursions
the reservation could be ringed with army posts and a fort constructed in the Navajos' midst.[44]

Carleton disagreed with most of these assertions. The Indians
at Fort Sumner did not seem dissatisfied; rather they were the
happiest people he had ever seen, industrious and looking forward
to supporting themselves on their new reserve. Steck also misrepresented the army's subsistence costs. The quartermaster never
employed sixty men, the statistics gathered by the military board
incorporated transportation expenses, and the total figure for
nearly a year, not four months, was $414,852.66.[45]

The controversy took on another dimension when Bosque Redondo became a major political issue in the territory. Proponents
of Carleton's plan, such as Governor Connelly, Delegate Francisco Perea, and ex-superintendent Collins, wanted to open up
the mineral lands of the Navajo country. Collins advanced their

43. Steck to Dole, May 20, and October 29, 1864, OIA, LR, New Mexico
Supty.; Steck to Dole, June 25, 1864, enclosed in Dole to Usher, July 16, 1864,
CIA, pp. 358–59.
44. Steck to Dole, October 10, 1864, CIA, pp. 327–30.
45. Carleton to Usher, August 27, 1864, JSC, pp. 192–93.

views in the columns of his Santa Fe *Weekly Gazette* and in lengthy letters to Secretary of the Interior John P. Usher and Commissioner Dole. One editorial suggested that Carleton's antagonists merely wished to make a few thousand dollars by returning the Navajos, whence they would again prey on New Mexicans. Judge Kirby Benedict, William H. Manderfield, editor of the Santa Fe *New Mexican*, Secretary Arny, and Judge Joseph G. Knapp, unwilling to sacrifice the choice agricultural and grazing land of the Pecos, supported Steck.[46] In the 1865 delegate contest, Bosque Redondo polarized the candidates, with anti-Bosque Colonel J. Francisco Chavez defeating the pro-Carleton incumbent Perea by a vote of 8,511 to 6,180.[47]

The government could not prudently permit such a divisive controversy to continue. In November 1864 Senator James Harlan recommended that the Indian Office dispatch a reliable and intelligent investigator to examine the reservation site and ascertain the number of Indians at Fort Sumner, their personal condition, attitudes, means of support and the needs for permanent settlement. He should also determine the number of Indians still in the Navajo country, their circumstances, their attitude toward the United States, and what force would be required to drive them from the mountains. For the assignment the senator suggested T. W. Woolson of Mt. Pleasant, Iowa, a minor state politician.[48] Dole accepted the advice and appointed Woolson.

On January 10, 1865, the investigator arrived by coach in Santa Fe and with a military escort proceeded to Bosque Redondo. After a personal investigation of the site, he asked Steck, Collins, Arny and others to submit detailed statements. Though Woolson's final report is not among the papers of the Indian Office, his correspondence with Steck reveals that the special agent adjudged Fort Sumner a pleasant place for an Indian colony.[49] Two post-

46. Santa Fe *Weekly Gazette*, October 22, 1864; Lawrence R. Murphy, "William F. M. Arny, Secretary of New Mexico Territory, 1862–1867," *Arizona and the West*, 8 (Winter, 1966): 330.

47. Tegeder, "The Territories and the Lincoln Administration," p. 95.

48. Harlan to Dole, November 15, 1864, OIA, LR, New Mexico Supty.

49. Santa Fe *Weekly Gazette*, January 14, 1865; Woolson to Steck, January 9 and 23, 1865, Steck Papers.

war investigations supplemented Woolson's work. The findings of Congressmen James R. Doolittle, Lafayette S. Foster, and Lewis W. Ross proved inconclusive due to conflicting testimony, yet they observed Navajo suffering and seemed pessimistic about the success of Carleton's experiment. Julius K. Graves, whom the Secretary of the Interior appointed in 1865 to gather additional information about the Navajos, deemed Bosque Redondo a wise choice for them and recommended that the Apaches be reassigned.[50]

The Navajos remained at Bosque Redondo for three more years, doubtless as a result of these reports. Meanwhile, two other combatants in the drama departed the scene: Michael Steck resigned in 1865 and public pressure from New Mexico terminated Carleton's command in 1866. Shortly thereafter the Interior Department took charge of the Navajos. Since it could not bear the annual expense of almost three quarters of a million dollars to provision the tribe, the department resolved to settle them on a reserve where they could feed themselves. Furthermore, disease, Comanche raids, poor food, and a lingering homesickness so demoralized the Navajos that sizeable numbers had left Bosque Redondo.[51] In the summer of 1868 government commissioners negotiated a treaty in which the Navajos, who were to be returned to their canyoned homeland, vowed never to fight again.[52] The tribe honored its word.

In another blow to Carleton's plan, 335 demoralized and discontented Mescaleros fled from Fort Sumner in November 1865. Some returned to the Sacramento mountains; others joined the Gila Apaches west of the Rio Grande. In 1873 the government assigned the Mescaleros to a reserve in their own country in south-central New Mexico.[53]

General Carleton's foremost problem at Bosque Redondo had been to change his captives' way of life, to make self-supporting

---

50. Reeve, "The Federal Indian Policy in New Mexico," pp. 15–21.

51. Underhill, *The Navajos*, pp. 140–41; Dale, *Indians of the Southwest*, p. 59; Bailey, *The Long Walk*, pp. 209–10.

52. Kappler, *Indian Affairs* 2:1015–20.

53. Beck, *New Mexico*, pp. 191–92.

farmers of them. Time, a hospitable environment, patience, and flexibility on the part of Indian and white were crucial to the success of the general's experiment. Yet all were noticeably absent. Also troublesome was the ambiguity of the Indian Office's role in relation to the military. To some extent this was the Indian service's fault; it refused to assume responsibility for the army's captives, though it wished a voice in their management. Burdened with the cost of provisioning the Navajos and Mescaleros at Bosque Redondo, the military determined to keep Indian Office interference to a minimum. Carleton's affronts to the Indian Office in the Labadi affair, expenditure of the congressional appropriation and the Comanche campaign, precipitated a serious quarrel with Superintendent Steck, who appeared content at first to play a limited role regarding the Navajos and Mescaleros. The Steck-Carleton duel, concerned outwardly with the nonjurisdictional matter of the suitability of the Bosque Redondo, added another dimension to interdepartmental discord and further disrupted the effective administration of the reservation policy. Both men claimed to promote the territory's welfare, but the thrust and parry and counterthrust of their correspondence suggest more subjective motives. Not until these antagonists passed from the scene and the Interior Department assumed complete control of Bosque Redondo was the Indian Office's function in New Mexico clarified.

CHAPTER IV

Conclusion to Part I

The superintendencies discussed thus far experienced similar administrative problems, triggered by the swift influx of whites and the resultant destruction or dispersion of game, the seizure of choice land, the pollution of streams, and the spread of disease. In mineral-rich Nevada, Colorado, and Montana, the movement of miners was particularly rapid and troublesome. From New Mexico to Montana, the consequences of such change were the same: vicious cycles of retaliatory raids perpetrated by red men and white. Indian hostiles confined their attacks to the overland immigrant routes and to isolated ranches, farms and mines, for these were not wars of extermination. Under the circumstances the Indian Office chose to separate the races and confine the nomadic peoples to isolated reservations. Yet in trying to do so, it foundered dreadfully.

In addition to these general similarities, Governor Evans of Colorado shared some specific administrative burdens with other superintendents. For officials trying to preserve the peace in Montana and on the Colorado-New Mexico border, delayed annuities proved irksome. Outside Colorado, bureaucrats generated little interest in Indian agriculture or instruction of the young in such techniques. Accusations of fraud were leveled at Indian Office personnel only in New Mexico and Colorado, and only in Montana did the army post as few troops as in Colorado.

More widespread were the inconveniences of disrupted communications with the East and growing public pressure to chastise and even exterminate hostile Indians. Following a series of attacks on the overland trail in eastern Nevada early in 1865, the Gold Hill *Daily News* decried the eleven-day disruption of communications with the East. Though they had championed Indian rights and tribal reservations just a year before, editorialists now called for the elimination of all Indians between Canada and Mexico, and denounced the treaty-making efforts of eastern sympathizers and congressmen. In September 1865 Utah Superintendent Irish noted that former renegades had so prejudiced the territory's settlers, soldiers, and certain government officials that most favored genocide.[1] By taking a consistently hard line toward red hostiles, the Virginia City *Montana Post* doubtless spoke for many local citizens. In January 1865 the following editorial comment appeared: "His [Chivington's] is the true way to settle Indian difficulties. A savage cannot be trusted. The lust for blood and rapine never is eradicated." Nor was much sympathy expressed for the views of humanitarians who had never seen the mutilated bodies of close friends. To the *Montana Post* editor writing in February, the Indian was incorrigible, a trained killer who could neither be civilized nor Christianized. All praise to Chivington and the Colorado troops! Let us have "*More powder and less ink.*" Physical danger alone did not motivate this editorialist. Indian wars slowed territorial development: emigration would be interrupted, outside capital cut off, prices inflated. Montana's red men must either be destroyed or put under military guard on isolated reservations.[2]

Numerous as these common administrative problems seemed, the Indian Office faced its most diverse and most serious challenges with the Cheyennes and their Arapaho allies. Relations with them led to the most tragic finale.

Notable difficulties avoided by Governor Evans occurred in the Southwest, where the Indian Office felt the direct impact of the Civil War and the Steck-Carleton feud. The general's colonization

1. Gold Hill (Nevada) *Daily News*, February 26, 1864, and February 11 and March 18, 1865; Irish to Dole, September 9, 1865, CIA, pp. 314–15.
2. *Montana Post*, January 21 and February 4, 1865.

scheme, to which Steck objected so strongly, had dire implications for the Indian Office. Since Bosque Redondo was the only reserve on which an important nomadic tribe was segregated during the Civil War years, the vicissitudes that Carleton faced in trying to change their way of life in a strange, barren land would later confront the Office of Indian Affairs when other hostiles surrendered. Of equal import was the enduring effect of life at Bosque Redondo on the Navajo people. Two noted anthropologists have written: "Even today it seems impossible for a Navajo of the older generation to talk for more than a few minutes on any subject without speaking of Fort Sumner. . . . One can no more understand Navajo attitudes—particularly toward white people—without knowing of Fort Sumner than he can comprehend Southern attitudes without knowing of the Civil War."[3] Finally, the Steck-Carleton controversy demonstrated the problems of interdepartmental cooperation when jurisdictional lines were unclear, and showed the disruptive effects of such a quarrel on the reservation policy. In Colorado, on the other hand, civil and military officers at times became too closely aligned. "No governor or legislature of State or Territories," wrote the Indian Peace Commission in 1868, should "be permitted to call out and equip troops for the purpose of carrying on war against Indians. It was Colorado troops that involved us in the war of 1864–'65, with the Cheyennes."[4]

Other rifts within the white community, which Colorado avoided, included Mormon quarrels with Lincoln's first civil appointees and with General Connor. Fortunately too for the Cheyennes and Arapahos, white interlopers in eastern Colorado did not as seriously deplete the game as in Utah, Nevada, and southern Colorado. Nor did Colorado Superintendency officials experience the fiscal difficulties shared by Utah, Nevada, and Montana, or the serious intertribal warfare and whiskey problem which so concerned Montana's Agent Upson.

3. Clyde Kluckhohn and Dorothea Leighton, *The Navajo* (rev. ed., Garden City, New York, 1962), p. 41.
4. Report of the Peace Commission, *House Exec. Doc.* 97, 40 Cong., 2 Sess., II: 21–22.

What made the Indian Office so impotent, unable either to stop the depredations of warlike bands or to care adequately for more peaceful nomads who at least agreed to restrict their wanderings? James L. Collins of New Mexico remarked on the smallness of a superintendent's staff and the absence of any police force under his control. The futility of negotiating with powerful and self-sufficient nomads who did not wish to walk the white man's road was demonstrated forcefully in Montana, Colorado, and New Mexico. If a few bands tried reservation life, the Indian Office frequently chose a bleak location for them, went back on its promises of presents and technical aid and appeared too narrow minded to consider anything but agriculture as a fitting occupation for an Indian. In justice to the Indian Office it should be noted that General Carleton made many of the same mistakes. Finally, one must recall that this was a time of rapid change in the West, as George Bent depicted in the land of the Cheyennes (see page 25).

The Cheyenne and Arapaho treaty concluded on the Little Arkansas in October 1865 proved scarcely more than a truce, for hostiles north of the Platte River did not sign it. The next decade was one of frustration and turmoil for the Indian Office as well as the southern bands. Unhappiness with their restriction to a reserve south of the Arkansas generated a fruitless cycle of raids by uncontrollable Cheyennes and Arapahos, chastisement by the United States Army, and more honeyed words from federal peace commissioners. The wars of the Southern Cheyennes and Southern Arapahos ended in the mid-1870s. The slaughter of vast buffalo herds by white hunters convinced even the young warriors that they must accept some sort of new life on the 4,297,771-acre reservation set aside for them by President Grant in 1869 in what is now western Oklahoma.[5]

In May 1868, following the Red Cloud War, the Northern Cheyennes and Northern Arapahos signed a treaty of peace and friendship with the United States, agreeing thereby to accept as their home part of the land assigned to the Brulé Sioux in April or a portion of the southern bands' reserve. The Indian Office

5. Berthrong, *Southern Cheyennes*, pp. 243ff.

pressed for the latter, but the approximately three thousand members of the northern bands adamantly refused to move south of
the Arkansas. George Bent noted that forty years of separation
had made the northerners more and more like their Sioux allies.
Too, they considered the north country their home, and no
amount of government cajoling in the early 1870s could con-
vince them otherwise. Federal officials decided to let the steady
migration of whites into their homeland and the consequent destruction of game force the Indians to accept the Oklahoma
reservation. Yet events moved faster than anticipated. The discovery of gold in the Black Hills and the army's inability to keep
miners out of Sioux country brought war, which involved the
Northern Cheyennes in the Custer massacre. Consequently they
forfeited any voice in deciding where their future home would be.
After rounding up the camps of Dull Knife and Two Moons in
1876 and 1877, federal officers herded the remaining northern
bands south to the Indian Territory.[6]

In the wake of fifteen discouraging and profitless years of
negotiation, the Indian Office finally had all the Cheyennes on
a reserve. Bureaucrats now faced some different managerial problems. To understand them, we need not pursue the Cheyennes
into the closing years of the nineteenth century, for the Office of
Indian Affairs experienced similar difficulties in the Civil War
years with the reservation people.

6. Kappler, *Indian Affairs: Laws and Treaties* 2:1012–15; Hyde, *Life of George Bent*, pp. 197, 348-50; Edward Adamson Hoebel, *The Cheyennes: Indians of the Great Plains* (New York, 1960), pp. 2-3.

PART II

The Reservation People

CHAPTER V

The Uprooted Santees

On May 4 and 5, 1863, more than thirteen hundred Santee Sioux Indians, mainly women and children, left their compound below Fort Snelling, Minnesota, and boarded the steamboats *Davenport* and *Northerner*. The destination of the steamers was unknown to the frightened Sioux. Two missionaries aboard the vessels, John Williamson and Samuel Hinman, conducted hymn singing and prayers but could not allay the Indians' fears.[1] If Sioux braves had been present in greater numbers they could have comforted their families, but by May of 1863 most of the warriors who eluded capture after the uprising of 1862 had fled to the Dakota country with Chief Little Crow. Tribesmen left behind were imprisoned either at Davenport, Iowa, or at Fort Snelling. Thus, as the *Davenport* and *Northerner* steamed southward down the Mississippi in May 1863, they carried with them from Minnesota virtually the last remnants of the mighty nation which once had dominated the entire state.

The removal of the Sioux evoked mixed responses from white citizens of Minnesota. Some, like those who hurled rocks at the *Davenport* as it docked at St. Paul levee for supplies, hated the Indians.[2] The majority of whites regarded the removal of Indians

1. Stephen R. Riggs, *Mary and I: Forty Years With the Sioux* (Chicago, 1880), pp. 196–97; Roddis, *Indian Wars of Minnesota*, p. 197.
2. William E. Lass, "The Removal from Minnesota of the Sioux and Winnebago Indians," *Minnesota History* 38 (December, 1963): 358.

as an opportunity to open for white settlement the rich bottomlands of the Minnesota River, formerly part of the Sioux reserve. This thought, not hatred for the Indian, excited land speculators and frontier farmers.

When Congress organized the Territory of Minnesota in 1849, the Santee Sioux roamed its southern and western prairies. The name Santee, a shortened form of *Isanyatee*, derived from a time when they lived at Isantamde, or Mille Lacs as it is called today.[3] The Santee or Eastern Sioux included four tribes: the Sissetons, Wahpetons, Mdewakantons, and Wapekutes. Together with the Tetons, Yanktons, and Yanktonais they formed the Sioux confederacy of seven council fires. Tall, bold, warlike, the Sioux were referred to in plains sign language by moving a hand across the throat daggerlike. The ferocious fighting qualities of the confederacy first manifested themselves in its conquest of the upper-Mississippi Valley in the sixteenth and seventeenth centuries. By the 1730s and 1740s, however, Chippewas, armed with European rifles and perhaps advised by the French, dislodged the Sioux from northern and eastern Minnesota, including Mille Lacs. The Sioux in turn drove the Cheyennes onto the Dakota plains. Henceforth the Chippewas controlled the coniferous woodlands, while the Santees found a new home in the fertile Minnesota Valley, former hunting grounds of the Cheyennes.[4] The Tetons, Yanktons, and Yanktonais migrated to the valley of the Missouri.

Western Minnesota is a land of transition, where wood becomes sparse and prairie land prevails. In the mid-nineteenth century the Stone Age culture of the Santees embraced elements of both their woodland past and the nomadic ways of buffalo-hunting cousins to the west. The Eastern Sioux still cultivated maize, and during the planting and harvesting seasons dwelt in permanent, bark-covered houses. While crops matured or when necessary to supplement a skimpy yield, bands packed their belongings in canoes or on horses and went off in quest of buffalo,

3. Stephen R. Riggs, *Tah-koo Wah-Kan; or the Gospel Among the Dakota* (Boston, 1869), pp. 3–4.

4. Theodore C. Blegen, *Minnesota: A History of the State* (Minneapolis, 1963), pp. 20–23; Roddis, *Indian Wars of Minnesota*, p. 4.

deer, elk, small game, waterfowl, fish, wild fruits, and edible roots. Like the Cheyennes, the Santees followed a strict division of labor under the direction of a band chief and council.[5] A fun-loving people, they filled leisure moments with dancing, song fests, games, gambling, and feasts. Sioux braves were inveterate pipe smokers, a custom stimulated no doubt by the famed red pipestone quarries in southwestern Minnesota and the belief that tobacco, obtained from traders, was an especially pleasing offering for their gods. Pipes were lit at ceremonies and on solemn oc-casions. When two Santees met on the prairie they usually smoked before exchanging greetings and gossip.[6]

Hunger and the threat of death from wild beasts or a Chippewa raiding party were the constant companions of nomadic Santee hunters. Yet there was a thrill to danger and to fighting. And, as with the Cheyennes, courage brought its rewards. Steel knives, hatchet heads, needles, and firearms obtained from white mer-chants increased the hunter's efficiency but also led to a rapid depletion of fur-bearing animals, for whose skins the trader paid handsomely, and to intertribal struggles for new hunting grounds.[7] Santee-Chippewa skirmishes, for example, persisted well into the nineteenth century.

White contact somewhat improved the lot of the Santee wom-en, who found many uses for metal items such as iron and brass cooking pots. Women did all the field work and by custom the crops belonged to them. When on the trail they performed duties similar to their Cheyenne counterparts.[8]

Strong religious beliefs governed much of the everyday life in camp and during the hunt. For the Indians the natural world exuded mystery and power. Like the Cheyennes, the Santees at-tributed supernatural powers to nearly everything in nature and believed that even such common objects as rocks and trees de-manded reverence. Because spiritual forces continually threat-

5. Riggs, *Tah-koo Wah-kań*, p. 5; Wissler, "The North American Indians of the Plains," pp. 438–44.

6. Riggs, *Tah-koo Wah-kań*, pp. 21–22, 36.

7. Folwell, *History of Minnesota* 1:85–86.

8. Roy W. Meyer, *History of the Santee Sioux: United States Indian Policy on Trial* (Lincoln, Neb., 1967), pp. 20–21; Riggs, *Tah-koo Wah-kań*, p. 18.

ened, the Santees tried to placate these divinities with dances,
formal worship, and other expressions of gratitude.[9]

While the Santees clung stubbornly to their woodland-prairie
culture, beautiful, fertile Minnesota developed rapidly as a territory. Lake Superior, the Minnesota and Mississippi Rivers, and
the Red River of the North stimulated its commerce; its farmlands
lured husbandmen westward to reap rich harvests of corn and
wheat. In 1858 Minnesota achieved statehood, and within two
years its population had reached 172,023.[10]

As the frontier line pushed across the state in the 1850s, the
Santees withdrew. In 1851 at Traverse des Sioux and Mendota
they surrendered valuable portions of their domain in southern
and western Minnesota and accepted a new reserve: a 150-mile
strip of land along both sides of the Minnesota River. Technically
the Santees became reservation Indians for the first time; in practice they enjoyed much of their former freedom because the
government could not immediately contain them. By the mid-
fifties, with game fast disappearing from the Santees' old haunts
and numerous pioneer families settling ceded land, whites insisted that the Indians stay on their reservation. They had little
choice but to comply.[11]

In the late 1850s Santee Agent Joseph R. Brown persuaded
several of his charges to become full-time farmers, despite the
stigma of its being women's work. He equipped converts with
white men's clothing, their own cattle, houses, and eighty-acre
allotments, and made them cut their hair. Catholic and Protestant
missionaries also promoted the white man's way among the Santees. Besides preaching Christianity they studied the Sioux language, translated the Bible into the native tongue, established
elementary schools, and provided medical aid. The Reverend
Stephen R. Riggs encouraged one Santee group to form the
Hazelwood Republic, whose associates farmed individual tracts

9. Riggs, *Tah-koo Wah-kan*, pp. 55–57; 102–3; Blegan, *Minnesota*, pp. 23–25.
10. Charles S. Bryant, *A History of the Great Massacre by the Sioux Indians
... (Cincinnati, 1864), p. 415; *Population of the United States in 1860*, p. 14.
11. Kappler, *Indian Affairs* 2:588–93; Meyer, *Santee Sioux*, p. 88.

of reservation land.[12] The government reasoned that when all the Santees accepted severalty, they would require much less territory. Therefore the Indian Office negotiated two new treaties in 1858 by which the Eastern Sioux ceded that half of their reservation which lay north of the Minnesota River.[13]

The "civilization" clauses of the treaties of 1851 and 1858 directed the president to establish farms and manual labor schools and to erect mills and blacksmith shops on the Santee reservation. Certain other monies from the sale of Indian land were to be invested for the red men so that each year, for fifty years, they would receive an annuity payment. Accordingly, the government built sawmills and constructed two villages on the reservation: the Lower or Redwood Agency, to which the Wahpekutes and Mdewakantons were assigned, and the Upper or Yellow Medicine Agency for the Sissetons and Wahpetons. The Yellow Medicine River served as the dividing line between the Upper and Lower Sioux, as whites called them. In or near the agency towns lived Indian Office officials and their families, clergymen, doctors, teachers, interpreters, traders, carpenters, clerks, and millwrights.[14]

Several factors undermined Agent Brown's work in the late 1850s. One was the Santees' loss of respect for the federal government. Looters who broke into agency warehouses in 1855, 1856, and again in 1858 went unpunished. Nor did Washington chasten Inkpaduta's renegade band of Wahpekutes, which in 1857 massacred several whites in nearby northwest Iowa. Trouble within the Indian community also frustrated Brown.[15] To curtail the Santee-Chippewa feud, the Indian Office in 1846 had settled the Winnebago tribe from Iowa on an 800,000-acre buffer reserve in central Minnesota. The plan failed miserably. The luckless Winnebagos dreaded attacks from both sides and grew increasingly homesick for their prairie lands to the south. There were

12. Meyer, *Santee Sioux*, pp. 102ff; Roddis, *Indian Wars of Minnesota*, pp. 13–17.

13. Meyer, *Santee Sioux*, pp. 102ff; Kappler, *Indian Affairs* 2:781–89.

14. C. M. Oehler, *The Great Sioux Uprising* (New York, 1959), pp. 15–16.

15. Meyer, *Santee Sioux*, pp. 97–101, 105.

so many who forsook the reservation that in despair the government relocated them just below the Sioux lands, on a tract in what is now Blue Earth County.[16] Though the Santees and Winnebagos became quite friendly in the late 1850s, the Chippewa-Sioux rivalry continued. Even more disruptive to Indian Office economic plans was antagonism between the "farmer" and "blanket" Santees. Approximately nine-tenths of the Eastern Sioux steadfastly refused to abandon their old ways. Moreover, they so harassed the "cut-hairs" that the Hazelwood Republic collapsed in 1860.[17]

Despite this setback, missionaries and government officials remained optimistic about the Indians' future "progress." Too, the commissioner of Indian affairs emphasized the significance of such efforts among the Santees. "It will, indeed, be remarkable," he wrote in his annual report of 1859, "if the great and hitherto unsolved problem of the civilization and regeneration of the 'Red man,' shall be successfully worked out in the case of one of the wildest, most warlike, and, as heretofore believed, most untamable portions of this singular race."[18]

Many obstacles hindered the Sioux from achieving the civilization and regeneration of which the commissioner spoke. Thomas Galbraith discovered the serious factionalism between "farmer" and "blanket" Indians when he assumed charge of the Santee Agency in June 1861. An able agent, though inexperienced and a bit bullheaded, he continued Brown's severalty program even though it intensified the hostility of traditionalists. They complained, with some reason, that the government favored the landed "farmer" Indians, who by the summer of 1861 had 2,140 acres under cultivation on 145 farms, 124 of which were severalty farms. Perhaps this hostility to the government's "civilization" policy was unavoidable, but it made the agent's job more difficult since he lacked sufficient force to protect the unpopular farmer faction. Galbraith also reported that certain whites encouraged

16. Roddis, *Indian Wars of Minnesota*, pp. 7–8.
17. Meyer, *Santee Sioux*, pp. 105–8; Oehler, *Great Sioux Uprising*, pp. 15–16.
18. CIA, 1859, pp. 375–76.

the rift between the Indians and weakened his effectiveness.[19]

The most troublesome of those whites who for their own profit fomented discontent among the Sioux was the whiskey peddler. Bishop Whipple enumerated two reasons why "firewater," the curse of the Indian country, continued to flow across its borders. Annuity payments lured the peddler who knew the tribesman was unable to handle large sums of money and that a quick profit could be realized. The exposed location of the reservation abetted whiskey sales, too. In theory a reserve should be situated in a remote area and have natural boundaries; instead, the Upper and Lower Santee reservations, a scant ten miles wide after 1858, extended ribbonlike for 150 miles. "They nearly solved the problem of embracing the smallest area within the longest boundaries," wrote one historian. "An hour's walk brought the Indian to the edge of his country, to meet his deadliest foe, the white man with his whiskey jug."[20]

Collusion between the whiskey dealer and Indian accomplices swelled the flow of whiskey onto the reservation. According to Clark W. Thompson, head of the Northern Superintendency, which included Minnesota's Indians, the trader merely set up a store on the edge of the reserve and employed a Sioux as his clerk. Because the trader personally did not introduce spirituous liquors onto the reserve, he averted prosecution under federal trade and intercourse acts. Sometimes the huckster sold alcohol outside the reserve to an Indian middleman, who was encouraged to carry it back to his thirsty tribesmen. In this way the trader violated no statute and, according to Thompson, the Indian was also immune from punishment.[21]

If a bold hawker ventured onto the reservation to sell whiskey,

19. Galbraith to Clark W. Thompson, July 15, 1861, enclosed in Thompson to Dole, July 27, 1861, OIA, LR, St. Peter's [or Santee] Agency; Galbraith to Thompson, January 27, 1863, enclosed in Thompson to Dole, January 27, 1863, CIA, pp. 397–400.

20. Whipple to Buchanan, April 9, 1860, in Henry Benjamin Whipple, *Lights and Shadows of a Long Episcopate* ... (New York, 1912), pp. 51–52; Folwell, *History of Minnesota* 2:227–28.

21. Thompson to Dole, July 3, 1861, OIA, LR, Northern Supty.

it was difficult to apprehend him and to obtain his conviction, for
the agent had no security force to assist in the enforcement of
federal statutes. Should an arrest be made, the case was tried in
a nearby district or circuit court of the United States. This was
tantamount to acquittal. Juries composed of citizens of frontier
towns had little concern for the red man's welfare and, like the
defendent, frequently participated in some form of illegal trade
with the Sioux.[22]

Annuity money was a source of other problems for the Indian
Office besides encouraging the alcohol trade. The Santees claimed
that the government reneged on its treaty obligations by paying
a large part of their annuities to traders and others who presented
claims against the Sioux for damages or for yearly credit purchases.[23] Whether submitted in Washington or at the local agency,
the illiterate Indians had no recorded evidence to dispute such
claims.[24] Stephen Riggs testified that in 1861 the Upper Sioux
should have received $45,000 from Washington rather than
$36,000. The government paid $9,000 of the Santees' money to
white creditors and over half of it to the trading company of
Blake and Carruthers, which accused the Indians of stealing $5,500
worth of goods from their store at Big Stone Lake. The Indians
confessed that two tribesmen took some groceries worth no
more than two or three hundred dollars.[25]

Another cause of Indian discontent was the delay of an annuity
shipment from Washington. In mid-July 1862 the Upper Sioux
gathered as usual at the Yellow Medicine Agency. They brought

22. Whipple to Buchanan, April 9, 1860, Whipple, *Lights and Shadows*, pp.
51–52.

23. Galbraith to Thompson, January 27, 1863, enclosed in Thompson to
Dole, January 27, 1863, CIA, pp. 399–400; Asa W. Daniels, "Reminiscenses of
Little Crow," *Collections of the Minnesota Historical Society* 12 (St. Paul,
1908): 527–28.

24. Robert I. Holcombe, ed., "Chief Big Eagle's Story of the Sioux Outbreak
of 1862," *Collections of the Minnesota Historical Society* 6 (St. Paul, 1894): 835;
Return I. Holcombe and Lucius F. Hubbard, *Minnesota in Three Centuries*
(4 vols., New York, 1908) 3:280.

25. Deposition of Riggs to Commissioners on Sioux Indian Depredations
in Minnesota, *House Exec. Doc.* 58, 38 Cong., 1 Sess., 9:10 (Ser. 1189).

few provisions since the agency warehouse was known to be full and their money would soon be distributed. Unbeknownst to the waiting Santees, Washington officials still were wrangling over whether to substitute greenbacks for coin in the Sioux payment. As the days slipped by the five thousand Indians grew uneasy. A clerk told those who sought credit at the agency store that traders had claimed their entire annuity. As supplies dwindled, squaws dug roots for food or sold their husbands' weapons to white settlers. Agent Galbraith appeased the hungry Santees for almost three weeks by doling out small amounts of provisions. On August 4 the braves revolted, hacking their way into the warehouse to get goods for the needy families and threatening to drive all the whites from the reservation. Soldiers stationed at the agency restored order. Galbraith issued additional supplies to the Indians and sent them back to their homes with instructions to remain there until notified that the annuity payment would be made. No riots occurred at the Redwood Agency of the Lower Sioux, but the delay in payment caused sullenness and distrust. By the eighteenth when $71,000 in coin arrived at neighboring Fort Ridgely, five whites lay dead near Acton and the uprising had begun.[26]

The convulsion of Civil War, which caused the delay of the Sioux' annuity money, also generated restlessness among the Indians who sensed the excitement of April 1861 and Minnesota's concern for the survival of the Union. Newspapers kept on the counter at the trader's store pictured scenes of the war and proved a constant source of fascination and anxiety for the Sioux. Moreover, Civil War among the whites undermined Galbraith's efforts to preserve peace between the Indian nations. He reported "Often, when I have upbraided them for going to war with their hereditary enemies, the Chippewas, have they replied to me thus:

26. Mrs. N. D. White, "Captivity Among the Sioux, August 18 to September 26, 1862," *Collections of the Minnesota Historical Society* 9 (St. Paul, 1901): 396–97; Whipple, *Lights and Shadows*, p. 106; Willoughby M. Babcock, "Minnesota's Indian War," *Minnesota History* 38 (September, 1962): 94–95; Holcombe and Hubbard, *Minnesota in Three Centuries* 3: 283–84.

Our Great Father, we know, has always told us it was wrong to make war; now he is making war and killing a *great many*; how is this? We don't understand it." Some contemporaries attributed the Santees' restiveness to Confederate agents, who supposedly provoked the Indians with reports that only old men and boys remained to defend Minnesota's exposed frontiers. Galbraith and other officials reported no such meddling.[27]

Despite such administrative problems as delayed and reduced annuity payments, intra- or intertribal conflicts, and whiskey dealers, as long as the Santees remained at peace with the whites, acculturation was difficult but not an impossibility. By 1862 progress in agriculture and "civilization" was discernible at the Upper and Lower Agencies. Then on a beautiful Sunday afternoon in August 1862, four young braves shattered the peace between red man and white. By brutally taking the lives of five whites near the town of Acton, they created insurmountable problems for those concerned with their welfare.

During the early morning hours of Monday, August 18, the Lower Sioux chiefs and several warriors met in council. Fearing reprisals for the Acton murders, the majority of the bands voted for war against the whites. Little Crow (Taoyateduta), a chief of the Kaposia band of the Mdewakantons and the most powerful man present, opposed the action, but before dawn he yielded to the demands of angry young braves.[28]

Minnesota was caught by surprise when the Indians arose on its western border. A few newspaper reports of "Indian rumors" during August elicited no alarm. "We were beginning to regard the poetry of the palisades as a thing of the past," wrote one observer, "when, suddenly, our ears were startled by the echo of the warwhoop, and the crack of the rifle, and our hearts appalled by the gleam of the tomahawk and the scalping knife, as they descended in indiscriminate and remorseless slaughter, on defense-

27. Whipple, *Lights and Shadows*, p. 108; Galbraith to Thompson, January 27, 1863, enclosed in Thompson to Dole, January 27, 1863, CIA, p. 401. To the author's knowledge, no evidence exists that the Confederacy had paid-agents in Minnesota.

28. "Taoyateduta is Not a Coward," *Minnesota History* 38 (September, 1962): 115; Babcock, "Minnesota's Indian War," pp. 95–96.

less women and children on our border."[29] A few days after the uprising began, refugees choked all roads leading to the safety of St. Paul. Terrified women and children with their belongings and emigrants chattering in German, French, and Swedish greeted the advancing federal troops who marched westward to the scene of slaughter. Even St. Paul residents grew skittish as more survivors and refugees arrived each day. About midnight on August 28, reported Indian sightings in the northern part of the city caused a panic. Citizens armed themselves and made their way toward Third Street, but a thorough search uncovered no hostiles.[30]

From the onset disorganization characterized the Indians' attack on the Minnesota frontier. Independent bands refused to cooperate, and many braves seemed more interested in plunder than attacking enemy strongholds. The Santees planned first to destroy Fort Ridgely and the town of New Ulm, both near the southern tip of the Sioux reservation, then press down the Minnesota River to the Mississippi. Little Crow's unwise deployment of warriors, the loyalty of some "farmer" Indians to the whites, and the successful defense by volunteers of New Ulm and Fort Ridgely defeated the first objective. After a month-long series of minor clashes, Little Crow was decisively beaten in the Battle of Wood Lake, on September 23, 1862. His warriors and the Upper Sioux, who played a minor role in the massacres, fled to the plains of the Dakota country.[31]

Most knowledgeable officials agreed with Minnesota's lieutenant governor Ignatius Donnelly that the Sioux uprising was un-

29. Blegen, *Minnesota*, pp. 259–60; John G. Nicolay, "The Sioux War," *Continental Monthly* 3 (February, 1963), p. 195.

30. Charles W. Johnson, "Narrative of the Sixth Regiment," *Minnesota in the Civil and Indian Wars, 1861–65* (2 vols., St. Paul, 1890–93) 1:304; St. Paul *Pioneer and Democrat*, August 29, 1862.

31. Many histories of the Sioux uprising of 1862 may be consulted for a detailed account of military events. The best are: Kenneth Carley, *The Sioux Uprising of 1862* (St. Paul, 1961); Robert Huhn Jones, *The Civil War in the Northwest: Nebraska, Wisconsin, Iowa, Minnesota and the Dakotas* (Norman, 1960); Oehler, *The Great Sioux Uprising*; and Roddis, *Indian Wars of Minnesota*. An analysis of the number of civilians massacred during the outbreak appears in Appendix D of the last work. Roddis estimated the dead at 360.

premeditated. Others viewed the Santee War as part of a general uprising of Northwest Indians. Panic stricken settlers in Dakota Territory, Iowa, Kansas, and Nebraska Territory, for example, fled to more populated areas. "From all indications and information we are likely to have a general Indian war all along the frontier," wrote General John Pope who, fresh from humiliation at Bull Run, had been transferred to Minnesota to fight the Sioux. Washington officials, likewise uneasy, arranged for the California mails to be sent by sea rather than the overland route.[32] The fear of a widespread outbreak plus a latent hatred for the red man aroused a demand for revenge against all Minnesota Santees.

Shortly before the Battle of Wood Lake, friendly Sioux who had not participated in the massacres rescued 269 white captives from the hostile camp and under the leadership of Chief Wabasha escorted them to a village now called Camp Release, close by the Upper Agency. Word was sent to Colonel Henry Hastings Sibley, experienced frontiersman and commander of the Minnesota troops, that the hostages were safe. On September 25, 1862, Sibley's force reached Camp Release, where it took charge of the former captives and accepted the surrender of those hostiles who did not flee with Little Crow as well as the friendly Indians of Wabasha's band. General Pope instructed Sibley to treat all the Santees as "maniacs or wild beasts." Instead, the colonel appointed a military commission to try only those Indians accused of committing crimes during the outbreak. In early November 1862 the commission completed its work, having sentenced 307 to death and 16 to imprisonment.[33]

The verdicts met with public approval. Since mid-August newspaper editors and state officials had clamored for vengeance against the Sioux. "Exterminate the wild beasts," wrote Jane Swisshelm, editor of the St. Cloud *Democrat*, "and make peace with the devil and all his hosts sooner than with these red-jawed

32. Report of Donnelly, August 29, 1862, CIA, pp. 204–5; Pope to General-in-Chief Henry W. Halleck, September 16, 1862, *Minnesota in the Civil and Indian Wars* 2:232; *New York Times*, August 28, 1862.

33. Pope to Sibley, September 28, 1862, Rodis, *Indian Wars in Minnesota*, p. 141; Carley, *The Sioux Uprising of 1862*, pp. 60–61; Folwell, *History of Minnesota* 2:196.

tigers whose fangs are dripping with the blood of the innocents."
The commission decisions satisfied Sibley, too. Senator Henry M.
Rice of Minnesota, knowledgeable in the ways of the red man,
assured Bishop Whipple that the peace required execution of the
condemned Indians. So vehemently did the state's western residents concur, that when a rumor reached New Ulm that all the
convicted Indians would not be executed, its citizens attacked
Sibley's prisoners as he transferred them from the Lower Agency
to Mankato.[34]

The uprising of August 1862 forced government officials like
Agent Galbraith to yield authority to the army, and not until the
hostiles' defeat did the Indian Office and humanitarians again become active. Father Pierre De Smet, the famous black-robed Jes-
uit, cautioned that the execution of the condemned Sioux might
trigger reprisals against white prisoners in Dakota. It would be
far wiser, he advised, to keep the 307 Indians as hostages. Congregational missionaries John P. Williamson and Stephen R. Riggs
protested against the hasty and unfair actions of the military commission. "Four hundred have been tried in less time than is gen-
Williamson said.[35] Such pleas were not warmly received in Mineral[ly] taken in our courts with the trial of a single murderer,"
nesota. The Indian Office and the missionaries therefore concentrated on winning a presidential pardon.

On November 8, 1862, President Lincoln received a long telegram from General Pope, listing the names of the Santees condemned to be hanged. The president, who thought the figure
excessive, requested the trial transcripts be sent to him. No sooner
had Lincoln taken the matter into his hands than appeals for the
Indians' release and petitions for their execution deluged the

34. Jane Grey Swisshelm, *Crusader and Feminist: Letters of Jane Grey Swiss-
helm, 1858–65*, ed. by Arthur J. Larson (St. Paul, 1934), pp. 26–27; Sibley to
Whipple, December 7, 1862, Henry B. Whipple Papers, Minnesota Historical
Society, St. Paul; Rice to Whipple, November 19, 1862, Whipple Papers; St.
Paul *Pioneer*, November 13, 1862.

35. Galbraith to Thompson, January 27, 1863, enclosed in Thompson to
Dole, January 27, 1863, CIA, pp. 407–8; De Smet to Mix, December 12, 1862,
OIA, LR, Northern Supty.; Williamson to S. B. Treat, November 5, 1862, Correspondence of the American Board of Commissioners for Foreign Missions,
typed copies in the Minnesota Historical Society.

White House. Commissioner Dole periodically informed Secretary of the Interior Caleb Smith and the president of pleas for mercy received by the Indian Office, and recommended personally that not all the convicted Sioux be executed. Bishop Whipple journeyed to Washington to present his case for clemency.[36]

Petitions from various Minnesota towns and cities urged execution of all 307 Sioux. Politicians and the state press reflected public opinion with unusually bad taste. The St. Paul *Press* went so far as to warn the president: "We have hopes that the government will yet consent that capital punishment shall be meted out to all the condemned by the proper authorities, but, should another course be adopted, we feel very confident that the people will take the matter into their own hands, and do substantial justice." Governor Alexander Ramsey, one of the state's most influential Republican politicians, volunteered to order the execution of the Santees if the president wished to avoid the painful decision. No less patronizing was the letter from Minnesota's Senator Morton S. Wilkinson and Congressmen Cyrus Aldrich and William Windom, which began, "Mr. President, let us relate to you some facts with which we fear you have not heretofore been made acquainted." After chronicling a few hideous occurrences of the uprising, the legislators warned that a pardon of the Sioux prisoners would be odious to their constituents.[37]

In the face of such political pressure—not to mention the demands of civil war—Lincoln acted with restraint. It was his duty, he later wrote, to act not "with so much clemency as to encourage another outbreak, on the one hand, nor with so much severity as to be real cruelty, on the other." After a careful examination of the trial records, he ordered the execution of only those Indians who had violated females or participated in massacres. On De-

36. Message of the President of the United States in Answer to Senate Queries about Indian Barbarities in Minnesota, December 11, 1862, *Sen. Exec. Doc.* 7, 37 Cong., 3 Sess., 1:1 (Ser. 1149); Dole to Smith, November 10, 1862, CIA, p. 213; Dole to Smith, OIA, Report Books, 12: 511–12; Belgen, *Minnesota*, p. 280.

37. St. Paul *Press*, November 22, 1862; Ramsey to Lincoln, November 28, 1862, Lincoln Papers; Message of the President to the Senate, December 11, 1862.

cember 26, 1862, thirty-eight Santees were hanged at Mankato.[38]

Before the Interior Department could repair the damage done to the reservation program, Minnesotans demanded complete removal of the Sioux. Many residents believed peace would never be theirs until all Indians were driven from the state. The fiery owner of the St. Cloud *Democrat*, Jane Swisshelm, continued her campaign for extermination or removal. On an eastern lecture tour she raged before one audience, "We cannot breathe the same air with these demon violators of women, crucifiers of infants," and she called upon every Minnesota man "who has a soul" to take up his rifle and shoot every Indian he could find.[39]

Other appeals for removal of the Santees were less vindictive. Lieutenant Governor Donnelly feared that the Sioux would retard the state's growth. The economic argument for removal, though not easily distinguishable from pure hatred of the Indian, was prominent in the speeches and writings of Minnesota's congressmen and state officials. In his annual message to the Legislature at St. Paul in January 1863, Governor Ramsey warned that the welfare of the state required removal of the Indians.[40]

In Washington, Minnesota's representatives officially voiced these and other reasons for removal. Few opposed their demands. In mid-February 1863 Congress declared that the Santees, because of their uprising against the whites, must forfeit all lands within Minnesota. A subsequent act of March 3, 1863, authorized their removal from the state.[41] Only twice had the United States government extinguished Indian titles by right of conquest: in 1814 after the Creek war and following the Santee outbreak in Minnesota.[42]

In its removal bill of March 3, 1863, Congress required that the Sioux be relocated outside the limits of any state. In mid-

38. Message of the President to the Senate, December 11, 1862; Sibley to Lincoln, December 15 and 27, 1862, Lincoln, *The Works of Lincoln* 6:6–7n.

39. Portland *Daily Oregonian*, April 14, 1863.

40. Donnelly to Ramsey, August 29, 1862, St. Paul *Pioneer and Democrat*, September 2, 1862; Governor's Message, January 7, 1863, State of Minnesota, *Executive Documents for the Year 1862* (St. Paul, 1863), n.p.

41. *United States Statutes at Large* 12:652–54, 819.

42. Hodge, *Handbook of American Indians* 2:804.

December 1862, Secretary of the Interior Smith, in response to a query from Cyrus Aldrich's House Committee on Indian Affairs, recommended they be located on the unoccupied lands of the upper Missouri. Apparently this was acceptable, for the following March Dole and John P. Usher, the new Secretary of the Interior, chose for the Sioux the Fort Randall area, six hundred miles north of St. Louis. Few whites lived in the region and steamboats could conveniently supply a reservation. The presence of a fort seemed to assure protection for the Santees and for agency employees.[43]

Dole ordered Superintendent Clark Thompson to work out the details of removal, which were enough to overwhelm the most imaginative and resourceful administrator. He was to provide for miscellaneous exigencies occurring en route and supply the uprooted Indians until they became self-supporting, as well as hire blacksmiths and carpenters to fashion tools and to build the new agency near Fort Randall.[44]

The superintendent proceeded immediately to St. Louis to procure the necessary supplies, transportation facilities, and laborers. On April 16, 1863, he entered into a contract with P. Chouteau, Jr., and Company to ship the Sioux at twenty-five dollars per person from Fort Snelling to a point within a hundred miles of Fort Randall. Food would be provided at a cost to the government of ten cents a day per Indian. Mechanics and laborers were scarce because of the demands of the war and the mobilization of Missouri's Home Guards. When his work in St. Louis was completed, Thompson journeyed northward with men and equipment to Crow Creek, the site he would choose for the Sioux's new reservation, some 160 miles above Fort Randall on the Missouri River.[45]

The more than two hundred convicted Indians not executed in December 1862 were transferred in April 1863 from Mankato to

43. Smith to Aldrich, December 16, 1862, *House Report* 13, 37 Cong., 3 Sess. (Ser. 1173); Lass, "Removal from Minnesota of the Sioux and Winnebago Indians," p. 354.

44. Dole to Thompson, April 9, 1863, CIA, p. 419.

45. Dole to Thompson, April 8, 1863, CIA, pp. 417–18; Thompson to Dole, April 16 and May 28, 1863, OIA, LR, Northern Supty.; Thompson to Dole, April 28, 1863, CIA, p. 423.

Camp McClellan at Davenport, Iowa, and were not immediately affected by Congress's removal bill of March 1863.[46] The act applied only to the "friendlies" and those Sioux free of criminal convictions. In November 1862 the army had marched the latter group of Lower Sioux to Fort Snelling, located on a rocky bluff at the confluence of the Minnesota and Mississippi. On the river flats a fenced compound awaited them, where they pitched their tepees and passed the dreary winter of 1862–63. The Santees under guard in December numbered 1,601. Measles and other pestilences afflicted the incarcerated Indians, and 130 succumbed by mid-March 1863.[47]

During the first week in May 1863, the task of transferring the Santees from Fort Snelling to the Dakota country began. Though the overland route was a good deal shorter, the Indian Office favored cheaper and safer water transport. In Thompson's absence, his brother, Benjamin, acted as special agent in charge of removing the Sioux. Those on board the *Davenport* steamed all the way to St. Louis; the *Northerner* sent its Indians by rail from Hannibal to St. Joseph. There the Indians camped in army tents and awaited the *Davenport*'s passengers to be brought up river by the *Florence*, a steamer large enough to accommodate all the Santees. On May 17 the *Florence* reached St. Joseph and took the rest of the Sioux on board. Crowded conditions forced half the Indians to remain on the hurricane deck, and still there was not room enough for all of them to lie down at once. Their food, half-rations, consisted of hard bread and uncooked mess pork. For the sick there were few medicines on board and no doctor. The *Florence* docked at the mouth of Crow Creek on June 1, 1863, after a twelve-day voyage from St. Joseph.[48]

46. Lass, "Removal from Minnesota of the Sioux and Winnebago Indians," p. 356.

47. John P. Williamson to Thomas S. Williamson, November 17, 1862, Thomas S. Williamson Family Papers, Minnesota Historical Society; Sibley to Usher, March 14, 1865, OIA, LR, St. Peter's Agency; Folwell, *History of Minnesota* 2:252.

48. J. P. Williamson to Mrs. T. S. Williamson, May 13, 1863, Francis H. Relf, "Removal of the Sioux Indians from Minnesota," *Minnesota History* 2 (May, 1918): 420–25; J. P. Williamson to Riggs, May 14, 1863, Stephen R. Riggs

It is difficult to comprehend the suffering, confusion, uncertainty, and sense of loss the Santees felt during the forced emigration from their Minnesota homeland in the spring of 1863. The successive shocks of national military defeat, forced marches, imprisonment, and deportation have no comparable parallels in our modern American life. "The journey … put me somewhat in mind of the children of Israel journeying to the land of Canaan," the Reverend John P. Williamson wrote, "only it is just the reverse. Instead of taking them straight through[,] God led them around by the way of the wilderness—so that the desire might not rise to return. The Government is taking these Indians almost as round about a way from one wilderness to another around by the way of civilization—steamboats and railroads—in order I suppose that the Indians may think that they can never find the way back."[49]

Considering conditions, the commissioner and his officers did a respectable job. Unlike similar removals in the 1830s there was no "Trail of Tears." Twenty-four of the 1,318 Sioux died between May 4 and June 3, but on such a long journey under crowded conditions this must be expected. The cost to the government: $36,322.10, not an unreasonable sum.[50] This much, then, was to the office's credit; it helped to save the Santees from angry and vengeful Minnesotans. However, the problem of settling them on a reservation and teaching them the white man's way of life was not solved, but merely transferred from Minnesota to the upper Missouri. Here, the relocation of nearly thirteen hundred refugees created new administrative problems in addition to the old.

The sight which greeted the Indians at Crow Creek on June 1, 1863, was a stark and dismal contrast to the green prairies of western Minnesota. A serious drought gripped the Dakota Territory, scorching the plains grass. A cottonwood grove along the

Family Papers, Minnesota Historical Society; J. P. Williamson to T. S. Williamson, May 25, 1863, T. S. Williamson Papers; Testimony of J. P. Williamson, JSC, pp. 413–15.

49. J. P. Williamson to Riggs, May 14, 1863, Riggs Papers.

50. J. P. Williamson to T. S. Williamson, June 3, 1863, Williamson Papers; Certificates of Receipt given to P. Chouteau and Company, June 1863, JSC, pp. 394–95.

river formed the only greenery visible; the only arable soil, a thin strip of bottomland. Wild life existed but few Indians possessed the guns or the horses necessary for hunting.[51] Superintendent Thompson called the Santees' new home the best one available on the upper Missouri;[52] to most other observers it seemed a poor choice. An old French woodchopper warned the Reverend Williamson about the unpredictability of a Dakota crop. "Sometime she grow, & sometimes she grow not," was his sagacious observation after forty-five years on the plains. Williamson reported that a second pioneer recalled that he had once spent four hundred dollars trying to farm a strip north of Fort Randall and could not "raise a potatoe as large as the end of his thumb, or enough nubbins for his corn—so he gave it up."[53]

Despite the agricultural disadvantages the Indians at Crow Creek had to be fed, so the superintendent ordered that all arable land near the river be prepared for planting. The hard soil and tree roots splintered the plows, which were not designed for such sod. Nevertheless, the Indians planted potatoes, corn, and other vegetables in the inhospitable soil.[54] By the first of July the corn crop looked promising, but as summer drew on, lack of moisture and the intense heat of the sun proved too much for the young stalks, which curled and shriveled into a dull brown. The other vegetables did not come up at all.[55]

The Indians' inability to catch game and the failure of the summer crop forced Thompson to feed the thirteen hundred disconsolate Santees on imported flour and meat. Since the Missouri River was navigable only during a short period in the spring, the superintendent hauled provisions overland. At first he purchased goods at Sioux City or St. Louis, but inflated prices made the cost prohibitive. The Indian Office judged that the most practical way to feed its charges during the winter was to freight provisions overland from Mankato. The army agreed to escort the wagon

51. J. P. Williamson to T. S. Williamson, June 3, 1863, Williamson Papers; Samuel Hinman to Whipple, June 8, 1863, Whipple Papers.

52. Thompson to Dole, May 28, 1863, OIA, LR, Northern Supty.

53. J. P. Williamson to T. S. Williamson, June 9, 1863, Williamson Papers.

54. Thompson to Dole, July 1, 1863, CIA, p. 441.

55. Testimony of J. P. Williamson, JSC, pp. 413–15.

train. The "Expedition to Moscow," as the servicemen dubbed it, traversed the three-hundred-mile expanse in the dead of winter, arriving at Crow Creek on December 2, 1863.[56]

Finances were such that the quantities of flour and meat brought from Minnesota had to last until May 1864. To stretch the daily ration as far as possible, agency employees served the Indians a thin gruel prepared in a specially constructed vat. Flour, a few beans, pork, and sections of slaughtered cattle, including the heads and entrails, were dumped into it. A steampipe which ran from a boiler into the vat cooked the conglomeration. In communal fashion each Indian family received a measured amount of the mixture per day, though some refused to eat the foul-smelling stew. Dr. S. C. Haynes, a surgeon at the nearby military post, recalled that he once passed by the apparatus during a cleaning and "the settlings smelt like carrion—like decomposed meat."[57]

Those Santees who refused the contents of the vat had limited alternatives for obtaining food. Some women and children cut wood along the river and sold it to government workers in exchange for flour.[58] Other tribesmen stole horse feed. Poisoned wolves and dead army mules supplied meat in addition to skins for warm clothing. Starving females prostituted themselves for food.[59]

Thompson's inability to provide for all the Indians at Crow Creek partly resulted from insufficient funds. There were two reasons for this. First, the Indian Office expected that the Sioux would be self-supporting on their new reservation. When their agricultural efforts failed they became dependent upon the government. Second, Congress planned to finance any additional needs of the Sioux by selling their reservation lands in Minnesota, but as late as March 1864 the General Land Office had not yet surveyed the old reserve. Survival of the Crow Creek Indians thus

56. J. P. Williamson to T. S. Williamson, August 4, 1863, T. S. Williamson Papers; Johnson, "Narrative of the Sixth Regiment," pp. 317–18; Willim E. Lass, "The 'Moscow Expedition,'" *Minnesota History*, 39 (Summer, 1965): 235–40.

57. Testimony of Dr. S. C. Haynes, September 2, 1865, JSC, pp. 401–2.

58. The Reverend Edward R. Pond claimed that this flour came from the Indians' own rations, Testimony of Edward R. Pond, JSC, pp. 408–9.

59. Testimonies of Dr. S. C. Haynes, September 2, 1865, and Judson Lamoure, JSC, pp. 401–2.

hinged on appropriations from Congress, which were tardy and inadequate.[60]

By January 1864 it was obvious that the Indians would starve before spring unless some left the reservation. Even government officials and the missionaries encouraged them to disperse. About two hundred Indians journeyed downstream to the vicinity of Fort Randall where they grubbed food and shelter from white soldiers and farmers and from their cousins the Yankton Sioux, who camped near the post. Soon thereafter a scout reported large herds of buffalo on the plains a hundred miles north of Crow Creek. Fifty rifles purchased by Superintendent Thompson were distributed to the Santee hunters. They and their families left immediately in pursuit of the herds with instructions to return in time for the spring planting. The six hundred Indians who remained on the reservation received adequate nourishment during the rest of the winter.[61]

In mid-July 1864 clouds of hungry grasshoppers, borne by northerly winds, destroyed all hope for another year of sustaining the Indians by agriculture. The insects even devoured wild berries and edible roots which the squaws gathered. The destitute Santees returned to their monotonous diet of flour and meat. An occasional fish from the river was all that highlighted an otherwise drab menu. Winter snows and winds of 1864–65 might have produced another tragedy at Crow Creek, but by then disease and migration had so decimated their numbers that those on the reservation received adequate food and clothing.[62]

As long as most of the Indians remained, the constant scarcity of food and clothing at Crow Creek contributed to sickness. Their health steadily deteriorated after their arrival in Dakota, where the change in climate and water caused diarrhea and dysentery.

60. Dole to Usher, March 30, 1864, OIA, Report Books, 13:354; CIA, 1864, p. 184. Annuity payments had been forfeited according to the act of February 16, 1863, which dissolved treaties with the Sioux.

61. J. P. Williamson to T. S. Williamson, December 24, 1863, Williamson Papers; J. P. Williamson to Editor of *Missionary Herald*, April 4, 1864, *Missionary Herald of the American Board* 60 (July, 1864): 203–4.

62. Testimony of Edward R. Pond, JSC, pp. 408–9; J. P. Williamson to Riggs, July 5, 1864, Riggs Papers.

Lack of nourishment further weakened them. Dr. John S. Wakefield, an old employee from the Minnesota reservation, came to minister to the sick, but discouraged by the lack of medical supplies and afraid of unsettled conditions, he left Crow Creek for Fort Randall early in June. The Angel of Death replaced the good doctor at the Dakota reservation. By June 9, fifteen Indians were dead. During the first week of August the death rate climbed sharply. All the children had whooping cough; others suffered from a variety of illnesses the missionaries could not diagnose. On September 26, 1863, Williamson estimated that 137 Indians had died since June 1, and noted further that there were only a few babies and small children left. Harsh winter winds chilled the thinly clad people. Death from exposure took its toll. By midwinter one hundred and fifty more perished from freezing and starvation. The Indians' health improved after they scattered from the reservation, but only three-fourths of the Sioux lived to return for the spring planting.[63]

Hostile partisans of Little Crow who surrounded the Crow Creek reservation threatened Indian Office employees as well as the Minnesota Santees. Captain Miner of Company A, Dakota Cavalry, was stationed at Crow Creek with forty men, yet residents felt insecure with such a small force.[64] Beginning in July 1863, Superintendent Thompson sent periodic requisitions to Washington for adequate military support but received no sympathetic response. To protect the outpost in the meantime, he built a four-hundred-foot-square cedar log stockade which was completed, with most of the agency buildings, by mid-September 1863. Minor raids continued with the resultant loss of horses and cattle. Early in October Chester Adams, acting agent at Crow Creek, reported the resignation of more than three-fourths of his employees because of the danger of Indian attack. And as late as the winter of 1863–64, the superintendent and his agent still entreated the War Department and Indian Office to post additional

63. J. P. Williamson to T. S. Williamson, June 9 and August 4, 1863, Williamson Papers; J. P. Williamson to Mrs. S. R. Riggs, September 26, 1863, Riggs Papers; T. S. Williamson, H. D. Cunningham, J. P. Williamson and Edward R. Pond to Usher and Dole, September 8, 1864, CIA, p. 565.

64. J. P. Williamson to T. S. Williamson, June 9, 1863, Williamson Papers.

troops at Crow Creek.[65] The threatened assault by the plains tribes never materialized, yet the reservation's precarious location contributed to the low morale and inefficiency of all who lived there.

The relocation at Crow Creek of 1,945 Winnebagos expelled from Minnesota made more difficult, if not impossible, the solution to the Indian Office's problems of agriculture, supply, disease, and protection. Few if any Winnebagos participated in the uprising of 1862, but Minnesota whites made no distinction between peaceful and hostile Indians.[66] As early as October 1, 1862, one St. Paul paper called for the speedy removal of the Winnebagos on the grounds that Minnesotans would be endangered as long as they remained in the state. A desire for Winnebagos' land also provided a strong motive for expulsion. Situated like an island in the midst of a white population, their reservation covered four and one-half townships of rich farmland.[67]

Secretary of the Interior Caleb B. Smith suggested to Cyrus Aldrich of the House Committee on Indian Affairs the passage of a bill to relocate the Winnebagos. On February 21, 1863, Congress enacted a statute for their peaceful exodus from Minnesota.[68]

Seven weeks later Commissioner Dole instructed Winnebago agent St. André Durand Balcombe to arrange for the transportation of the Indians to Crow Creek. Balcombe was also to persuade his charges that eviction from Minnesota was for their own protection and that the Indian Office would find them a satisfactory new home.[69] The Winnebagos gave up the reservation, though

65. Thompson to Dole, July 1, 1863, CIA, p. 348; Adams to Sibley, October 7, 1863, Clark W. Thompson Papers, Minnesota Historical Society; Thompson to Mix, September 15, 1863, OIA, LR, Northern Supty.

66. Pope to Lincoln, November 17, 1862, Records of the Legislative Branch, House Committee on Indian Affairs, Wartime Records, 37 Cong., National Archives; Smith to Cyrus Aldrich, December 16, 1862, *House Report* 13, 37 Cong., 3 Sess., n.p.

67. St. Paul *Pioneer*, October 1, 1862; Gideon Welles, *Diary of Gideon Welles; Secretary of the Navy Under Lincoln and Johnson*, ed. by Howard K. Beale (3 vols., New York, 1960), 1, October 14, 1862: 171.

68. Smith to Aldrich, December 16, 1862, *House Report* 13, 37 Cong., 3 Sess., n.p.; *United States Statutes at Large* 12:658–60.

69. Dole to Balcombe, April 10, 1863, OIA, LS, 70:256–57.

they hated to leave their crops and houses, and gathered at Camp Porter on the Minnesota River near Mankato to await their departure. During the second week in May, river boats took them down to Fort Snelling. From there they followed the route taken by the Santees: to Hannibal by steamer, across to St. Joseph in freight cars and up the Missouri to Crow Creek. By June 24, nearly two thousand Winnebagos disembarked at their new reservation, located next to that of the Sioux.[70]

From the moment of their arrival the Winnebagos were disheartened. The presence of forty soldiers and the small stockade offered little protection against Little Crow's scavenging Sioux. "What preparations had been made to receive so many wretched beings, who saw themselves forced to leave their tents, cabins, fields, gardens, mills, fishing-grounds?" asked Father De Smet. "They were given in exchange a portion of desert, comparatively uncultivated and miserable, destitute of animals and game."[71]

The Winnebagos also quarrelled with the Santees refugees, whom they blamed for their expulsion from Minnesota. The previous autumn the Winnebagos attempted to curry favor with the whites by killing two Sioux who sought asylum on their reservation. Though the whites were unimpressed, the grisly deed caused additional ill will between the two nations.[72]

Life at Crow Creek became intolerable for the Winnebagos. The nightmare took on the grim proportions of reality as winter struck the Dakota country. To escape starvation and death over five hundred fled their reservation in late September 1863, so that only 1,382 remained in December to receive supplies brought by the "Expedition to Moscow."[73] Agent Walter A. Burleigh

70. Balcombe to Thompson, May 12, 1863, OIA, FOR, Northern Supty. For a more detailed description of the Winnebagos' removal, see Lass, "Removal from Minnesota of the Sioux and Winnebago Indians," pp. 360–63.

71. Thompson to Dole, October 1, 1864, CIA, p. 539; De Smet to [Editor of the *Précis Historiques?*], May 17, 1864, Hiram M. Chittenden and Alfred T. Richardson, eds., *Life, Letters, and Travels of Father Pierre-Jean de Smet, S.J., 1801–1873 . . .* (4 vols., New York, 1905), 3:821.

72. Thompson to Dole, October 1, 1864, CIA, p. 542; Lass, "Removal from Minnesota of the Sioux and Winnebago Indians," p. 361.

73. Thompson to Dole, October 1, 1864, CIA, p. 539.

reported that seventy-five to one hundred starving, ill-clad Winnebagos journeyed downstream to his Yankton reservation in November 1863.[74] The army fed and put to work those who made their way to Fort Randall. At the request of Agent Balcombe the military later ordered the Winnebagos to return to the reservation. They refused; to go back meant starvation or murder by the hostile Sioux. Instead, these resourceful and desperate Indians traveled overland to Nebraska Territory and Iowa.[75]

Attempts to locate the runaway Winnebagos and minister to their needs exposed other Indian Office administrative problems, such as faulty communications and confusion over responsibilities. After receiving a House Resolution about the plight of the Winnebagos, Thompson admitted to Commissioner Dole in May 1864 that he had not received an official communication from Crow Creek since he had left in mid-December to find an answer to his supply problem. Private letters from Crow Creek assured him there were sufficient provisions. Apparently, Thompson explained, only those Winnebagos who left the reservation suffered hunger.[76] Chester Adams was probably the superintendent's source of information. Thompson employed him to oversee the civilian work force, and in the spring of 1864 he was also acting agent for the Sioux and Winnebagos. But why put Adams in command? What became of Balcombe, to whom Thompson had delegated this authority?[77]

When Thompson first journeyed to Washington in the summer of 1863 to arrange for feeding the Crow Creek Indians, Balcombe

74. Burleigh to Alfred Sully, November 6, 1863, enclosed in Edward R. S. Canby to Usher, December 8, 1863, OIA, LR, Northern Supty.

75. Sully to J. F. Meline, Acting Assistant Adjutant General, Department of the Northwest, November 21, 1863, enclosed in Canby to Usher, December 8, 1863, OIA, LR, Northern Supty.; Sully to Assistant Adjutant General, Department of the Northwest, May 28, 1864, enclosed in Edwin M. Stanton to Usher, June 14, 1864, OIA, LR, Winnebago Agency.

76. Thompson to Dole, May 3, 1864, OIA, LR, Winnebago Agency.

77. The Office of Indian Affairs deemed it unnecessary to have agents for both the Santees and the Winnebagos at Crow Creek, because of their adjoining reserves. Galbraith was thus recalled to Minnesota to serve with the Sioux claims commission, Lass, "The 'Moscow Expedition,'" pp. 229–30.

had gone to Sioux City, ostensibly to attend to a family illness. Thereafter he spent most of his time in that city while Adams looked after things at Crow Creek.[78]

This arrangement proved unsatisfactory. In February 1864 Balcombe received a curt letter from the commissioner, who had just learned from Agent Burleigh of the Winnebagos' destitute situation and their wanderings in Iowa and Nebraska Territory. Why, Dole asked, must the Indian Office rely upon agents of other tribes for information about the Winnebagos? The commissioner sent a second inquiring letter to Balcombe in May and another to Thompson in June, requesting information so that he could inform Congress, the military, and irate citizens in the Midwest.[79] Communications were hopelessly snarled, with the commissioner as well as the superintendent ignorant of the tribe's condition and whereabouts.

Balcombe attributed the Winnebagos' unfortunate condition to their own stubbornness. They refused to farm, to hunt, or to accept Crow Creek as their new home. They could get food and supplies at Crow Creek or they could do without; it was not government policy to maintain them anywhere else. If Indian agents and the military drove them away from other reservations instead of feeding them, the starving Indians might be encouraged to return to their reservation.[80]

When the Winnebagos left Crow Creek a majority made their way south to the Omaha Indians' reservation in Nebraska Territory. A Winnebago delegation had initiated negotiations with this tribe after the failure of their first summer crop at Crow Creek. Omaha chiefs agreed to receive their impoverished neighbors when the Winnebagos promised to pay their own expenses from annuities. However, instead of a few hundred as the Omahas anticipated, more than twelve hundred Winnebagos arrived by August 1864. The problems engendered by their mass migration

78. *Ibid.*

79. Dole to Balcombe, February 11, 1864, OIA, LS, 73:151; Dole to Balcombe, May 12, 1864, OIA, LS, 74:116; Dole to Thompson, June 17, 1864, OIA, LS, 74:324.

80. Balcombe to Thompson, June 21, 1864, OIA, Records of the Northern Supty.; Balcombe to Dole, June 21, 1864, OIA, LR, Winnebago Agency.

taxed the skills of the Omaha agent, Robert W. Furnas, as well as the entire Indian Office, now that it had established their whereabouts.[81]

Subsistence of the Winnebagos was as much a problem on the Omaha reserve as at Crow Creek. Balcombe continued to live in Sioux City, thirty-five miles away, and ignored his charges. When Agent Furnas complained about feeding the Indians until June 1864, at a cost of over $10,500 to the government, Balcombe responded that if Furnas would not feed the Winnebagos so well they might return to Crow Creek.[82] In July Superintendent Thompson visited the Omaha Agency to scrutinize the Winnebago subsistence accounts and to inquire about the possibility of concentrating the entire tribe there. The disagreement continued over who was responsible for the Winnebagos' welfare, although Thompson instructed Furnas to continue to feed the refugees.[83] Balcombe maintained that he could do nothing about gathering them together at Crow Creek; moral suasion had failed and he was not provided with a military force or the means to transport and feed his Indians. Thompson noted that he too lacked the power to drive the Winnebagos back to Crow Creek. If, at great expense, the Indians were returned, what would prevent their scattering again at the first opportunity? Perhaps the money might better be spent in subsisting them in Nebraska until the government could devise a method to keep the Winnebagos at Crow Creek.[84]

The problem of subsistence became serious when more Winnebagos arrived at the Nebraska agency during the late winter months of 1864. Furnas wrote: "They have had no clothing furnished them since they have been here and [are] now [at] *mid-*

81. Furnas to Dole, May 3, 1864, OIA, FOR, Northern Supty.; Robert C. Farb, "Robert W. Furnas as Omaha Indian Agent, 1864–1866," *Nebraska History* 32 (September, 1951): 189–91.

82. Furnas to William M. Albin, June 8, 1864, OIA, LR, Winnebago Agency; Abstract of Disbursement for Winnebagos Subsistence, Furnas Papers, Nebraska State Historical Society, Lincoln; Balcombe to Dole, June 21, 1864, OIA, LR, Winnebago Agency.

83. Thompson to Dole, September 13, 1864, OIA, LR, Winnebago Agency.

84. Balcombe to Thompson, September 23, 1864, *ibid.*; Thompson to Dole, October 1, 1864, CIA, p. 541.

winter so nearly universally naked, that one half of them pos-
itively cannot get out of their tents, and the young and old and
feeble, are *actually freezing to death*."[85]

Dole wired the Omaha agent authorization to spend $3,000 to
clothe the Winnebagos.[86] The commissioner then informed Balcombe that the Office had learned from reliable sources that the
Winnebagos on the Omaha reservation were dying from the
cold. This was incomprehensible since provisions had been sent
for the Winnebagos. Why had Balcombe taken no action on behalf of his Indians? Why had he failed to keep the department
advised of their condition? If the Indians' goods had not reached
him, where were they? Finally, the commissioner remarked, "I
understand that you do not consider them [Winnebagos] under
your charge, and that it is not your duty to visit them and keep
this office advised of their condition."[87] If this were true, and
Balcombe's actions suggest it was, then the breakdown of the
lines of authority and communication within the Indian Office
was indeed serious. Who had responsibility for the Winnebagos
on the Omaha reserve, their appointed agent or the local one? The
question was never clearly answered during Dole's administration.

Because of complaints about wandering Winnebagos in Iowa
and elsewhere,[88] the commissioner decided to purchase a portion
of the Omaha reserve on which to settle the scattered Winnebagos permanently. The Indians agreed to the plan and promised
to pay the Omahas $50,000 for 153,600 acres of good farmland
on the north side of their reservation. In March 1865, Dole
authorized Balcombe to remove all agency property and any
Winnebagos from Crow Creek to their new home, to procure
agency buildings and to break up five hundred acres on the northern third of the Omahas' land.[89]

---

85. Furnas to Thompson, November 1, 1864, Thompson Papers; Furnas to
Dole, December 19, 1864, OIA, LR, Winnebago Agency.

86. Furnas to Dole, January 5, 1865, OIA, LR, Winnebago Agency.

87. Dole to Balcombe, December 27, 1864, OIA, LS, 76:81.

88. B. D. Holbrook to Dole, July 22, 1864, OIA, LR, Winnebago Agency.

89. CIA, 1864, pp. 183–84; Edward B. Taylor to Dennis N. Cooley, August
23, 1865, CIA, pp. 593–94; Dole to Balcombe, March 25, 1865, OIA, LR, Winnebago Agency.

The Office of Indian Affairs reorganized the Northern Super-intendency shortly after the death of Lincoln. The Winnebagos continued to live on their new reserve under the jurisdiction of the northern superintendent. The Dakota Superintendency took charge of the Lower Sioux at Crow Creek.[90] In the spring of 1865 they numbered 1,043, of whom 900 were women and children.[91] Still discontented with the barren country of the upper Missouri they asked to be assigned to a new reservation.[92] This the government did the following year for its own convenience, placing them near the mouth of the Niobrara River in Nebraska, where an additional 247 Santees, mainly men released from the Davenport prison, joined them.[93]

The difficulties engendered by the relocation of the Santees and Winnebagos severely taxed the resources of the Indian Office and ultimately proved more tragic than the process of removal. In the first place, the location of the reservation was a poor choice. As the Santees and Winnebagos viewed their new, drought-stricken homeland, then witnessed the failure of the first crops, they lost all desire to farm the land. To survive they ventured out onto the plains to hunt the buffalo as they had done in the past or begged food from the whites. This undermined a basic policy of the Indian Office: to encourage the red man to abandon the chase and to adopt white man's ways.[94] Though Balcombe shirked his duties, the most attentive agent probably could not have kept the Winnebagos at Crow Creek without a large military force.

A second factor that contributed to the relocation difficulties at Crow Creek was the lack of warriors in the total Santee population. Three-fourths of the Indians were women and children, com-

90. CIA, 1865, pp. 215–16.

91. James M. Stone to Newton Edmunds, October 3, 1865, CIA, pp. 412–13.

92. A. W. Hubbard to James R. Doolittle, n.d., JSC, p. 365.

93. Taylor to Cooley, December 30, 1865, OIA, LR, Dakota Supty.; Meyer, *Santee Sioux*, p. 156. The Indians in Davenport prison were those President Lincoln saved from hanging in December 1862. Thomas S. Williamson and Stephen R. Riggs ministered to them, and their papers in the Minnesota Historical Society describe prison conditions. For details about the removal of the Sioux in 1866, see OIA, Special File No. 235.

94. Hinman to Whipple, June 6, 1864, Whipple Papers.

paratively defenseless if attacked by plains tribes. Morale was lower and the death rate higher than if more warriors had been present. Women were inexperienced hunters, and in order to obtain food they had to journey to Fort Randall where they sold wood to the soldiers or prostituted themselves.

The presence of the Winnebagos did little to improve conditions at Crow Creek. They believed their removal from Minnesota was unjust and refused to live on their new reserve. Their rivalry with the Santees attracted hostile warriors from the west, exposed the military weakness of the outpost and made the Santees increasingly restless. Yet, unlike the Sioux, the Winnebagos had a balanced population. Their warriors provided the leadership to escape the confinement of Crow Creek and to migrate to the Omaha lands in Nebraska. While at Crow Creek, however, the mutual incompatibility of Santees and Winnebagos compounded the problems of the Indian Office.

A fourth reason for the failure at Crow Creek was its isolation. The poor soil, imbalance in the Sioux population, and the resentful attitude of the Winnebagos meant that supplies and dispatches had to flow freely from the East if the Indian Office were to avoid a tragedy. The Crow Creek reservation, it was hoped, would insulate the Indians from harmful white influences. Ironically it frustrated help from the whites when it was most needed. Supplies shipped overland were delayed, executive and congressional officials seemed unsure of conditions in Dakota Territory, and Superintendent Thompson had to travel back and forth between the upper Missouri and the nation's capital.

Two additional factors contributed to the failure at Crow Creek. The Civil War inflated the price of goods and services throughout the West, which meant that congressional appropriations fell short of the amounts required and that goods had to be hauled overland from Minnesota rather than purchased at Sioux City or St. Louis and shipped upstream. Second, the Office of Indian Affairs was beset by problems contingent to the Santee uprising: the fate of Winnebagos and Eastern Sioux not removed from Minnesota and the irksomeness of outspoken critics of Indian policy. Such troubles, aside from diversionary effects, were not themselves of great significance; but, like a small rock out-cropping that exposes large formations to the geologist, they reveal to the historian other problems of Indian administration in the Old Northwest.

In the spring of 1863 Benjamin Thompson transferred 1,318 Indians from Fort Snelling to the steamers *Davenport* and *Northerner.* The 283 Santees left within the compound were, for the most part, the Lower Sioux who had helped to save the lives of countless whites in the bloody months of August and September 1862.[95] Their salvation from the fate of their Dakota-bound brethren was due to the efforts of humanitarians like Bishop Whipple and favorable recommendations from the Indian Office. Many of these warriors became scouts for General Sibley and, with their families, settled near Big Stone Lake, where they patrolled the border along the protective cordon of forts and stockades on Minnesota's western frontier.[96] Others who had been farmers before the outbreak turned to hunting for a living, since the government offered no economic aid.[97]

The fate of an Indian named Taopi was illustrative no doubt of the Lower Sioux. In September 1863 he journeyed to Faribault, Minnesota, to inform Bishop Whipple of the friendly Indians' impoverishment. Since Taopi planned to seek aid from General Sibley in St. Paul, Whipple wrote to the commander asking him to provide a home for Taopi. Sibley responded sympathetically to Whipple's entreaties, emphasizing that he was powerless to help Taopi. Since the friendlies had severed relations with their tribe, all he could do was to place them west of his outside military line and provide them with rations. Taopi refused to go. When he asked if Sibley would permit some of them to hunt in the vicinity of Fort Ridgely, the reply was, "No." Too many trappers in the area could not resist the temptation of collecting the $200 bounty for each Santee scalp. All the general promised was to

95. Charles Mix to Dole, May 18, 1863, OIA, LR, Northern Supty.; Roddis, *Indian Wars of Minnesota,* p. 197.

96. Mix to Dole, May 18, 1863, OIA, LR, Northern Supty.; Winifred W. Barton, *John P. Williamson, A Brother to the Sioux* (New York, 1919), pp. 90–91.

97. Hinman to Dole, March 15, 1865, OIA, LR, St. Peter's Agency.

allow the outcasts to care for themselves and not to send them to Crow Creek.[98]

Early in 1865 the Secretary of the Interior proposed to settle the wandering Santees on eighty-acre plots provided by the removal act of March 1863 for the friendly Indians who had rendered outstanding service. Yet Minnesotans could no more accept a friendly Sioux than an unfriendly one, and before the secretary could assign them to allotments along the upper Minnesota, white settlers elbowed their way onto the land and refused to have red men as neighbors. Therefore those Santees who did not join Sibley's scouts remained homeless. Many of the outcasts eventually settled near Faribault and Mendota, on the private lands of Alexander Faribault and General Sibley.[99]

The destiny of a third Santee group requires some annotation. Sisseton and Wahpeton bands of the Upper Agency scattered following Little Crow's defeat at Wood Lake in September 1862. For five years they wandered over the trackless Dakota plains, causing havoc among the Indians at Crow Creek and leading in a merry chase the punitive expeditions sent out in 1863 and 1864. Equally alarming to the federal government was the hostiles' occasional gravitation toward Canada, where some found refuge, or in the direction of their former homeland. The meanderings were significant to the Office of Indian Affairs because they rekindled the fires of fear and Indian hatred in the Minnesota Valley, and increased the difficulty of providing for friendly Sioux such as Taopi. In 1867 Washington negotiated a treaty with most of the Sissetons and Wahpetons which provided reservations for them in Dakota Territory on the south side of Devil's Lake and between Lake Traverse and Lake Kampeska.[100]

---

98. Whipple to Sibley, September 21, 1863, Henry H. Sibley Papers, Minnesota Historical Society; Sibley to Whipple, October 13, 1863, and February 17 and July 23, 1864, Whipple Papers.

99. Hinman to Dole, March 15, 1865, OIA, LR, St. Peter's Agency; Folwell, *History of Minnesota* 2:263–64.

100. Folwell, *History of Minnesota* 2:418; Kappler, *Indian Affairs* 2:956–59. For an analysis of the impact of the Sioux War on United States relations with Great Britain, see Alvin G. Glueck, Jr., "The Sioux Uprising: A Problem of International Relations," *Minnesota History* 34 (Winter, 1955): 317–24.

Though most of the Winnebagos were removed from Minnesota in June 1863, some went in small groups to Wisconsin and Iowa to avoid deportation.[101] In Wisconsin they wandered unattended, joining other stray Winnebagos and Potawatomis who had been roaming at will for years. The government had long since officially removed the tribes from Wisconsin, but some returned and so were not under the supervision of an Indian agent. The presence of the newcomers alarmed Wisconsin residents, already jittery over events in Minnesota the previous fall. After General John Pope telegraphed the Office of Indian Affairs about various Minnesota Winnebagos who were robbing Wisconsin citizens, the commissioner informed the Secretary of the Interior that the general must be mistaken. They were wanderers who had not lived in Minnesota for years. Dole further advised that the Indian Office had no funds for their removal. Besides, the low waters of western rivers presently made a transfer impossible.[102] The secretary suggested that Dole telegraph Pope and apprise him of the Indian Office's position.[103] Pope replied that since no state of war existed with the Indians of the state, it was thus the duty of the Indian Office to take charge of the Winnebagos. If it refused, matters would be left to the state.[104]

Whiskey peddlers easily victimized the Wisconsin Winnebagos, for according to the 1862 amendment of the Indian Intercourse Act, only those tribesmen under the care of an agent were protected. Unless the Indian Office assumed responsibility for them, United States Attorney John B. Cogswell could not prosecute those engaged in the whiskey traffic.[105] The presence of intoxicated red men was of course doubly dangerous. The "demoralized, vile, drunken, savage people" threatened the lives and property of Wisconsin residents, a citizens' group of Monroe

101. Balcombe to Dole, May 12, 1863, OIA, LR, Winnebago Agency.

102. Milo M. Quaife, "The Panic of 1862 in Wisconsin," *Wisconsin Magazine of History* 4 (1920–21): 170; Dole to Usher, July 2, 1863, OIA, Report Books, 13:199.

103. Usher to Mix, July 2, 1863, OIA, LR, Winnebago Agency.

104. Pope to Governor Edward Salomon, July 3, 1863, enclosed in Salomon to Usher, July 10, 1863, OIA, LR, Winnebago Agency.

105. Cogswell to Dole, September 27, 1863, OIA, LR, Winnebago Agency.

County said. Already the Indians had killed Mrs. George Slater and assaulted another white woman.[106]

In July 1863 the Indian Office accepted the offer of Wisconsin congressman Walter D. McIndoe to visit the troubled regions of his state in order to quiet the stray Indians until the government could make plans for their relocation. By late September McIndoe confirmed the tales of Indian depredations. He also believed that many Winnebagos were Minnesota refugees. Due to the coming of winter and the ease with which the Indians could be tracked in the snow, little danger existed at present. In the spring there would be trouble unless the Indians were removed. But such was not the will of Congress.[107] In June 1864 it authorized the Secretary of the Interior to take charge of stray Winnebago and Potawatomi bands and it allotted money for their subsistence. The following month Secretary Usher appointed a special agent, with headquarters at Stevens Point, Wisconsin, to assume responsibility for the troublesome red men.[108]

The management of Winnebago and Santee affairs illicited some harsh criticism of Indian Office administrators. If the critics were influential men, such as generals Alfred Sully and John Pope, the Indian Office felt the censure most sharply. In the spring of 1863, Sully led a column of troops against the hostile Santees in Dakota. During the campaign he observed conditions at Crow Creek and reported Winnebago complaints about the reservation site and their treatment there. In several communiques Sully noted what an expensive failure Crow Creek was.[109] Thompson denied Sully's charge about Winnebago starvation. Ample food existed after the supply train arrived in December 1863. On occasion he also purchased food from the army at Fort Randall; perhaps this

106. Petition from the Citizens of Tomah, Monroe County, enclosed in Salomon to Usher, July 28, 1863, CIA, pp. 484–85.

107. Dole to McIndoe, July 31, 1863, CIA, pp. 485–86; McIndoe to Dole, September 25, 1863, CIA, pp. 491–92.

108. Quaife, "The Panic of 1862 in Wisconsin," p. 170; Usher to Dole, July 7, 1864, OIA, LR, Winnebago Agency.

109. Sully to Assistant Adjutant General, Department of the Northwest, November 22, 1864, "Official Correspondence Pertaining to the War of the Outbreak, 1862–1865," *South Dakota Historical Collections*, 8 (Pierre, 1916): 343–44.

created the impression that the Indians went hungry. Thompson insisted that the army shared responsibility for Sioux and Winnebagos leaving the reserve, since General Sully's soldiers encouraged discontent among Crow Creek red men by openly sympathizing with them and by lifting the blockade against the Winnebagos at Fort Randall.[110]

Sully stopped at Crow Creek again in 1864, and was astonished that the agent had allowed two or three hundred Santees to move eastward to farm and fish on the James River. Sully knew of the Indians' destitution; still, the agent should have notified the military authorities. How would the people of Minnesota react when informed that two or three hundred former enemies wandered about the border of the state?[111]

Sully's report infuriated General Pope, commander of the military Department of the Northwest. He penned an endorsement of Sully's charges against the Indian Office and sent them both to General-in-Chief of the Army Henry W. Halleck. How can the military accomplish anything in the Northwest under such circumstances, he wrote? First the army captured these Indian murderers in western Minnesota in September 1862 and took them to Fort Snelling for the winter. The next year the Indian Office removed them to Crow Creek and then turned them loose to threaten the Minnesota frontier for a second time. "I trust," wrote Pope, "that the military authorities will be relieved from responsibility for results."[112]

Pope did not let the matter drop with an official protest. He was too immersed in a campaign for the reform of Indian policy to allow so propitious an opportunity to escape. He sent copies of Sully's June 17 letter and the department commander's endorsement to General Sibley in Minnesota. "It will be well for the people of Minnesota to understand the course pursued in this matter by the Indian Department," Pope wrote. All the work and

110. Thompson to Dole, May 3, 1864, OIA, LR, Winnebago Agency; Thompson to Dole, October 1, 1864, CIA, pp. 539–40.

111. Sully to Assistant Adjutant General, Department of the Northwest, June 17, 1864, enclosed in Pope to Sibley, June 30, 1864, Sibley Papers.

112. Endorsement of Pope, enclosed in Pope to Sibley, June 30, 1864, Sibley Papers.

expense of ridding Minnesota of the Santees had been undone by this extraordinary performance, and the people should know those responsible for it. The general suggested that Sibley unofficially communicate the details of Sully's letter to the St. Paul newspapers, which in turn would arouse the populace. John Pope was indeed intent upon preserving the military's honor in this affair.[113]

To the historian, Pope's correspondence is important for several reasons. Besides revealing a serious blunder by the Indian Office, it shows the extent to which the military would go in the rivalry over Indian matters. Also, Pope's method of informing the public of the army's position undoubtedly created more administrative problems for the Northern Superintendency.

The unyielding westward expansion of the Northwest frontier gave rise to many of the Indian Office's difficulties in Minnesota. Greedy whites who coveted the land of the Santees and Winnebagos or who sought profits from illegal trading practices helped to precipitate the outbreak of 1862, which in turn gave Minnesotans a legitimate excuse to be rid of the red man. The tragedy of relocation acted out on the barren plains of Crow Creek epitomized the Indian Office's inability to mitigate the suffering of its uprooted wards.

The sorrowful story of Minnesota's Indians lacked no impassioned raconteurs. But even they could not slow America's westward march. Even they could not prevent tragedy from being repeated elsewhere.

113. Pope to Sibley, June 30, 1864, Sibley Papers.

CHAPTER VI

Difficulties with Other Tribes

As with the uprooted Santees at Crow Creek, the Indian Office faced a major challenge in caring for those Indians loyal to the Union who were driven from homes in the Indian country south of Kansas. When the Interior Department learned of their skirmishes with Confederate pursuers, the secretary sent Dole to Kansas to help General David Hunter organize a volunteer force to protect the loyal Creeks, Seminoles, Cherokees, and Delawares, led by Creek chief Opothle Yahola. When Dole reached the general's camp, he learned that the rebels, reinforced by Texas troops, had routed the loyalists in an engagement late in December 1861.[1]

Confusion reigned among Opothle Yahola's men, who fled northward with their families up the valley of the Verdigris. They had little time to rest and no shelter from bitter winter winds which cut through their thin clothing and piled snow drifts across the line of retreat. When they reached Fall River, sixty miles west of Humboldt, Kansas, the old chief called a halt. Dotting the trail for three hundred miles behind them lay the bodies of their dead and the bloody tracks of the barefooted.[2]

Confederate and Union armies also overran the loyal Quapaw, Seneca, and Seneca and Shawnee reserves in the northeastern

1. CIA, 1862, p. 181.
2. George A. Cutler to William G. Coffin, September 30, 1862, CIA, p. 283; Elijah Sells to Dennis N. Cooley, October 16, 1865, CIA, p. 438.

corner of the territory, forcing the tribes to withdraw early in
1862 to the Ottawa reservation in Kansas, where the government
subsisted them.[3] Since about 1800 the Wichitas and several affiliated bands had made their homes on lands leased from the
Cherokees in the western part of the Indian territory near Fort
Cobb. Pressure from the south and east forced nearly two-thirds
of the Wichitas north to Belmont, Kansas, where they received
Indian Office aid until 1863; the kindly Osages then permitted
them to hunt buffalo on their lands near the mouth of the Little
Arkansas.[4]

The desperate condition of the loyalists encamped at Fall River
shocked Union officials. An army surgeon reported "many have
their toes frozen off, others have feet wounded by sharp ice or
branches of trees lying on the snow; but few have shoes or moc-
casins. They suffer with inflammatory diseases of the chest, throat,
and eyes."[5]

The Southern Superintendency, which embraced southern
Kansas and much of what is now the state of Oklahoma, could
not provide immediate relief for the refugees, so unexpected was
their arrival. Without adequate clothing and shelter they perished at an alarming rate. Two hundred and forty Creeks succumbed to exposure and starvation during the first sixty days.
Doctors amputated more than a hundred frozen limbs.[6]

Commissioner Dole was in Kansas on February 6, 1862, when
General Hunter advised him that the military could supply the
refugees only until the fifteenth. Unable to communicate with
Superintendent William G. Coffin in southern Kansas, Dole ap-
pointed Dr. William Kile, an Illinoisian on General James H.
Lane's staff, a special agent to supply the needs of the destitute
Indians. At Dole's request, Congress later authorized the In-
terior Department to use the Southern Indians' unspent annuities

3. Coffin to Dole, September 24, 1863, CIA, p. 292.
4. James R. Mead, "The Wichita Indians of Kansas," *Transactions of the Kansas State Historical Society* ... (Topeka, 1904) 8:175; Coffin to Dole, September 24, 1864, CIA, p. 449.
5. Dr. Archibald B. Campbell to Dr. James K. Barnes, February 5, 1862, CIA, p. 296.
6. CIA, 1862, p. 181.

for the refugees' relief, which Coffin estimated would cost $167,000 for the first 135 days.[7]

To sustain Opothle Yahola's loyalists, Special Agent Kile contracted for the necessary supplies in the Leavenworth area, and Superintendent Coffin transported them to the Verdigris Valley for distribution by the agents. Kile was handicapped by fiscal formalities which demanded that supplies be procured by advertisement, and because the war forced steadily upward the price of cattle and other goods, while the value of government vouchers plunged. In September 1862 Secretary of the Interior Smith terminated Kile's temporary association with the Southern Superintendency; it was Coffin's personal responsibility to purchase provisions as well as to distribute them.[8]

The confiscation of letter books, census rolls, tribal files, and other field records by disloyal employees proved another hindrance to Coffin and his staff.[9] Furthermore, when estimating their expenses for the next quarter, neither the agents nor the superintendent knew precisely how many Indians they would have to feed; the number continually changed. Indians drifted in and out of the Verdigris camp, while the death rate continued high among those who remained. Nor did the Indian Office know how long it would have to support the refugees; that would depend on the course of the war. For two years the uncertainty continued, each rumor of the Indians' imminent return more positive than the last, more disruptive to fiscal planning.

To care for thousands of loyal Indians scattered over a hundred mile expanse of Osage and Cherokee Neutral Lands in southern Kansas, between the Verdigris and the Arkansas, Superintendent Coffin decided to gather them on the Verdigris, and sent out supply wagons to bring in the hungry and the homeless. When spring winds warmed the valley the refugees had to be moved again; the stench of two hundred dead and decaying

7. Dole to Caleb B. Smith, June 5, 1862, CIA, p. 292; Smith to Dole, February 14, 1862 (telegram), ID, LS; Coffin to Dole, February 13, 1862, OIA, LR, Southern Supty.

8. Kile to Dole, April 1, 1862, OIA, LR, Southern Supty.; Smith to Mix, September 22, 1862, ID, LS.

9. Coffin to Dole, October 5, 1862, CIA, pp. 279–80.

horses made the site uninhabitable.[10] Where next to send them? The question seemed answered when a Sac and Fox delegation invited the loyalists to their lands in Osage County. In accepting the offer the superintendent did not foresee the opposition of Opothle Yahola and his obstinate Indians who wanted to be escorted south to their homes, not further north.[11] They balked when the agents moved them almost thirty miles from the Verdigris, and so Coffin settled them on the Neosho River, near the town of LeRoy in Coffee County.[12] When autumn leaves carpeted the valley, heralding the approach of winter, Chief Opothle Yahola reluctantly consented to move his people to the Sac and Fox reservation. Obviously they could not return to their homeland before spring. Coffin safely transferred two thousand Creeks by the end of November 1862.[13] Five months later he sent a census for the Southern Superintendency to the commissioner:

Creeks at the Sac and Fox Agency	3290
Chicasaws at the Sac and Fox Agency	170
Cherokees at the Sac and Fox Agency	250
Seminoles at Neosho Falls	901
Wichitas and other affiliated Tribes at Belmont	1789
Quapaws, Senecas, and Senecas and Shawnees (at Ottawa Reservation)	690
Total number	7090

Though the Indians hoped during the spring and summer of 1863 to leave Kansas before cold weather came, circumstances did not favor their return. In January 1864 Superintendent Coffin forwarded another census to Washington, substantially the same as the first.[14]

To locate the Southern Indians in convenient areas accomplished but part of Coffin's task; more demanding was the need

10. *Ibid.*

11. Coffin to Dole, March 28, 1862, OIA, Special File No. 201.

12. George C. Snow to Coffin, September 29, 1862, CIA, pp. 286–87; Isaac Coleman to Coffin, September 30, 1862, CIA, p. 285.

13. Coffin to Dole, November 14, 1862, OIA, LR, Southern Supty.

14. Censuses enclosed in Coffin to Dole, April 9, 1863, and January 25, 1864, *ibid.*

to feed, clothe, and care for them after the army withdrew its aid in mid-February 1862. Coffin proposed to give each individual shoes, a pair of socks, and a blanket or its equivalent in coarse clothing. Before the end of the month he sent five wagon loads of these articles down to the Verdigris; other teams hauled corn and condemned army meat. Upon arrival at the refugee camp, the superintendent's staff realized that army reports did not exaggerate pitiful conditions there. Coffin's supply trains had not yet arrived when he wrote on March 3 that some of the weak Indians had to be hauled in wagons when they left camp.[15] The Southern Superintendency faced another tragedy when winter descended late in 1863 and the Indians still had not returned to their homes in the south. The Indian Office was simply unprepared to sustain them through another season. Choctaw and Chickasaw Agent Isaac Coleman reported from the Sac and Fox reserve that the Indians' shoes, issued more than a year ago, were worn out.[16] Tribesmen under the charge of Creek Agent George A. Cutler and Wichita Agent Edwin H. Carruth lacked adequate clothing and shelter for protection against the numbing winter blasts.

Inadequate diet, clothing and shelter inevitably brought on disease and death. During late March 1862 three to seven Indians succumbed each day at the Verdigris camp. Two to four hundred lay sick.[17] Dr. S. D. Coffin, brother of the superintendent, and a Dr. Carter cared for the ill, but by July the former reported one-fifth of the Indians on the sick list. Frostbite, measles, mumps, diphtheria, and pneumonia, contracted during the cold and rainy winter months, took their toll. Superintendent Coffin estimated that 10 percent of the red men who reached Kansas died by October 1862.[18] The Indians' health improved somewhat in the

15. Coffin to Dole, February 13, 1862, CIA, p. 290; Coffin to Dole, March 3, 1862, OIA, LR, Southern Supty.

16. Coleman to Coffin, October 30, 1863, enclosed in Coffin to Dole, November 24, 1863, OIA, LR, Southern Supty.

17. Kile to Dole, April 1, 1862, *ibid.*

18. Coffin to Dole, March 28, 1862, OIA, Special File No. 201; Dr. S. D. Coffin to Dole, July 5, 1862, enclosed in Coffin to Dole, August 28, 1862, OIA, LR, Southern Supty.; Coffin to Dole, October 5, 1862, CIA, p. 280.

course of their second year in Kansas. The most prevalent diseases were "gastric or gastro-enteric" in nature and pneumonia. Dr. Archibald V. Coffin's report, filed in August 1864, told a grim tale: the exceptionally severe winter of 1863–64 again victimized the inadequately clothed and sheltered Indians. Many perished. Smallpox raged at the Neosho and Belmont reservations. The Indian Office vaccinated the refugees immediately, but the virus used for immunization proved inert and the disease spread to all the camps at both reserves. The Seminoles had to burn the few articles of clothing they had. Fortunately the loyalists on the Sac and Fox lands escaped the epidemic. Though the general condition of the Indian improved with the arrival of spring, the doctor cautioned that every effort must be made to supply and shelter the Indians sufficiently before November 1, lest the tragedy be repeated a third time.[19]

The uncooperativeness of many refugee Indians undermined the Indian Office's efforts to aid them. Their diet was one source of discontent. Grumbling red men and white troublemakers demanded that the natives be given sugar, coffee, tobacco, and other nonessentials. Both white and Indian observers regarded condemned bacon, purchased by the Office of Indian Affairs for the refugees, as "not fit for a dog to eat."[20] When they reached the Neosho the loyalists also wanted to manage their own affairs. The Seminoles and Creeks, for example, reorganized, elected chiefs, and asked to be recognized as independent nations entitled to all their property and annuities under former treaties.[21] Complaints about their clothing and shelter were common; whiskey peddlers infested the Sac and Fox reserve and Indians refused to testify against them in the courts; rebel emissaries infiltrated the camps, seeking to turn the loyalists against the

19. A. V. Coffin to W. G. Coffin, September 25, 1863, CIA, p. 307; A. V. Coffin to W. G. Coffin, August 25, 1864, CIA, pp. 451–52; Snow to Dole, August 8, 1864, OIA, LR, Seminole Agency.

20. Coffin to Dole, April 9, 1862, OIA, LR, Southern Supty.; George W. Collamore to Dole, April 21, 1862, CIA, pp. 299–301.

21. Billy Bowlegs et al. to Dole, April 14, 1862, enclosed in Coffin to Dole, April 15, 1862, OIA, LR, Seminole Agency; Creek Chiefs to Dole, April 5, 1862, OIA, LR, Creek Agency.

United States; Indians from the Central Superintendency, disguised as refugees, tried to draw subsistence; and the Sac and Fox nation presented Superintendent Coffin with a $14,688 bill for the rental of buildings on their reservation.[22]

The fate of these seven thousand refugees from the Indian country was as uncertain as the course of the Civil War on the border. To some degree the Indians must be blamed, for they failed to cooperate with any plan of aid. Each year their hopes of returning south rose and fell with the advancing armies. Finally, biting winter winds, empty stomachs and, in some cases, death overwhelmed them. Caught unprepared, the Indian Office succored the destitute red men as best it could, but never quite successfully. Each spring it too expected that the Indians would be returned to their homes and become self-supporting. When they were not, Superintendent Coffin was unable to sustain them for another winter on the bleak Kansas plains. Freezing bodies huddled in threadbare tents bore grim testimony to the inadequacy of the Indian service and to the war on the border.

The whiskey problem caused restlessness among the Minnesota Chippewas and the Indians of Wisconsin and the Pacific Northwest. In 1855 the Chippewas ceded tracts of land in Minnesota in exchange for several reservations and a guarantee that the government would provide large annuity payments and numerous services. The Mississippi bands received reservations on Mille Lacs and on Sandy, Rabbit, Gull, Pokegama, and Rice Lakes. The federal government assigned the Pillager and Winnibigoshish bands to tracts on Leech Lake, Lake Winnibigoshish, and Cass Lake.[23] With villages scattered so far from his headquarters on the Gull Lake reserve, the Chippewa agent had difficulty suppressing the whiskey traffic, which reached such proportions that hardly a night passed without some drunken disturbance. Three Indians killed one another and a fourth burned

22. Pas-co-pa to Dole, August 29, 1863, OIA, LR, Seminole Agency; Cutler to Coffin, September 5, 1863, CIA, p. 300; Collamore to Dole, April 21, 1862, CIA, pp. 299–301; Dole to Coffin, June 1, 1863, OIA, LS, 70:511; Henry W. Martin to Coffin, February 28, 1865, enclosed in Coffin to Dole, March 6, 1865, OIA, LR, Southern Supty.

23. Kappler, *Indian Affairs* 2:685–90.

to death within one week in January 1862. When the annuity shipment arrived the next month, officials arrested five persons on the first day of distribution for introducing liquor onto the reservation.[24]

The Wisconsin Indians, like those of Minnesota, retreated in the face of the expanding white population. During the first half of the nineteenth century they surrendered virtually the entire state. The Interior Department concentrated the remaining tribes on widespread, sometimes isolated reservations. On the eve of the Civil War about eight or nine thousand Wisconsin Indians maintained relations with government agencies.[25]

Journeying north from the more populous regions of southern Wisconsin, a traveler would first come upon the Oneida Indians, located at the southern tip of Green Bay on a 61,000 acre reserve in Brown and Outagamie Counties. The tribe migrated from New York during the 1820s and 1830s, and by 1862 numbered 1,128. Their reservation contained six thousand acres of good soil cleared for farming, but there was much poverty.[26] Prior to 1854 the peaceful Menominees roamed the northeastern part of the state near the river which bears their name on the Michigan-Wisconsin border. That year the government set apart for them twelve townships on the upper Wolf River. Though valuable stands of timber covered much of the reserve, it was poor for farming purposes: too many lakes and ponds and too much sandy soil. There were 112 frame houses, 75 log structures, and about 150 wigwams dotting the reserve.[27] In 1856 the Menominees sold two townships to the Stockbridge and Munsee nation, which previously occupied a tract on the eastern shore of Lake Win-

24. Lucius C. Walker to Thompson, September 25, 1861, OIA, FOR, Northern Supty; John H. Enmegahbowh to Mrs. Henry B. Whipple, January 12, 1862, Whipple Papers; Walker to Thompson, February 20, 1862, enclosed in C. W. Wycoff to Dole, February 27, 1862, OIA, LR, Chippewa Agency.

25. Quaife, "The Panic of 1862 in Wisconsin," p. 170.

26. Moses M. Davis to Dole, September 27, 1862, CIA, pp. 473–74, 476; Quaife, "The Panic of 1862 in Wisconsin," p. 169.

27. Davis to Dole, September 27, 1862, CIA, pp. 472–73; Hodge, *Handbook of American Indians* 1:842; Walter James Hoffman, "The Menomini Indians," *Fourteenth Annual Report of the Bureau of Ethnology*, Pt. I (Washington, 1896), p. 31.

nebago. The new reserve, with its rolling, sandy surface and restricted growing season, so displeased the united tribes that by
September 1861 more than half had scattered from it rather than
await relocation on good farming land.[28] In the mid-1850s the
Interior Department assigned the Wisconsin Chippewas to areas
in the northern portion of the state, but this in no way restricted
their hunting, trapping, and berry picking.[29]

Whether the Indians lived on or off the southern Wisconsin
reservations, white liquor merchants easily found them. A perus-
al of Agent Moses M. Davis's reports during the war years leaves
little doubt that he considered whiskey the Indian Office's chief
problem and the red man's major obstacle to self-improvement.
Davis estimated that one-fourth of the adult Menominees and
Stockbridges and Munsees used spirituous liquors. As for the
Oneidas, farther south and thus closer to the supply, about one-
half the adult males imbibed.[30] In exchange for alcohol the
Indians bartered annuity monies, annuity goods, and forest products stolen from their own reservations.[31] Besides the loss of communal property, some tribesmen burned or froze to death while
intoxicated. In 1865 Agent Davis blamed whiskey for most
crimes committed by Indians on their reserves. Furthermore, it
compounded the task of mission teachers and others interested in
changing the red man's lot.[32]

Evidence suggests that the courts were a major hindrance in
eliminating Wisconsin whiskey trade. United States District
Court Judge Andrew G. Miller described liquor cases brought
before him as useless attempts to end the traffic and an unnecessary expense for the government as well as for the defendants,

28. Hoffman, "The Menomini Indians"; Dole to William Windon, March
7, 1864, OIA, Report Books, 13:330–31; Davis to Dole, September 27, 1861,
CIA, p. 803.

29. William F. Raney, *Wisconsin: A Story of Progress* (New York, 1940),
p. 79; Quaife, "The Panic of 1862 in Wisconsin," p. 169.

30. Davis to Dole, September 27, 1861, CIA, p. 804; Davis to Doolittle,
August 31, 1865, JSC, p. 462.

31. Davis to Dole, September 27, 1861, CIA, p. 803; Davis to Dole, September
27, 1862, CIA, p. 475.

32. Davis to Dole, September 27, 1862, CIA, p. 476; Davis to Dole, September
25, 1865, CIA, p. 622.

who had to travel long distances to stand trial. Though the testimony in one case was "positive and uncontroverted" according to Agent Davis, Miller instructed the jury that the district attorney failed to prove that the defendants knew they had sold whiskey to Indians. The trial ended in acquittal.[33]

An apparent breakdown in tribal government, particularly among the Oneidas, also abetted the whiskey trade. In 1863 about a hundred Oneidas gradually stripped their reservation land of timber, which they bartered for alcohol at Fort Howard, De Pere, and Green Bay, or sold to a nearby railroad line.[34] Though the chiefs opposed this waste, they were too weak to protect either private or communal property. To conserve tribal wealth and curb the whiskey business, the headmen asked that state statutes be extended over their tribe so that Indian criminals could be punished. According to their agent many Oneidas were "civilized" enough to accept the surveying and allotment of tribal lands and to abide by Wisconsin laws.[35]

The headlong penetration of whites into the Pacific Northwest and their encroachments on reservation land gave rise to the Indian Office's most serious administrative difficulties there during the Civil War years. A case in point was the never-ending battle with aggressive and troublesome whiskey dealers.

During the 1850s the United States relegated Pacific Northwest Indians to reservations. The Walla Walla Council of 1855 established restricted locations for seven tribes east of the Cascades. The spirited and industrious Nez Percés accepted a well-watered, three-million-acre tract in the valleys of the Grande Ronde, Clearwater, Snake, and the Salmon. The Cayuses, Umatillas, and Wallawallas received a fertile, 800-square-mile reserve at the headwaters of the Umatilla River, in the genial climate of the Blue Mountains. The Yakimas abandoned their claim to lands north of Ahtanum Creek and joined the Klikitats and Pa-

33. Davis to Dole, September 26, 1864, CIA, p. 583.
34. Davis to Dole, August 25, 1863, OIA, LR, Green Bay Agency; Davis to Dole, September 26, 1863, CIA, p. 467.
35. Davis to Dole, September 26, 1864, CIA, pp. 580–81; E. A. Goodnough to Davis, September 4, 1862, CIA, p. 480; Davis to Dole, September 25, 1865, CIA, p. 619.

loos on a reservation on the upper drainage of the Yakima River.[36] The government assigned other eastern tribes to restricted areas the same year. The Flatheads, Upper Pend d'Oreilles, and Kutenais met with United States representatives in July near present-day Missoula, Montana. The Indians ceded about twenty-five thousand square miles of what is now western Montana and agreed to settle on a million-and-a-quarter-acre reserve bordering the southern shores of Flathead Lake. The Kutenais did not live on the general reservation but roamed the country north of Flathead Lake and into Canada. The Flatheads continued to range along the Bitterroot Valley.[37] The confederated tribes of central Oregon, including the Tyighs, John Days, Teninos, and Wascos, gathered on the Warm Springs reservation. According to the terms of the Wasco treaty of 1855, this sanctuary of excellent grazing land was bounded on the west by the summit of the Cascades, on the north by the Mutton Mountains and on the south by the Deschutes River.[38] Tribesmen west of the Cascades were also collected on reserves. Between 1853 and 1856 treaties extinguished most land holdings of Oregon's western tribes, organizing two reservations and a subagency for them.[39] The Grande Ronde, in the upper Yamhill Valley east of the Coastal Range, became the permanent home for a part of the Rogue River tribe and for remnants of various bands from the Willamette and upper Umpqua valleys. Warriors of southwestern Oregon settled on the Siletz (or Coastal) reserve which extended along the shoreline from Cape Lookout to the Tsiltcoos River.[40] Some fertile soil existed, streams teemed with fish, and the mountains abounded with game. A forty-five mile long

36. Merrill D. Beal, *"I Will Fight No More Forever": Chief Joseph and the Nez Perce War* (Seattle, 1963), p. 26.

37. William H. Wallace to Dole (?), November 17, 1863, William H. Wallace Papers, University of Washington Library, Seattle; Hoopes, *Indian Affairs*, p. iii.

38. William Logan to J. W. Perit Huntington, August 3, 1863, CIA, p. 193.

39. Royal A. Bensell, *All Quiet on the Yamhill: The Civil War in Oregon; The Journal of Corporal Royal A. Bensell, Company D, Fourth California Infantry*, ed. Gunther Barth (Eugene, Ore., 1959), pp. 198–99.

40. Charles Florus Coan, "The Federal Indian Policy in the Pacific Northwest, 1849–1879," doctoral dissertation, University of California, Berkeley, 1920, pp. 265–66, 279–80.

mountain range separated the aborigines from white men and their attendant vices. The Alseas, Kusas, Umpquas, and Suislaws not moved to Siletz resided at the Umpqua subagency eight miles south of Alsea Bay.[41] During this period Washington's coastal tribes were allocated twelve reservations on the Pacific and along Puget Sound from Bellingham to Commencement Bays, though the government did not force them to live there. Their assignment to agencies was solely for the jurisdictional and financial convenience of the Washington Superintendency.[42]

The Interior Department did not allot reservations to all the Indians who roamed the Pacific Northwest in the fifties. The Klamaths and Modocs of southern Oregon, the Snakes (or Western Shoshonis) of eastern Oregon's high desert country, and miscellaneous Washington tribes such as the Colvilles, Spokans, Lower Pend d'Oreilles, and Coeur d'Alênes had to be dealt with in the 1860s and later.

The Umatilla reservation was most vulnerable to whiskey dealers because of its proximity to white settlements and its location on the main wagon road to the farming towns in the Grande Ronde and Powder valleys and the mines of Boise and Owyhee. Agent William H. Barnhart noted the passage of thousands of travelers during the summer of 1862. From these men, from whites in Walla Walla, and from pesky traders camped close by the reserve, the Indians obtained alcohol. Many law-abiding whites near the agency lived in constant fear of attacks from drunken natives.[43]

Suppressing the whiskey trade was a formidable task. Barnhart reckoned only military force could prevent the traffic in his area. Though reduced in strength in the Pacific Northwest during the war, the army helped to track down and arrest some hucksters. As a warning to Washington citizens ignorant of the

41. CIA, 1863, pp. 132–33. Later called the Alsea Subagency.

42. Coan, "Federal Indian Policy in the Pacific Northwest," pp. 297–99; James R. Masterson, "The Records of the Washington Superintendency of Indian Affairs, 1853–1874," *Pacific Northwest Quarterly* 37 (January 1946): 40–41.

43. Barnhart to Calvin H. Hale, June 13, 1862, enclosed in Hale to Rector, June 30, 1862, OIA, FOR, Oregon Supty., LR, 1862; Barnhart to William H. Rector, August 5, 1862, CIA, pp. 413–14.

law or the penalties for selling spirituous liquors to Indians, Superintendent Calvin H. Hale issued a public notice in June 1862.[44] In the final analysis the problem lay not so much with an ignorant populous as with the failure of white juries to convict men engaged in this illicit business and the difficulty of getting government witnesses to a court room, due to primitive transportation facilities and inadequate procedures for paying witnesses' expenses. The Neah Bay agent notes, for example, that to win a conviction a white prosecution witness must not only have seen the accused give or sell whiskey to Indians but also have tasted the beverage to prove that it was spirituous liquor or wine.[45] Though admissible, Indian testimony could never convict a white huckster.

Prostitution, too, degraded the Indian and subverted the work of the Indian Office in the Pacific Northwest. Reports of agency physicians detailed the ravages of venereal disease among their patients. Superintendent William W. Miller of Washington Territory ordered all subordinates in August 1861 to prohibit "open prostitution and concubinage" between Indians and whites in their districts. The prostitution of native girls by their parents, a common practice along the coast, was less prevalent in eastern Washington and Oregon where red men were freer of the corrupting influence of unscrupulous whites.[46]

Unhealthy conditions on Pacific Northwest reservations must have contributed to Indian restlessness and the tendency to scatter to old hunting grounds. Even before the overland migration to Oregon in the 1840s, the white man's diseases swept away a majority of area tribesmen.[47] Physicians sent to Washington and Oregon agencies during the Civil War reported high incidences

44. Barnhart to Rector, August 5, 1862, CIA, pp. 413-14; Notice of Hale, June 25, 1862, enclosed in Hale to Dole, July 1, 1862, OIA, LR, Washington Supty.

45. Henry A. Webster to Hale, n.d., 1862, CIA, pp. 551-52.

46. Circular of Miller, August 12, 1861, in Olympia *Washington Standard*, September 21, 1861; W. J. Trimball, "American and British Treatment of the Indians in the Pacific Northwest," *Washington Historical Quarterly* 5 (January, 1914), pp. 44-45.

47. Leslie M. Scott, "Indian Diseases As Aids to Pacific Northwest Settlement," *Oregon Historical Quarterly* 29 (June, 1928): 144.

of venereal and respiratory infection. Much sickness resulted from the Indians' unsanitary habits and their superstitions regarding medicines, yet the government's failure to supply the red men with hospital facilities, sufficient food, clothing, medicine, and adequate dwellings once it brought them together on reservations, contributed to the magnitude of the problem.[48]

For those Wisconsin Indians who remained on their allotted tracts, Indian Office care was equally feeble. Many eruptive diseases such as smallpox and measles afflicted the tribesmen, but the most common as well as the most fatal was pneumonia, which the Indians called "quick consumption." The lack of medical help compounded the danger of illness. The Stockbridges and Munsees, for example, harbored few suspicions about the white man's doctors,[49] but because of their isolation from medical services, disease ran rampant. During the summer of 1865 smallpox struck the Stockbridge and Munsee as well as the Menominee reservations. Many families fled northward, carrying the virus with them. By June 1 a hundred cases were reported and a total of eight hundred vaccinated. Among the hundred and fifty known Menominee sufferers, seventy-nine died.[50]

Indian discontent with reservation conditions caused part of the Indian Office's imposing array of administrative problems. In 1861 and again in 1864 Agent Davis reported that approximately half of the Stockbridges and Munsees had abandoned their lands.[51] One reason was the isolation of their reserve. Indians seeking employment could not find work as day laborers near their homes, and had to go where their skills were in demand. Such dispersion reduced the government's influence over them. Stockbridges and Munsees who abandoned many of their old ways and tried to be good farmers grew disillusioned because

48. See for example Dr. Nathaniel Hudson to James B. Condon, August 1, 1863, CIA, p. 205; and E. H. Spinning to Alfred R. Elder, June 30, 1864, CIA, p. 207.

49. Davis to Dole, September 26, 1863, CIA, pp. 469–70; Davis to Doolittle, August 31, 1865, JSC, p. 462.

50. Davis to Dole, September 25, 1865, CIA, pp. 619, 621–22.

51. Davis to Dole, September 27, 1861, CIA, p. 803; Davis to Dole, September 26, 1864, CIA, p. 580.

their reserve lacked enough arable land to support them.[52] They were bitter, too, because the Interior Department had tricked them into ceding their former home on Lake Winnebago.[53] The commissioner of Indian affairs acknowledged Stockbridge and Munsee dissatisfaction, recommending in 1863 that their reserve be sold and the tribe permitted to purchase part of the Oneida reserve farther south.[54] The proposal was never implemented, and the Stockbridges and Munsees may still be found on the same lands.

Restless reservation tribes were not confined to Wisconsin. With headquarters at St. Joseph, Missouri, the Central Superintendency embraced what is today southeastern Wyoming, Nebraska, and Kansas north of the New York Indian lands. Some sixteen tribes under the superintendent's jurisdiction numbered about thirteen thousand and represented a striking variety of cultures, since many of them were not native to the area, having been uprooted at an earlier time from eastern free states. The Indians ranged from the fierce nomads of the western plains portion of the superintendency to the more acculturated who lived on reserves in central and eastern Nebraska and Kansas.[55]

The federal government set aside land for three agencies in east-central Kansas. At the Osage River Agency the Miamis and four small confederated tribes maintained nominal tribal ties. Of approximately 360 members, most farmed and lived in cabins located on head-rights and wore European dress.[56] Immediately to the west on a twelve-mile-square reserve dwelt the Sac and Fox, who numbered 1,341 in 1861. They too had a severalty program. The Sac and Fox agent also exercised jurisdiction over the confederated Chippewa and Munsee Indians and the Ottawas,

52. Davis to Dole, September 26, 1863, CIA, p. 466; Davis to Dole, September 26, 1864, CIA, p. 579.
53. Dole to Windon, March 7, 1864, OIA, Report Books, 13:330–31.
54. CIA, 1863, p. 152; Dole to Davis, December 26, 1863, OIA, LS, 72:268–69.
55. CIA, 1862, p. 178; Annie Heloise Abel, "The Indians in the Civil War," *American Historical Review* 15 (October, 1909): 281.
56. Gustavus A. Colton to Harrison B. Branch, August 19, 1862, CIA, pp. 260–61.

neither of which were numerous.[57] In 1863 the Indian Office established an Ottawa Agency. On the Neosho River about twenty miles west of the Sac and Fox were the Kansa lands where 146 families lived, mostly in stone or log houses.[58]

Northeastern Kansas was a crazy quilt of reservations. More than 2,200 Potawatomis resided north of the Kansa Agency. Shawnee lands on the south side of the Kansas River adjoined the state of Missouri. Until 1863 their agent supervised the 430 Wyandots as well as his own charges; the Indian Office then transferred the Wyandots to the Delaware Agency, immediately to the north.[59] By the terms of an 1854 treaty the Northern Kickapoos, after ceding 618,000 acres, retained 150,000 just west of Horton. The southern bands migrated to Texas in the 1850s and lived by the chase. When the Civil War broke out they refused a rebel alliance. About six hundred found new homes in Kansas and with Union encouragement raided against the Confederacy.[60] Four hundred Iowas and the Sac and Fox of Missouri farmed individual patches on the fertile Great Nemaha reserve, north of the Kickapoos on the Kansas-Nebraska border.[61]

Nebraska Indian reserves in the eastern part of the territory were also scattered. On the gently rolling prairie along the Big Blue River south of Beatrice dwelt the 470 members of the confederated Oto and Missouri tribes. Their land was fine for grazing, but high winds and long droughts made agriculture uncertain.[62] The Pawnee reserve was an irregularly shaped fifteen-by-thirty mile strip of fertile bottomland on the Loup River. Villages of circular lodges fifty-to-sixty feet in diameter lay between the Loup and Beaver Creek.[63] In 1860 the Omahas num-

57. Clinton C. Hutchinson to Branch, October 1, 1861, CIA, pp. 670–71.

58. H. W. Farnsworth to Dole, January 20, 1863, OIA, LR, Kansas Agency.

59. William W. Ross to [Dole?], September 30, 1863, OIA, LR, Potawatomi Agency; Fielding Johnson to Branch, September 25, 1863, CIA, pp. 353–54.

60. A. M. Gibson, *The Kickapoos: Lords of the Middle Border* (Norman, 1963), pp. 119–20, 197–98.

61. John A. Burbank to Branch, October 1, 1862, CIA, p. 278; Taylor to Cooley, December 6, 1865, OIA, LR, Great Nemaha Agency.

62. Census of June 11, 1862, enclosed in John Baker to Dole, November 28, 1862, OIA, LR, Oto Agency; Baker to Dole, *ibid.*

63. Henry W. De Puy to Branch, July 30, 1861, OIA, LR, Pawnee Agency.

bered about 950. They hunted and harvested corn, wheat, potatoes, and other vegetables on a 300,000 acre reserve, fifteen miles
south of Sioux City, Iowa. The Upper Platte agent resided in the
vicinity of Fort Laramie[64] and looked after the affairs of the
Northern Cheyennes, the Northern Arapahos, and certain Sioux
bands.

Organized in March 1861, Dakota Territory took in the gently
rolling plains region north of the forty-third parallel and west of
Minnesota to the Continental Divide. The principal tribes native
to the Dakota Superintendency included the Poncas, Gros Ventres, Mandans, Arikaras, Assiniboins, Crows, Blackfeet, and Sioux.
Disregarding amity agreements, the government had treaties solely
with the Blackfeet, Yankton Sioux, and Poncas, and only the latter two lived on reservations.[65] Looking north from Nebraska,
the first agencies were for the Poncas and Yankton Sioux. The
former bordered the Niobrara River, near the Nebraska-Dakota
line; the Yankton lands lay on the northeast side of the Missouri,
above Chouteau Creek. The majority of both tribes forsook the
hunting life in 1858 and with their agents' help broke land for
farming.[66] Prior to 1864 the Mandans, Gros Ventres, Arikaras,
Assiniboins, Crows, and Sioux (excluding the Yankton and those
bands attached to the Upper Platte Agency) belonged to the
Upper Missouri Agency. In that year the Indian Office assigned
the non-Sioux tribes to the new Fort Berthold Agency. As bitter
foes of the Sioux, the two to three thousand peaceful Mandans,
Gros Ventres, and Arikaras lived for mutual protection in a farming village of dirt lodges close to Fort Berthold, though they
claimed most of western Dakota.[67] Poor but friendly, the Assiniboins ranged from the lower Yellowstone to Canada. The Crows
roamed the entire Yellowstone Valley.[68] The hostility of many
Sioux bands toward whites prevented much contact with the
Indian Office except when their agent delivered presents. The

64. Orasmus H. Irish to Branch, October 29, 1861, CIA, p. 673; John Loree
to Branch, September 30, 1863, CIA, pp. 374–75.
65. CIA, 1862, p. 183.
66. William Jayne to Dole, October 18, 1861, CIA, p. 727.
67. De Smet to Dole, September 23, 1864, CIA, p. 426.
68. Testimony of Mahlon Wilkinson, September 12, 1865, JSC, p. 415.

Blackfoot Agency was transferred to the new Idaho Superintendency in 1863. With the organization of Montana Territory the following year, the Interior Department placed the Blackfoot under the jurisdiction of this superintendency.[69]

The diminishing game supply from Kansas to Canada necessitated that the reservation tribes become self-supporting farmers. However, drought and insects during the growing seasons of 1863 and 1864 brought starvation to the agencies, undermined the Indians' loyalty and friendliness toward the United States, neutralized the agricultural expenditures of the Office of Indian Affairs as well as the work of its agents, and discouraged those red men whom the government sought to settle. In fact, field officials urged some Indians to resume their hunting trips to procure provisions for the winter.[70]

Communal land ownership was another obstruction to agricultural progress and a major cause of Indian idleness and discontent. The Indians' reluctance to abandon tribal ways could be seen in the widespread opposition to regular manual labor. Fathers wanted their sons to become warrior-hunters, and young men found it difficult to farm when ridiculed by women.[71] A schism developed in the Potawatomi tribe between the pro-severalty "mission band" and the "prairie band," which opposed any change from traditional customs.[72] It also proved difficult during a drought to demonstrate the advantages of severalty. In fact, many of the "mission band" Potawatomis had to leave their allotments in search of subsistence, while at the Ponca reservation funds budgeted for a manual labor school were diverted to purchase provisions.[73] Nevertheless, the government had some success with private farms on the Delaware, Great Nemaha, Kansa, and Potawatomi reserves, and with manual labor schools at all the

69. Hill, *Preliminary Inventory of the Records of the Bureau of Indian Affairs* 2:312.

70. Edmunds to Dole, September 20, 1864, CIA, pp. 404–5.

71. CIA, 1863, p. 148; John B. Hoffman to Edmunds, August 20, 1864, OIA, FOR, Dakota Supty., 1864, Correspondence with Agents.

72. CIA, 1861, p. 629.

73. Luther R. Palmer to Thomas Murphy, September 14, 1865, CIA, p. 559; Dole to Edmunds, September 8, 1864, CIA, pp. 436–37.

Central Superintendency agencies except the Osage River and the Kickapoo.[74]

Because the Yakima Indian War of 1855–58 delayed the ratification of most treaties concluded with Pacific Northwest tribes in the mid-fifties, many Indian Office difficulties during the following decade derived from the preliminary implementation of the reservation system. A major task was restricting Indians to their reservations. Some returned to former homes, where the threat of starvation prompted them to steal from pioneer families; others loitered near the settlements, creating a nuisance. Scheming whites offered them whiskey so that braves would prostitute their wives and young girls or hire out as cheap farm labor. As long as the Indians meandered about the countryside, peaceful relations between the races were jeopardized. Moreover, if the practice continued among the Umatilla Agency Indians, noted Barnhart, the reservations would never become self-supporting economic units and the Indians never "civilized."[75] Besides homesickness, tribal wanderlust illustrated the Indian Office's inability to make reservations attractive.

Absenteeism and economic discontent went hand in hand. Some poorly situated reserves lacked either good fisheries or fertile soil; others were so small that in times of crop shortages the Indians could not subsist by the chase or other traditional methods. More often Indian obstinacy stemmed from their lack of interest in agriculture and the government's languid encouragement of them to change their old ways. Illustrative of the complexity of the problem were the coastal tribes of the Siletz reservation, which previously lived by fishing and the chase and from natural products of the region. They disliked regular manual labor and would escape to the woods to avoid it. Had the Indians shown more interest in such pursuits, they would still have been handicapped by their inexperience in agriculture, the unsuitability of much of the land for farming and the remoteness of the reservation, which made transportation a problem. By 1865 the

---

74. Murphy to Cooley, October 23, 1865, CIA, p. 543.
75. Coan, "Federal Indian Policy in the Pacific Northwest," pp. i–ii; Barnhart to Rector, August 5, 1862, CIA, p. 415.

first reports of agricultural success were reported at Siletz.[76] Washington's Superintendent Hale recommended in 1863 that some incentive be employed to win over the Pacific Northwest tribes from their old way of life to agricultural pursuits. Oregon Agent Benjamin R. Biddle thought it would also be wise to distribute annuity goods in compensation for labor on the reservation.[77] Other Oregon Superintendency officers suggested that the allotment of land in severalty would allow each Indian to enjoy the fruits of his own labor. Nevertheless, no major reforms resulted.

Press reports and agents' letters indicate that roving Indians posed as much a problem in California as in the Pacific Northwest. When the Lincoln administration took the political reins in March 1861, California natives occupied several reservations and agency farms. In the extreme northwest corner of the state, above Crescent City, lay the Smith River reserve, walled in on the north and east by uninhabitable mountains and protected by the Pacific on the west. Yearly salmon catches, game from the mountains and arable fields yielded adequate subsistence for the two thousand Humboldt, Bald Hill, and Bear River tribal inhabitants. Nestled on the Klamath River, the Klamath Indians lived under similar conditions.[78] The federal government assigned five to six hundred Yukis and about two thousand Wailakis to the Mendocino reservation, slightly larger than a township, on the northern coast above Point Arena. About fifty miles to the northeast lay Round Valley, nineteen thousand acres of well-watered land surrounded by high mountains. The mild climate was especially suited for growing cereals. The twelve thousand Yukis, Wailakis, and members of bands from the Sacramento Valley and Pitt River lived together in harmony. During the summer they dwelt in brush

76. Benjamin R. Biddle to Dole, June 30, 1862, CIA (1863), p. 179; Biddle to Rector, August 13, 1862, CIA, pp. 420–21; Sub-report of James W. Nesmith, JSC, p. 2.

77. Hale to Dole, September 1, 1863, CIA, p. 558; Biddle to Rector, August 13, 1862, CIA, p. 421.

78. George M. Hanson to Dole, October 10, 1862, CIA, pp. 453–54; Hanson to Dole, July 15, 1861, CIA, p. 757.

huts and for the winter constructed houses of oak slats.[79] On the western edge of the Sacramento Valley the sprawling Nome Lackee reserve encompassed over twenty-five thousand acres, although the proximity of white settlements and the amount of money needed to fence Indian farm lands somewhat reduced its suitability for Indians.[80] From William and Edward Campbell, the Indian Office rented the Kings River Farm, located on the river of that name in central California, ten miles from the Sierra Nevada foothills. Officials fenced and irrigated over three hundred acres, but the farm was too small for the number of Indians assigned to it, and there was excessive contact with advancing whites. Similarly, the government rented the 1,280-acre Tulé River Farm east of Tulare Lake. In 1863 about seven hundred Owens River and Tulé River Indians raised cereals, corn, and vegetables there and enjoyed the fruits of a vineyard and orchard.[81] Situated at the juncture of the Sierra Nevada and Coastal Range, the twenty-five-thousand-acre Tejon reserve was surrounded on three sides and guarded from a northern approach by the Kern River desert. The soil was well suited for farming and the fine range for stock grazing. About 1,370 Caruanas, Tataguas, and Castakes lived there in 1862. An estimated ten thousand warlike tribesmen, such as the Yumas, Mohaves, Walapais, and Kawias, roamed the Colorado district of southern California, which ran east and west between the Mojave and Colorado Rivers and south to the Mexican border.[82]

The superintending agent for the southern district of California, John P. H. Wentworth, noted in July 1861 that many natives had abandoned the Tejon, Kings River, and the Tulé River farms in search of food. George M. Hanson, Wentworth's counter-

79. Mendocino *Herald*, n.d., in San Francisco *Daily Alta California*, March 4, 1861; Elijah Steele to Dole, October 31, 1863, CIA, p. 521; Austin Wiley to Dole, September 1, 1864, CIA, pp. 261–62; Statement of B. L. Fairfield, July 25, 1865, in Sub-report of Honorable William Higby, JSC, p. 504.

80. Hanson to Dole, October 10, 1862, CIA, pp. 456–57.

81. John P. H. Wentworth to Dole, July 14, 1861, CIA, p. 752; Wentworth to Dole, September 1, 1863, CIA, p. 223.

82. Wentworth to Dole, July 14, 1861, CIA, p. 753; Wentworth to Dole, August 30, 1862, CIA, p. 468–70.

part for the northern district, filed a similar report the same month. Of the Nome Lackee reservation Indians, who formerly numbered between two and three thousand, all but two hundred scattered to former homes. In fact, Hanson received protests that fall about wandering Indians throughout northern California.[83] Resolutions adopted by citizens at Pinegrove and Parksville threatened that unless the government removed the red men between the Chico and Pitt Rivers by November 1, they would be treated as hostiles. Short of funds since assuming office, Hanson could only ask the Shasta county residents to be patient until the Interior Department appointed a special agent to gather up the Indians.[84]

Natural disasters upset federal plans for a few California reservations. In the southern district where many reserves were already of inadequate size, a drought caused serious subsistence problems in the spring of 1864. The unusually sluggish Colorado River had failed to overflow its banks and irrigate bottomlands the previous summer. Tribal hostility mounted as crops withered. In response to a telegraphic call for help, the Office of Indian Affairs authorized $3,000 in relief funds.[85] Flooding of the Klamath River reservation in December 1861 also brought emergency government action, but not before the lives of 2,200 Indians were temporarily disrupted. The surging waters totally destroyed the reservation, sweeping thirty to forty thousand dollars worth of government buildings and crops into the ocean. When the waters receded, cobble stones and three feet of sand covered the fields. Prompt aid from the Indian Office resulted no doubt from Hanson's warning of dire consequences should the refugees be allowed to return to their old haunts or prey upon whites. In February 1862 he proposed to move the Klamaths north to Smith

83. Wentworth to Dole, July 14, 1861, CIA, p. 753; Hanson to Dole, July 15, 1861, CIA, p. 757; Hanson to Dole, September 21, 1861, OIA, LR, California Supty.

84. Notice of Hanson, Sacramento *Daily Union*, October 14, 1861.

85. *Daily Alta California*, May 8, 1864; Wentworth to Dole, April 19, 1864 (telegram), OIA, LR, California Supty.; Dole to Usher, May 6, 1864, OIA, Report Books, 12:401–2.

River, which had plenty of room for all the Indians of the northern district who could not be moved to Nome Lackee or elsewhere.[86] The Office of Indian Affairs approved the purchase of five thousand acres on the north side of the river. Yet by the summer of 1863 the Klamaths still lacked adequate shelter and many suffered disease and death.[87]

Other California tribes suffered because the Lincoln administration had inherited reservations on the brink of ruin. Crops were inadequate, the Indians destitute and agency employees discontented with delays in pay. In the summer of 1861, for example, not one acre was under cultivation at the Nome Lackee reserve. Fencing was nonexistent, as were farm tools; only a few beef cattle grazed on agency land; the naked Indians were starving; and Hanson had no funds. As late as September 1865 peaceful reservation tribesmen still lacked necessary clothing.[88] Clearly, failure to care for the Indians' physical wants during the war years in part explains their unwillingness to colonize on reservations.

Sometimes Indian uncooperativeness escalated into open hostility which menaced both whites and nonbelligerent natives. The peace in northern California was threatened within weeks after Dole took charge of the Indian Office. In June 1861 seven citizens of Siskiyou County reported attacks by Modoc and Klamath Lake warriors who had plundered their farms and driven off stock. The law-abiding citizens of Eureka, in nearby Humboldt County, threatened to resist the collection of taxes unless the governor saw to their protection. To restore peace and return hostiles to their reserves, General Wright created the military District of Humboldt, which included all counties from Sonora to Del Norte, and placed it under the command of Colonel Francis J. Lippitt. Agent Hanson agreed to receive and subsist as many as possible of the

86. Hanson to Dole, December 31, 1861, CIA, pp. 457–58; Dole to Hanson, January 4, 1862, OIA, LS, 67:206; Hanson to Dole, February 14, 1862, OIA, LR, California Supty.

87. Dole to Caleb B. Smith, April 9, 1862, OIA, Report Books, 12:358; Hanson to Dole, July 18, 1863, CIA, p. 212.

88. Hanson to Dole, June 11, 1861, OIA, LR, California Supty.; Maltby to Cooley, September 15, 1865, CIA, pp. 278–79.

captured Indians.[89] With headquarters at Humboldt Bay, Lippitt's two companies faced an awesome task. Thousands of angry, armed Indians, scattered throughout the forests of northern California, owed allegiance to no single chief. Lippitt confessed that it would take about as long to round them up with cavalry detachments as it would to "bring in all the coyotes or squirrels."[90] Since the Colonel's command was too small for a concerted movement against the renegades, he established military stations at strategic locations. Post commanders, after giving hostiles a chance to surrender, pursued the rest relentlessly.[91]

By the fall of 1862 the army had imprisoned approximately eight hundred Indians, yet troops at Fort Humboldt could not protect their captives from irate whites until Lieutenant Colonel James R. Olney built a stockade. In mid-September Hanson loaded 840 Indians on the steamer *Panama*, which transported them to Smith River. Though a meager food supply existed for the Indians, who now numbered two thousand, the new arrivals lacked adequate clothing and shelter for the coming winter.[92] Such conditions no doubt caused these and other prisoners conducted to Round Valley to flee to the mountains and renew the fighting.[93]

Peace between the races became increasingly remote. Exasperated by Indian fickleness and the army's inability to strike a decisive blow at the hard-core hostiles, General Wright saw as the only alternatives extermination of the Indians or their removal from the district. The Indian commissioner likewise doubted that

89. John B. Rohrer et al. to Brigadier General E. V. Sumner, received June 10, 1861, OR, Ser. 1, 50, Pt. 1, pp. 507–8; Brigadier General James T. Ryan to Governor John Downey, July 31, 1861, Legislative Committee on Indian Affairs, Indian War Files, California State Archives, Sacramento; Wright to Hanson, December 24, 1861, OR, Series 1, 50, Pt. 1, p. 786; Hanson to Wright, December 31, 1861, *ibid.*, pp. 792–93.

90. Lippitt to Major R. C. Drum, January 12, 1862, OR, Series 1, 50, Pt. 1, p. 803.

91. Lippitt to Drum, March 5, 1862, *ibid.*, pp. 907–8.

92. Wright to Lorenzo Thomas, September 1, 1862, AGO, LR, 908-P-1862; Olney to Drum, June 8, 1862, OR, Ser. 1, 50, Pt. 1, pp. 69–70; Hanson to Dole, September 22, 1862, OIA, LR, California Supty.

93. Utley, *Frontiersmen in Blue*, p. 228.

northern California natives could ever live peacefully on their reserves.[94]

The year 1864 saw a conclusive termination of hostilities in the Humboldt District. Superintending Agent Elijah Steele arranged peace terms with the Modoc, Klamath, Shasta, Scotts Valley, and Hamburg Indians in mid-February 1864. Thereafter travelers passed safely through their country.[95] In October the Klamaths and Modocs ceded most of their land in northern California as well as southern Oregon and moved to a reservation established for them in southern Oregon. The remaining hostile bands of Hoopas, Redwoods, South Forks, and Grouse Creeks, which suffered severe hardship during the previous winter, gathered in Hoopa Valley to be fed by the army, though they refused to move to any existing reserve or to surrender their arms. Not until August did they turn over their weapons and accept peace terms offered by the new superintendent, Austin Wiley.[96] Both Wiley and the military commander of the Department of the Pacific preferred to move the hostiles to reserves south of San Francisco, but the Interior Department balked at the idea. Wiley therefore agreed to create a sanctuary in Hoopa Valley and colonize the bands there.[97]

Hostilities in the southern district centered in the Owens River Valley. Numerous wild and warlike tribesmen had maintained unchallenged possession of it for years. Not even the United States government established formal relations with them. Serious interracial bloodletting commenced in the early sixties when white farmers pushed into the valley, mines opened in nearby mountains, and Owens Valley became the chief southern route to the Esmeralda and Washoe districts of Nevada Territory. Late in April 1862 the army learned that about a thousand armed Owens Rivers, Tejons, Tulareños, Monos, and Paiutes had banded together to keep out the whites. They destroyed several dwellings,

94. Wright to Thomas, December 21, 1863, AGO, LR, 1005-P-1863; CIA, 1863, pp. 133–34.

95. Steele to John Conness, March 5, 1864, enclosed in Steele to Dole, March 8, 1864, CIA, pp. 264–65.

96. Statement of Wiley, 1865, in Sub-report of Higby, JSC, p. 500.

97. Wiley to Dole, August 2, 1864, CIA, p. 277.

slaughtered cattle and held the miners in check at Kern River.[98] Though the war still raged in June, many valley tribesmen were destitute. Agent Wentworth, in hopes of getting a truce, journeyed to Owens River with provisions. Upon arrival he counciled with Indian leaders of different tribes who promised peace in return for government protection and care.[99] Also temporarily sobering for the renegades was the construction of nearby Camp Independence by a company of troops from Fort Churchill, Nevada, and a squadron of cavalry from Los Angeles.[100] Like his northern Indian Office counterpart, Wentworth eventually doubted that the two races could ever live together in peace. Consultation with General Wright brought the removal of 850 Indian prisoners to the Tejon reserve and the abandonment of plans for a reservation on Owens River.[101] Meanwhile the remaining two-thirds of the hostiles continued to fight for their valley homes until white forces subdued them early in 1865.[102]

The incursions of predatory, non-treaty Indians so terrorized some reservation tribes in the Pacific Northwest that they were reluctant to remain in their assigned areas. The powerful Snakes, hereditary enemies of the central Oregon bands, launched numerous attacks on the Warm Springs reserve. During a raid in 1860 they killed or captured many women and children, drove off government and Indian stock, and sent red men and agency employees fleeing for their lives. The military pursued the renegades but failed to punish them. Only after much persuasion could Office officials induce the Warm Springs bands to return and resume their farming.[103] In October 1861 Agent William Logan reported another Snake attack. Unless the government provided arms for the protection of government employees at Warm

98. CIA, 1863, pp. 135–36; Lieutenant Colonel George S. Evans to Drum, April 29, 1862, OR, Ser. 1, 50, Pt. 1, p. 49.

99. Wentworth to Dole, June 13, 1862, OIA, LR, California Supty.; Wentworth to Dole, December 3, 1862, CIA (1863), p. 223.

100. Utley, *Frontiersmen in Blue*, p. 226.

101. Wentworth to Dole, September 1, 1863, CIA, p. 217.

102. Ralph J. Roske, *Everyman's Eden: A History of California* (New York, 1968), p. 348.

103. CIA, 1860, *Sen. Exec. Doc.* 1, 36 Cong., 2 Sess., 1:246 (Ser. 1078).

Springs, he warned, they and the friendly Indians would leave the reservation.[104] Logan had more success the following year; due to Superintendent William H. Rector's appeals the army stationed twenty-one soldiers from Fort Dalles at Warm Springs. Yet the Snake raids continued. In October 1863 they stole 140 horses and committed other minor depredations.[105]

For two years the Indian Office considered a Snake treaty indispensable to peace in Oregon and to keeping communications open with California. After the October 1863 attack on Warm Springs it consulted Oregon's Senator James W. Nesmith, who suggested a congressional appropriation of $20,000 for treating with the tribes. Congress voted funds in March 1864.[106] Unrest continued in central Oregon during the early months of 1864, and in the spring the army sent three expeditions against the hostiles. After the Battle of Crooked River in July the Yahuskin band of Snakes ceased depredations on United States citizens and signed a treaty in which it agreed to joint occupation with the Klamaths and Modocs of a reserve in southern Oregon. The following year the Walpapi band joined them, ending the Snake threat.[107]

An insidious threat to the reservation Indians of the Central and Dakota Superintendencies came from hostile bands to the west, which were either traditional enemies of the border tribes or felt that the friendly government wards no longer should be allowed to hunt on the plains. The wards had to hunt, since the drought had ruined their crops. Still, the government would neither arm them so they could protect themselves on the plains nor provide security for the agencies. During the Civil War years the hostiles harried the vulnerable Omahas, Delawares, Pawnees, Poncas, and lesser tribes of the upper Missouri.

In the Central Superintendency the plight of the Pawnees was

104. Logan to Rector, October 19, 1861, OIA, FOR, Oregon Supty., LR.

105. Colonel Justus Steinberger to Rector, July 5, 1862, OIA, FOR, Oregon Supty., LR; Huntington to Dole, October 23, 1863, OIA, LR, Oregon Supty.

106. Nesmith to Dole, February 1, 1864, OIA, LR, Oregon Supty.; *United States Statutes at Large* 13:40.

107. Kappler, *Indian Affairs* 2:865–68, 876–78; Coan, "Federal Indian Policy in the Pacific Northwest," pp. 387ff.

most serious. During the early 1860s the nomadic Sioux and Cheyennes drove the weaker Pawnees from traditional plains hunting grounds and so terrorized their reservation that the Pawnees dreaded to work in the fields. By 1863 life was increasingly insecure; in fact white agency employees were afraid to stay. In its 1857 treaty with the Pawnees the government promised them protection, but numerous Indian Office requests for arms and the permanent location of troops on the reserve went unheeded. Nor could Washington obtain an amity treaty between the Pawnees and their Indian enemies. Unable to procure adequate sustenance from any source, the destitute and disillusioned Pawnees blamed the federal government for their predicament.[108]

The condition of the Poncas was comparable. Bold Sioux raiders took advantage of their poverty and military weakness, the absence of nearby white settlements and the War Department's inability to spare weapons for the tribe's defense. Scared to do much farming, the Poncas spent the winters of 1863–64 and 1864–65 at the Omaha reserve. Not until 1865 did they produce a good crop on their own reservation.[109] Inadequate military protection enabled hostiles to intimidate the Assiniboins, Arikaras, Mandans, and Gros Ventres in the same manner. Furthermore, the United States lost the support of some friendly Sioux Bands. Agent Samuel N. Latta met with their leaders in May 1862 and learned that since the government could not defend the bands, the Sioux would break off relations and rejoin the hostiles. A decade of work with these people and thousands of dollars were wasted.[110]

Likewise bothersome were the hostiles of western Kansas and Nebraska, many of whom came under the jurisdiction of the

108. De Puy to Dole, December 29, 1861, OIA, LR, Pawnee Agency; Benjamin F. Lushbaugh to Branch, September 21, 1863, CIA, p. 369; Loree to Branch, September 30, 1863, CIA, p. 374; Lushbaugh to Mix, September 15, 1862, CIA, p. 267.

109. Hoffman to Jayne, February 2, 1862, OIA, FOR, Dakota Supty., 1862, Correspondence with Agents; Halleck to Caleb B. Smith, November 17, 1862, OIA, LR, Ponca Agency; Furnas to Albin, September 15, 1864, CIA, p. 499; Edmunds to Cooley, October 14, 1865, CIA, p. 372.

110. Latta to Dole, August 27, 1862, CIA, pp. 336–37.

Colorado Superintendency and the Kiowa Agency. Cheyenne, Arapaho, and Brulé attacks all along the central and western Platte Valley in August 1864 sent frightened Nebraskans eastward to Missouri. Full-scale war erupted in western Kansas, where Cheyennes and Arapahos descended on frontier settlements in the Little Blue Valley, while Kiowas, Arapahos, and Comanches struck the Santa Fe Trail. Throughout the rest of 1864 and 1865, the nomadic hostiles kept up their raids against ranches and stations of the overland lines.[111] Not until after the Appomattox peace could the nation turn its full attention to these frontier troubles.

Chippewa restlessness in 1862 resulted from several factors, including the previously noted whiskey problem. The tribe protested that the promises made in their 1855 cession treaties were not kept. No boxes of money came from the Great Father; agency blacksmiths lacked enough iron to do their work; carpenters never arrived to build houses for the chiefs and old men; cheap clothing failed to protect the women and children against winter winds.[112] Two individuals in particular helped to precipitate the events of August 1862. Lucius C. Walker, the Chippewa agent, prosecuted all persons engaged in the whiskey trade, discontinued his predecessor's practice of placating Indian chiefs with larger annuity payments than they deserved and refused to issue licenses to an old firm of Indian traders which he believed had a bad effect on the Chippewas. These reforms, particularly the agent's stern attitude toward the liquor trade, made him unpopular with many of his charges and produced an alliance between the discontented traders and chiefs.[113] Chief Hole-in-the-Day was Agent Walker's strongest opponent. The chief warned malcontents at Gull Lake and Leech Lake that the Great Father would force them to serve as soldiers against whites in the South. If the

111. James C. Olson, *History of Nebraska* (Lincoln, 1955), pp. 141–42; Albert E. Castel, *A Frontier State at War: Kansas, 1861–65* (Ithaca, N.Y., 1958), pp. 216–17.

112. Minutes of the Council at Crow Wing, September 1862, CIA, pp. 219–20.

113. Thompson to Dole, November 14, 1862, CIA, pp. 200–201.

Chippewas wished to save themselves they must war on the northern whites. When on August 18, 1862, three hundred Chippewas plundered private and government property in the Leech Lake area and threatened to attack the Gull Lake reservation as well, Walker assumed immediately that Hole-in-the-Day instigated the affair and ordered his arrest. Prompt action by the military and Indian Office prevented the outbreak from spreading. The evidence suggests that Hole-in-the-Day staged this hostile demonstration in the hope that Chippewa claims against the government and grievances against Agent Walker (whom they accused of fraud) might be appeased with a new treaty and appropriate bribes for himself. At any rate, he demonstrated how much trouble one chief could cause.[114]

Insufficient financial resources, unsatisfactory annuity goods, broken treaty promises, fraud: each impaired the Indian Office's ability to deal effectively with troublesome characters, be they red or white. Fiscal troubles constantly hobbled the Indian Office in the Pacific Northwest. The change of administration in 1861 and the government's absorption with the war delayed funds; this in turn caused employee dissatisfaction and heightened the Indian belief that the Great Father in Washington ignored his treaty obligations. Subagent George H. Abbott curbed his operations at Umatilla in 1861 and only kept employees and obtained supplies by incurring a $20,000 debt. The Yakima agent reported in December that his employees had not been paid for more than a year.[115] At least once the lack of money for transportation costs detained goods purchased on credit. Such financing was expensive, too. Superintendents and agents frequently paid 20 to 50 percent above the cash cost of supplies. Yet, in a country where interest rates ranged from 3 to 5 percent per month such high costs were to be expected. These transactions, even at such high rates, impaired the government's credit throughout the

114. John G. Nicolay, "Hole in the Day," *Harper's Monthly* 26 (January, 1863), reprinted in John G. Nicolay, *Lincoln's Secretary Goes West: Two Reports by John G. Nicolay on Frontier Indian Troubles, 1862*, ed. Theodore C. Blegen (La Crosse, Wisc., 1965), pp. 38–39.

115. Abbott to Rector, September 10, 1861, CIA, p. 776; Bancroft to Bion F. Kendall, December 31, 1861, OIA, FOR, Washington Supty., LR (Yakima).

Pacific Northwest, and by 1862 Indian Office officials in Oregon could obtain goods only if they guaranteed payment within a certain time.[116]

Money arriving from Washington quickly depreciated. Beginning in February 1862 the government issued about a half billion dollars in greenbacks whose value largely depended upon the people's confidence in the administration, since there was neither a gold reserve nor a specific redemption date for the bills. The Pacific Coast favored metallic currency and opposed the introduction of paper. California and Oregon, by passing statutes requiring certain contracts to be paid in gold, depressed the worth of greenbacks in the West. Government employees with fixed salaries paid in paper suffered a loss of real income.[117] Greenbacks furnished to Oregon's Superintendent J. W. Perit Huntington in 1863 circulated at only sixty to seventy-five cents on the dollar, equivalent to a 30 to 40 percent cut in appropriations. Huntington anticipated that unless the worth of paper currency appreciated or salaries increased, his best employees would leave the service by spring. The proximity of the gold fields and the news of daily mineral strikes irresistibly lured ambitious men.[118] Indian Office officials in Washington and Idaho grappled with the same fiscal dilemmas.

Because of price fluctuations west of the Rockies, the government policy of buying annuity goods in the East for Pacific Coast superintendencies proved unsatisfactory.[119] Many such items bore no relation to the Indians' needs or the requests of the agents and superintendents. To be given calico and trinkets in exchange for land only insulted shrewd dealers like the Nez Percés and Flatheads. Senator Nesmith learned of one transaction in which "forty dozen pairs of *elastic garters* were sent out to a tribe in which

116. Nesmith to Dole, December 13, 1861, OIA, LR, Oregon Supty.; Rector to Dole, March 16, 1862, OIA, FOR, Oregon Supty., LS, Vol. H, p. 116.

117. Joseph Ellison, "The Currency Question on the Pacific Coast During the Civil War," *Mississippi Valley Historical Review* 16 (June, 1929), pp. 50ff.

118. Huntington to Dole, December, 4, 1863, OIA, LR, Oregon Supty.; Huntington to Dole, December 21, 1863, OIA, FOR, Oregon Supty., LS, vol. H, p. 467.

119. Dole to Huntington, May 2, 1863, OIA, FOR, Oregon Supty., LR.

there was not a single pair of *stockings*."[120] Not only did annuity goods prove unsuitable in many cases but the date of their arrival was uncertain, sometimes leaving the Indians without essential winter clothing. The annuities for the Warm Springs reservation, shipped from New York in mid-June 1861, did not reach Portland until December 20.[121] The cost of so extended a journey also reduced the real value of the Indians' yearly allotment. Nesmith recalled that when he was a superintendent in the Pacific Northwest during the fifties, a shipment of annuity merchandise purchased in New York and worth about $9000 had cost, at twenty-five cents a pound, $10,000 to send to him, whereas "the same goods could have been bought in Oregon for less than the original cost in New York."[122] Similar improprieties occurred in the sixties if we accept the statements of West Coast Indian Office officials. These men wanted to invest Indian monies in locally purchased farm equipment, stock, and other items which would encourage reservation dwellers to become self-supporting.

Fraud likewise triggered Indian dissatisfaction. James H. Wilbur, who succeeded Ashley A. Bancroft at the Yakima Agency in 1864, accused his predecessor of paying Indians with their own annuity goods for work on government projects. Bancroft's wards believed he also took their provisions to sell to whites. Stationed among the coastal Indians, Corporal Royal A. Bensell noted in his journal that Siletz Agent Benjamin Simpson defrauded his charges by withholding annuities and selling the goods to red men at the agency store for three times their value. Timothy W. Davenport, Agent Barnhart's temporary replacement at the Umatilla reserve, recalled after the war some of the irregularities of his predecessor. Besides employing his brother as agency farmer, Barnhart used as his personal clerk a man listed on the rolls as a teacher. Davenport said that before departing, Barnhart remarked "that 'the place of agent at the Umatilla is worth $4,000

120. Trimball, "American and British Treatment of the Indians in the Pacific Northwest," pp. 38ff; Sub-report of Nesmith, JSC, p. 12.
121. Logan to Mix, December 25, 1861, OIA, LR, Oregon Supty.
122. Nesmith to Dole, December 13, 1861, *ibid.*

a year,' to which I [Davenport] responded by asking how that could be on a salary of $1,500. He made no reply but told the sutler, Mr. Flippin, that he 'could show me how easy it is to do such things.' "[123]

In the Central and Dakota Superintendencies corrupt agency officials intensified Indian poverty and suffering, and gave them another reason to reject the culture that produced such scoundrels. The "Indian Ring" operated efficiently on at least two Central Superintendency reservations. In 1865 Arkaketch and other Oto and Missouri chiefs detailed conditions on their reserve. Not only did their agent force them to buy supplies from the licensed trader, who charged twice as much as other merchants, but he did work for white citizens with the Indians' blacksmith shop and mill, keeping the profits for himself. Even the Indian owners had to pay a fee.[124] Another technique for robbing the Indians was to allow individual tribesmen to accumulate large debts at the trader's store, which they could never repay. The use of tribal funds to settle the accounts penalized the industrious members of the Indian community. As long as easy credit existed, two Delawares wrote in 1862, the young men would never work for a living.[125] Whites also coveted Indian land. Agent Charles B. Keith aided greedy Kansas railroad promoters in obtaining the fraudulent Kickapoo Allotment Treaty of 1863, thereby opening up over 125,000 acres of remaining Kickapoo land. And Yankton chiefs who testified before a congressional investigator in August 1865 felt that Yankton Agent Walter A. Burleigh had sought a maximum profit from his position. By withholding annuity goods and money, Burleigh, who arrived at the agency in 1861 with only a trunk, was "high up–rich" by 1865.[126]

123. Wilbur to William H. Waterman, July 22, 1865, CIA, pp. 251–52; Bensell, *All Quiet on the Yamhill*, pp. 183–84; T. W. Davenport, "Recollections of an Indian Agent," *Oregon Historical Quarterly* 8 (March, 1907):7.

124. Arkaketch et al. to Lincoln, March 17, 1865, OIA, LR, Oto Agency.

125. John Connor and Charles Journeycake to Smith, October 10, 1862, OIA, LR, Delaware Agency.

126. Gibson, *The Kickapoos*, pp. 124–240; Testimony of Yankton Chiefs, August 1865, JSC, pp. 368–70.

One reason, in addition to those noted in the Introduction, why such fraud persisted was the Indian Office's fear of embarrassing Lincoln's government. Filed in October 1864, Superintendent William Albin's first annual report pointed out some of the most common swindles at the agencies. The commissioner sharply rebuked Albin for making the objectionable statements, disparaging his agents, and furnishing ammunition to the enemies of the administration.[127] Albin's offensive remarks did not appear in the published version of his report.

127. Albin to Dole, October 1 and November 17, 1864, OIA, LR, Central Supty.

CHAPTER VII

Rebels, Rustlers, and Miners

Because of their location in the Old Northwest, the Santees escaped the direct impact which the North-South struggle had on the Central and Southern Superintendencies. Operating along the Kansas-Missouri border, Quantrill's raiders and other guerrilla bands attacked the Osage River, Kickapoo, Ottawa, Kansa, and Shawnee agencies. Hardest hit were the Shawnees, apparently because they furnished warriors for the Union army. By mid-September 1862 raiders had stolen $8,000 worth of horses and driven Black Bob's band from its home on the Missouri border, leaving many families destitute. At the close of 1864, border trouble still discouraged the Shawnees from extensive horse raising.[1]

As the storm clouds of civil war threatened the nation in 1861, Arkansas Governor Henry M. Rector dispatched a letter to John Ross, chief of the Cherokee nation:

It may now be regarded as almost certain that the States having slave property within their borders will, in consequence of repeated northern aggression, separate themselves, and withdraw from the federal government. . . .

Your people, in their institutions, productions, latitude, and

1. James B. Abbott to Branch, September 15, 1862, CIA, p. 256; Abbott to Branch, September 25, 1862, enclosed in Branch to Dole, October 3, 1862, OIA, LR, Shawnee Agency; Abbott to Dole, October 1, 1864. CIA, p. 523.

natural sympathies, are allied to the common brotherhood of the slaveholding States. Our people and yours are natural allies in war. . . .[2]

The Cherokees and the Chickasaws, Choctaws, Creeks, and Seminoles constituted the Five Civilized Tribes. Since their forced removal earlier in the century to the Indian territory south of Kansas, they had prospered as ranchers and farmers. Politically they resembled independent republics more than Indian tribes. Their vital interests were not at stake in a clash between North and South. But, as Governor Rector suggested in his January letter to John Ross, neutrality in the forthcoming conflict would be impossible; the Cherokees and their white neighbors were "natural allies." In less than a year the prophecy came true. The guns at distant Fort Sumter sounded the death knell for peace, and the reverberations from Charleston harbor staggered the Indian territory as they did the rest of the nation.

The bordering states of Texas and Arkansas, particularly anxious about the Indians' allegiance in the event of civil war, sent emissaries into the Indian territory to secure their support. Secessionist propaganda so alarmed the Chickasaws legislature that it called for an intertribal meeting to be held on February 7, 1861. John Ross, a staunch neutralist in the sectional quarrel, discouraged attendance at the February convention and no action was taken. A second convention in March proved equally unproductive. Secretary of War Simon Cameron doomed Indian neutrality on April 17, when he withdrew federal troops from the Indian country.[3]

The wartime panic which gripped Washington in part prompted the abandonment of Forts Washita, Arbuckle, and Cobb, and the retirement of Union troops to Fort Leavenworth, Kansas. The retrenchment also testified to the War Department's conviction that the West was of secondary importance to the eastern front. A holding action rather than an all-out offensive would be pursued beyond the Mississippi; if necessary, frontier posts might even be sacrificed temporarily. The Secretary of

2. Rector to Ross, January 29, 1861, CIA, p. 345.
3. Grant Foreman, *History of Oklahoma* (Norman, 1942), pp. 100–101.

the Interior opposed the strategy and urged the repossession of the Indian territory, but to no avail.[4]

The Confederacy quickly filled the vacuum created by the Union withdrawal. First came Texas troops. Then, in May, the South formed the District of the Indian Territory, under the command of Brigadier General Benjamin McCulloch. His fighting force included Texas, Louisiana, and Arkansas soldiers, and was to be expanded by the recruitment of Indian regiments. The Confederacy also planned to procure grain, lead, salt, horses, and cattle from the area. To marshal Indian support McCulloch journeyed west to Fort Smith late in May 1862, where he met Captain Albert Pike, the South's commissioner to the Five Civilized Tribes.[5] The two men then departed for the Indian country to parley with John Ross, whose cooperation was essential to the success of their mission.[6]

When civil war burst upon the nation, factionalism disrupted the Indian territory as it did most border areas. The Choctaws and Chickasaws lived in the "deep South" of the Indian country; few questioned their alliance with the rebels. The other three nations, deeply divided, preferred neutrality, but the Choctaws, Chickasaws, Creeks, Seminoles, and several plains tribes eventually signed alliances with the Confederacy. Ross, who had formally proclaimed Cherokee neutrality in May,[7] realized his nation could not stand alone. In October he too linked his people's fate with the Southern cause.[8]

Since military might begets political alliance, many federal officials understood the real reasons behind these treaties. "In-

4. Castel, *A Frontier State at War*, pp. 96–97; Edwin C. McReynolds, *The Seminoles* (Norman, 1957), p. 291.

5. Ohland Morton, "Confederate Government Relations with the Five Civilized Tribes," *Chronicles of Oklahoma* 31 (Autumn, 1953): 302; Edward Everett Dale and Gaston Litton, eds., *Cherokee Cavaliers: Forty Years of Cherokee History as Told in the Correspondence of the Ridge-Watie-Boudinot Family* (Norman, 1939), p. 98; A. M. Gibson, "Confederates on the Plains: The Pike Mission to Wichita Agency," *Great Plains Journal* 4 (Fall, 1964): 7.

6. McCulloch to Walker, May 28, 1861, OR, Ser. 1, 3:587.

7. McReynolds, *The Seminoles*, p. 292; Proclamation of John Ross to the Cherokee People, May 17, 1861, CIA (1863), p. 344.

8. Dole and Litton, *Cherokee Cavaliers*, pp. 99–100.

deed," wrote the commissioner of Indian affairs in November 1861, "the only matter of surprise to me is, that they have not more readily and heartily espoused the cause of the rebels."[9]

Lacking news from the North, the Indians had also been defenseless against Confederate distortions of fact: that England and France would aid the Confederacy, that the Indians' interests lay with the South, that the Union fought solely to end slavery and to steal Indian lands.[10] The latter was especially powerful propaganda since many of the tribesmen owned slaves.

Severed communications with the Indian Office also contributed to the vulnerability of the Five Civilized Tribes. Because of the nature of the patronage system, only Southerners held office in the Indian country, licenses were granted to none but Southern traders, and the federal government invested the Indians' trust funds in Southern stocks. When news of the war reached superintendency headquarters at Fort Smith in April 1861, Elias Rector and his agents, Southerners all, resigned their positions and were retained provisionally by the Confederacy to assist Commissioner Pike among the Indians.[11] William G. Coffin, a staunch Union supporter, replaced Rector as southern superintendent but could not carry out his duties; Confederates and disloyal natives blocked his access to the Indian country.[12] Hence Coffin and his staff established headquarters at Leavenworth, Kansas. Throughout the summer and fall of 1861 they could neither reach their charges nor obtain a military force to rescue them. When Commissioner Dole learned of the actions of rebel agents, he assured the chiefs of the Civilized Nations that the federal government would scrupulously observe its treaties, including the promise of protection: "in no event, and under no circumstances, shall your domestic institutions [slavery] be

9. CIA, 1861, p. 628.

10. Edwin H. Carruth to Coffin, July 11, 1861, enclosed in Coffin to Dole, September 26, 1861, OIA, LR, Southern Supty.

11. Annie Heloise Abel, *The American Indian as Slaveholder and Secessionist: An Omitted Chapter in the Diplomatic History of the Southern Confederacy* (Cleveland, 1915), pp. 59–62; Dale and Litton, *Cherokee Cavaliers*, p. 98.

12. *Leavenworth* (Kansas) *Conservative*, July 9, 1861, in the *New York Times*, July 20, 1861.

interfered with by any of its [the present administration's] officers and employés." But Caleb Smith failed to obtain troops from the War Department. Communications with the territory south of Kansas became so precarious that Dole eventually withheld the annuity payments of the Indians living there.[13] The inability of the United States to fulfill its treaty obligations frustrated the Indian Office's first efforts to rescue the Civilized Tribes.

Tribal feuds flared up anew when the North-South struggle spread to the Indian country, thus contributing to the South's triumph there. Since their removal from Georgia in the 1830s the Cherokees had been faction-ridden. The Ross party resented the Ridge party, led by Stand Watie, whose former leaders signed the fraudulent treaty of 1835 which removed the nation west of the Mississippi. Stand Watie recognized the opportunity for power which the war offered and organized a regiment of Cherokees in open disregard of Ross's neutrality statement. In August 1861 Confederate armies, with the help of Stand Watie's force, won the Battle of Wilson's Creek, in Missouri.[14] His neutrality policy bankrupt, John Ross committed himself to the Confederacy rather than lose political power to the triumphant Stand Watie.

No less severe was the Creek rift, which also originated at the time of the Creeks' removal from the Southeast. The McIntosh faction, dominant among the mixed-blood Lower Creeks, had favored removal; the Upper Creeks and their wealthy, full-blood Chief Opothle Yahola opposed it. Albert Pike won over the Lower Creeks in the summer of 1861. Opothle Yahola, steadfastly refusing a Confederate alliance, withdrew with the Upper Creeks to the North Fork of the Canadian River, near the present town of Eufaula, and rallied other Indians to support his loyalist faction.[15] In November he learned that Colonel Douglas H. Cooper, commanding a force of Indians and Texans, intended to attack the Upper Creeks' position. Hoping to avoid danger,

13. Dole to Ross et al., May 11, 1861, CIA, p. 650; CIA, p. 628.

14. Edward E. Dale, "The Cherokees in the Confederacy," *Journal of Southern History* 13 (May, 1947): 159–61; Foreman, *History of Oklahoma*, p. 104.

15. John Bartlett Meserve, "Chief Opothleyahola," *Chronicles of Oklahoma* 9 (December, 1931): 445–46.

Opothle Yahola's Creeks marched farther north. They were joined by a large number of Seminoles under chiefs Billy Bowlegs and John Chupco as well as some Cherokees, Delawares, and others from the southern plains. Numbering eight to twelve hundred warriors, the force fought a six-week campaign against Confederate pursuers before fleeing up the Verdigris to Kansas.[16]

Besides dispossessing the loyalists in 1861, the North-South conflict impeded the speedy return of the refugees—a problem the Indian Office did not face with the Santees. Three groups desired their restoration to the Indian country: the dispirited Indians, who longed for their homes in the South; the Interior Department, which bore the expense of feeding them in Kansas; and the army, which sought Indian help in reestablishing Union control west of Arkansas. When and how the Indians would be returned were points of contention.

Creek and Seminole chiefs made preliminary plans for their departure as early as February 3, 1862, when they met with General Hunter and agreed to support the Union army's invasion of the Indian territory. A grand council of all the tribes, meeting later the same month, confirmed the headmen's proposal. It cheered the Indians to know that soon they would be home; some even planned to plant a crop before the end of the season.[17] After it assumed control over the refugees, the Office of Indian Affairs likewise urged their return, and in March President Lincoln detailed two white regiments to escort them.[18] Two refugee regiments of mounted rifles were also organized for the Indians' defense. Confident they could "fight their way back," the native troops left for Humboldt in mid–June to join the regular army regiments. Coffin appointed Henry W. Martin and Edwin H. Carruth special agents to act as liaisons between the loyalist soldiers and the military, and to assure loyal tribesmen in the Indian

16. Foreman, *History of Oklahoma*, pp. 105–7; Kenneth W. Porter, "Billy Bowlegs (Holata Micco) In the Civil War (Part II)," *Florida Historical Quarterly* 45 (April, 1967): 395.

17. Leavenworth *Daily Times*, February 4, 1862; Coffin to Dole, March 3, 1862; OIA, LR, Southern Supty.

18. Smith to Halleck, March 21, 1862, ID, LS.

territory of the government's willingness to protect them.[19]

The expedition left Humboldt on June 28 under the command of Colonel William Weer, who had explicit orders from General James Blunt, commanding the military Department of Kansas: determine whether the corn crop in the Indian territory could support the refugees; protect the property, especially the cattle, of the loyal Indians living there; ascertain the strength and position of rebel forces from western Arkansas to Texas; and communicate with John Ross and other Confederate Indians, assuring them of the ability and willingness of the Union "to protect them and to fulfill all its treaty stipulations, while they remain loyal."[20] Though the army advanced as far as Tahlequah and Park Hill, Colonel Frederick Salomon, second in command, arrested Colonel Weer on July 18, charging him with misconduct as a result of intemperance and perhaps insanity. Salomon withdrew his white units to Fort Scott despite their victories in the Cherokee country. He left behind the Indian regiments under Colonel Robert W. Furnas to hold the upper portion of the Indian territory, which they did. When Blunt learned of Weer's arrest, he countermanded Salomon's mutinous orders and returned two Kansas regiments to reinforce the native troops.[21]

On July 7, before his arrest, Weer tried to arrange an interview with John Ross. The chief replied cautiously that he had signed a treaty with the Confederacy and must uphold it. Ultimately Weer's troops arrested Ross and took him to Kansas. The old chief, who later won a parole from the federal government, asked the president to pardon the Cherokees for their alliance with the rebels and to fulfill the stipulations of former treaties. At a special cabinet meeting it was agreed that no new promises should be made until the conclusion of the war.[22] Lincoln informed Ross

19. Burlington (Kansas) *Register*, in Leavenworth *Daily Times*, May 25, 1862; Coffin to Carruth, June 16, 1862, OIA, LR, Southern Supty.

20. Blunt to Weer, July 12, 1862, USAC, Department of Kansas, LS, 137:243–44.

21. Blunt to Smith, November 21, 1862, USAC, Army of the Frontier, LS (in the field), 136:117–18.

22. Grace Steele Woodward, *The Cherokees* (Norman, 1963), pp. 279–80;

of the government's determination to protect the loyal Cherokees, but did not clarify the precise relationship between the two nations. To curry favor with the United States as well as to encourage Union reoccupation of their country, Cherokee refugees in the North convened a national council at Cowskin Prairie, Missouri, in February 1863. They abrogated treaties with the Confederate states, abolished slavery in the Cherokee nation, and appointed a delegation headed by John Ross to represent them before the American government.[23]

When Colonel Salomon's troops withdrew from the Indian country, almost two thousand Indians followed in their wake, mainly Cherokee women and children whose menfolk had joined the Union troops after the defeat of a Southern force at Locust Grove on July 3. Destitute of food, clothing, and shelter and entirely dependent upon the federal government, the Cherokee families camped near Fort Scott, Kansas.[24] Superintendent Coffin visited the site late in October 1862, provisioned them and urged that they move north to the Sac and Fox reservation. Like the Creeks and Seminoles, the Cherokees hesitated to move farther from their homeland. Besides, General Blunt advised them that if the army reoccupied the Indian country the Cherokees could return.[25]

Coffin's report of his October visit was cool toward General Blunt, who the previous month had ordered Indian Office officials to enumerate the facilities for transportation and subsistence at each agency so that his quartermaster could supply needed wagons and food when the army returned the Civilized Nations to their homes. This infringement of authority piqued the Southern superintendent. The Indians enlisted in the army came under the general's command; the other refugees were under the care and

---

Salmon P. Chase, *Inside Lincoln's Cabinet: The Civil War Diaries of Salmon P. Chase*, ed. David Donald (New York, 1954), diary entry for September 24, 1862, p. 157.

23. Lincoln to Ross, September 25, 1862, in Lincoln, *The Works of Lincoln* 5:439; Ross to Dole, April 2, 1863, CIA, pp. 343–44.

24. Blunt to Smith, November 21, 1862, USAC, Army of the Frontier, LS (in the field), 136:117–18.)

25. Coffin to Dole, November 10, 1862, OIA, LR, Cherokee Agency.

control of the Department of the Interior, with Coffin as its appointed representative.[26]

In defense of his action the self-confident Blunt, a decisive and gifted soldier, wrote directly to the Secretary of the Interior:

> While I did not desire to interfere with the business of any Department, with which I was not legitimately connected, the interests of the Refugee Indians were so intimately blended with the military affairs of the Indian Territory, that I deemed it my duty to act in the premises, . . . and I have yet to be convinced that I committed any error. As the Military Commander, having jurisdiction over the Indian Territory, I regarded it as my duty to make every effort in my power to restore and protect its loyal people, and to save the country from rebel devastation. The Indians mustered into the Federal service were not willing to make a second expedition South, unless assurances were given them that their families should be taken to their homes, as soon as we obtained occupation of the country.

In addition to this rejoinder General Blunt insinuated that corruption existed in the Southern Superintendency. Obviously the Kansas refugees were victimized by "mercenary and unscrupulous speculators" bent on keeping them in the state as long as they could turn a profit. Even the Indians knew it. Blunt concluded his defense with a list of seven reasons why the Indians should be returned to their homeland, all of which hinged upon his resolute assertion that "the whole Indian Country is now substantially in our possession."[27]

In February 1863 Superintendent Coffin sanctioned the return of the refugee Cherokees at the request of Agent Justin Harlan and Colonel William A. Phillips, the new commander of the Indian Brigade. Blunt, who needed Coffin's cooperation for the year's military campaign, issued fifty serviceable army tents for the Indians' temporary use[28] and, when Agent Cutler wrote asking

26. Coffin to Blunt, September 28, 1862, enclosed in Coffin to Mix, September 29, 1862, OIA, LR, Southern Supty.

27. Blunt to Smith, November 21, 1862, enclosed in Smith to Dole, December 27, 1862, *ibid.*

28. Coffin to Dole, February 24, 1863, OIA, LR, Cherokee Agency; Colonel

when the other Civilized Nations would be restored to their homes, the general did not overstep his authority. The Kansas refugees were under the jurisdiction of the Southern Superintendency, he said; the army's role was to prepare the Indian territory for their return.[29]

Colonel Phillips's expedition to the Indian country succeeded initially. By April 1863 he had captured Tahlequah and occupied Fort Gibson. Indians sympathetic with the South fled to the Choctaw country along the Red River and to Texas where they lived as refugees and experienced many of the same hardships as the loyalists in Kansas. Behind Phillips came the Cherokees who settled, at the advice of General Blunt, in defensible colonies at Tahlequah, Park Hill, and Fort Gibson.[30] There remained ample time to put in a crop and all seemed well.

But the Union did not reckon with rebel Brigadier General Stand Watie, whose raiding parties assailed the refugee colonies throughout the summer and fall of 1863, forcing the loyalists to abandon their harvests and homes and to flee to Fort Gibson. Beyond the range of its cannon the Indian country lay ravaged: crops destroyed, houses burned, Cherokee cattle driven off. Public buildings at Tahlequah, the Cherokee capital, and Chief John Ross's house were leveled. Agency buildings near Tahlequah stood vacant, symbolic of federal impotence. As the upper Indian country became a no-man's-land of desolation and terror, circumstances at Fort Gibson also deteriorated. The fort commanded an area of one and one-half square miles into which were crowded three thousand soldiers and six thousand refugees. The Indian women and children who huddled outside the enclosure were "exposed to the hot sun, half starved and naked and a great many of them sick with dysentery and diarreah."[31]

Thomas Moonlight to Major L. C. Easton, March 3, 1863, USAC, District of Kansas, LS, 137:513.

29. Blunt to Cutler, February 24, 1863, USAC, *ibid.*, pp. 508–9.

30. Dale and Litton, *Cherokee Cavaliers*, p. 101; Blunt to Phillips, March 9, 1863, USAC, District of Kansas, LS, 137:548–51.

31. A. G. Proctor to Coffin, November 23, 1863, enclosed in Coffin to Dole, November 28, 1863, OIA, LR, Southern Supty.; Smith to Coffin, July 16, 1863, enclosed in Coffin to Dole, July 18, 1863, *ibid.*

The military's inability to protect the Cherokees touched off more bickering between the Indian service and the army. Colonel Phillips reported the Indian Office ill prepared to care for the Cherokees after their return. Harlan accused the army of wooing his Indians with a "syren song of security," only to abandon them in the face of rebel attacks. "Every promise has failed," he wrote. "I am now satisfied, that I committed an error in bringing them here."[32] Harlan also complained that the army tried to prejudice the red men against the Indian service, and Assistant Agent A. G. Proctor charged it with wanton and wasteful slaughter of stray Indian cattle. Coffin suggested to Washington that if the military had removed the rebels from the Indian territory instead of interfering with the Interior Department's affairs, the refugees would be happily settled in their homes.[33]

Because of the impracticality of provisioning the isolated Cherokees at Fort Gibson, Coffin, Proctor, and Harlan recommended that refugees not in the military service be sent back to southern Kansas.[34] But the weakness of General Blunt's command made this impossible. The Cherokees thus passed the winter of 1863–64 as virtual prisoners under the guns at Fort Gibson.

The loyalists in Kansas also spent a dismal winter, yet their exile neared an end. Late in January 1864, the chairman of the Senate Committee on Indian Affairs, James R. Doolittle, inquired of the Interior Department whether the refugees might be returned to their homes in time to raise a crop that season. Commissioner Dole solicited military support, but Blunt replied that because of a reorganization of the Department of Kansas, General Curtis had only the Indian Home Guard at Fort Gibson to patrol the country of the Civilized Nations.[35] However, Curtis convinced Dole that the Indians could be returned safely. On May 3 Congress appropriated the necessary funds: $52,000 for trans-

32. Phillips to Usher, May 15, 1863, OIA, LR, Cherokee Agency; Harlan to Coffin, May 26, 1863, OIA, LR, Southern Supty.

33. Henry Smith to Coffin, July 16, 1863, enclosed in Coffin to Dole, July 18, 1863, OIA, LR, Southern Supty.; Coffin to Mix, August 31, 1863, *ibid.*

34. Coffin to Mix, *ibid.*

35. Dole to Usher, February 9, 1864, OIA, Report Books, 13:302–3; Blunt to Dole, February 5, 1864, OIA, LR, Southern Supty.

portation and provisions during the removal, $153,000 for temporary subsistence after the tribes arrived in the Indian territory, and $18,000 for seeds, plows, and agricultural implements.[36]

Coffin arrived at the Sac and Fox reserve in mid–May 1864 to begin the removal. A week later he was still there, for the Indians hesitated to make the trip into what might be unsafe territory. Also Coffin underestimated the number of wagons needed. Instead of three teams per hundred Indians, he needed five.[37]

The refugee train stretched out for six miles when finally it snaked away from the Sac and Fox lands. Thousands of Indians walked ahead of the teams or meandered two or three miles behind. It was quite a sight, Coffin wrote, "and if I had no responsibility or care, I could enjoy it most hugely." An escort from Fort Scott later joined the Indian expedition, which lengthened the train to about six hundred wagons. On June 15, fifteen thousand Indian refugees arrived at Fort Gibson. The only loyalists yet to be returned included five hundred Seminoles quarantined with smallpox and six hundred Quapaws, Senecas, and Senecas and Shawnees whose farms in the Indian country were so infested with rebels that officials deemed it safer for them to remain in Kansas on the Ottawa reserve.[38] This delayed their restoration to the Indian territory until 1865.

Though safely delivered to Fort Gibson, the refugees arrived too late to plant a crop. Colonel Phillips's Home Guard still did not control the countryside, and the refugees had to congregate in protected areas like Fort Gibson. Extended and vulnerable lines of supply made sustaining the Indians at these strongholds enormously expensive.[39]

Coffin estimated late in September 1864 that fifteen thousand destitute refugees would have to be fed for at least another year. Shoes, blankets, pants, linsey, and calico must be shipped in before winter. Commissioner Dole recommended that a debt be created

36. Dole to Usher, March 21, 1864, OIA, Report Books, 13:346–47; *United States Statutes at Large* 13:67.

37. Coffin to Dole, May 22, 1864, CIA, pp. 482–83.

38. Coffin to Dole, June 3, 7, and 16, 1864, CIA, 484–86; Coffin to Dole, April 26, 1864, OIA, LR, Southern Supty.; CIA, 1864, p. 176.

39. Coffin to Dole, June 16, 1864, CIA, p. 486.

in anticipation of another congressional appropriation; otherwise the provisions could not be forwarded in time. President Lincoln authorized the Indian Office to expend an additional $200,000.[40] Nevertheless, nearly two months passed before Superintendent Coffin dispatched the needed provisions. Two thousand sacks of flour and 5,500 bushels of shelled and sacked corn stood ready for shipment by October 5, but because of Stand Watie's seizure of a wagon train the previous month and Confederate General Sterling Price's invasion of Missouri, no troops were available for escort duty until the next army train departed in mid–November.[41] As Coffin finally loaded his wagons a severe hail and snow storm struck the Leavenworth area, and many of the drivers refused to make the journey to Fort Scott. Only half the teams reached the post in time to join the caravan. As a final discouraging note the profligate escort troops openly looted Coffin's wagons.[42]

Demoralization of government employees on the border could be observed in the increasing quarrels between military and civil officials stationed at Fort Gibson. Phillips was so critical of the Indian Office that Washington could not ignore his charges. According to the colonel, Superintendent Coffin and his agents procured corn for Indians by fraudulent transactions with Cherokee farmers and paid contractors for beef stolen from Indian herds. Furthermore, Henry McKee, an Indian trader licensed by Superintendent Coffin and approved by Commissioner Dole, drove stolen cattle out of the Indian country to be sold in Kansas. Phillips proposed to arrest and try by military commission the Indian contractor, the McDonald and Fuller Company, for stealing cattle.[43] Secretary Usher directed Dole to investigate the allegations and to request explanatory reports from the superintendent and agents in question.[44]

Early in March Phillips again challenged the Indian Office and the firm of McDonald and Fuller by presenting a note of com-

40. Coffin to Dole, September 24, 1864, CIA, pp. 448–49; W. T. Otto to Dole, October 1, 1864, OIA, LR, Southern Supty.
41. Coffin to Dole, October 5, 1864, *ibid*.
42. Coffin to Dole, December 1, 1864, *ibid*.
43. Phillips to Usher, January 17, 1865, ID, LR Misc.
44. Usher to Dole, February 10, 1865, CIA, p. 456.

plaint signed by a Creek Indian, Mik-ko-hut-kay, together with a sample of inferior goods. Superintendent Coffin responded sharply to this second accusation: Mik-ko-hut-kay was but the "supple tool" of Phillips and his partners in the army sutler business, D. H. Ross and Company; not one Creek chief endorsed Mik-ko-hut-kay's letter; obviously Phillips and the sutlers sought by such erroneous statements to drive out all competition, specifically McDonald and Fuller; the sample of damaged goods came from one box, mistakenly sent by the contractors to the Creeks. Coffin had satisfactory assurances that the Indians received only high quality provisions. He concluded with some charges of his own: "it is clear in my mind, that the representation of Col Philips, is a miserable abortion, a desperate and dastardly effort, to retain his position, in which, he has shown himself so utterly inefficient and worthless...."[45] Reports from Coffin's agents further absolved the Indian Office.

Though existing records make it difficult to establish the validity of either Colonel Phillips's indictments or the recriminations of the Southern Superintendency field employees, the lack of cooperation between civilian and military officials doubtless worsened the refugees' lot. Charges and countercharges also revealed the illegal trading of Indian cattle.

This nefarious traffic flourished from the early days of the Civil War. Thousands of Indian cattle, loosed when plundering armies destroyed farms and fences, ran free over the land and multiplied. Not adverse to profiting from the misfortune of the Civilized Nations, enterprising Indians of the Wichita Agency and white Kansans ventured into the Indian country to round up strays and drive them north to market. While the refugees shivered on the Kansas plains the rustlers grew rich; when the refugees received provisions from Leavenworth they were most likely eating their own beef.[46] After they returned home and attempted to become self-sufficient again, the loss of cattle was even more serious. In October 1865 the southern superintendent estimated

45. Coffin to Dole, March 13, 1865, OIA, LR, Southern Supty.
46. Foreman, *History of Oklahoma*, p. 130; Milo Gookins to Coffin, October 20, 1864, OIA, LR, Wichita Agency.

that thieves rustled 300,000 head from the Indian territory during the previous four years—at the price of fifteen dollars a head, a loss of $4,500,000 to the Indians.[47]

To intercept stolen herds Superintendent Coffin assigned a special agent to patrol the Kansas border. General Curtis offered the full cooperation of the army, and Congress approved a special bill in March 1865 to punish cattle thieves.[48] Yet the rustling continued unabated. Coffin issued a few passes to cattle buyers which permitted them to enter the Indian country, so that the tribes might derive some benefit from the sale of their animals. This strategy proved equally ineffective. Though thieves still had difficulty driving cattle to Kansas, a license gave them free access to the Indian territory under the guise of buying cattle and allowed them to reconnoiter for the largest herds.[49]

Great portions of the Indian country lay in ruins when General Stand Watie surrendered his Indian force and signed articles of surrender with United States commissioners in June 1865. The physical condition of the Indians was distressing. Besides the fifteen thousand loyal Indians cared for during the winter of 1864–65, two other groups depended upon the government at war's end: the nearly four thousand members of the Indian regiments and numerous rebel refugees, on the brink of starvation since March. In addition there was the pressing need for materials to restore Indian self-sufficiency: axes to build homes and barns, plows and hoes to cultivate the soil, cattle to restock farms.[50] The fate of the Civilized Nations during Reconstruction is another story, however.

Whether starving and freezing in Kansas or trapped outside the walls of Fort Gibson, the lot of the Civilized Nations was grim during the Civil War. None save the contractors wanted them in Kansas, yet no one could protect them in the Indian

47. Elijah Sells to Cooley, October 16, 1865, CIA, p. 437.

48. Coffin to Dole, September 12, 1864, CIA, p. 491; *United States Statutes at Large* 13:563.

49. Coffin to Dole, September 24, 1864, CIA, p. 450; Harlan to Sells, October 1, 1865, CIA, p. 470.

50. Coffin to Dole, March 29, 1865, OIA, LR, Southern Supty.; Sells to Cooley, October 16, 1865, CIA, p. 438.

country. So they were herded like their own cattle, back and forth across the Kansas border. For three years the ridiculous rite was repeated. The military as well as the Indians must bear some of the blame, but the Indian Office was ultimately responsible for the refugees' well-being. The reasons for its striking lack of success included poor communications between southern Kansas and Fort Gibson, the low morale of government employees, quarrels over corruption and department jurisdiction, and the general inadequacy of Coffin's administrative machinery when confronted with a civil war. Many, too, were the results: disease, suffering, degradation, and death.

Like the Kansas cattle rustlers, other whites illegally entered Indian land in Arizona, California, and the Pacific Northwest for private profit rather than for the glory of Dixie or the Union. The organization of Arizona Territory in 1863 followed closely the withdrawal of Confederate troops; thus, overwhelming problems awaited the territory's first civil officials. Victimized by both Apaches and rebels, most of the dispirited non-Indian population of less than five thousand had fled to Tucson, abandoning their fields and the southern overland route to the plundering red men. Administrative stumbling blocks which hindered Charles D. Poston, Arizona's first superintendent of Indian affairs, included communications (replies from Washington to his letters took four or five months), inadequate appropriations, and jurisdictional misunderstandings with the army.[51]

During the Civil War years the military maintained authority over the territory's five thousand hostile Apaches; Poston offered no objections to that. His major complaint was the army's inability to protect exposed settlements and public highways from the roving marauders.[52]

Of the Indians under its management in Arizona, the industrious and peaceful Apache-Mohaves, Yumas, Pimas, and Papagos

51. Thomas Edwin Farish, *History of Arizona* (4 vols., Phoenix, 1915–16) 3: 217; Poston to Dole, September 30, 1864, CIA, p. 299; Poston to Dole, March 10, 1864, OIA, LR, Arizona Supty.

52. Poston to Dole, April 1, 1863, CIA, p. 510; Poston to Dole, September 30, 1864, CIA, pp. 298–99.

in the southern and western part of the territory caused the Indian Office the most concern. To aid their defense against the wild tribes and to enable them to continue producing agricultural surpluses for the army and miners, the military issued the Pimas, Papagos, and Maricopas a hundred muskets and ten thousand rounds of ammunition. Also, Dole authorized Poston to select a reserve for the Papagos south of Tucson and to set aside tracts for the Gila and Colorado River tribes.[53]

Meanwhile, rich mineral deposits along the Colorado, Gila, and Agua Fria Rivers lured hundreds of California miners to Arizona. One observer estimated in September 1863 that within a year ten to twenty thousand miners would be roaming the region.[54] The influx of whites together with the simultaneous destruction of game and the unusual drought of 1863 bred famine among the desperate tribes, who were urged by hostile warriors from the east to fight the intruders.[55] Poston and Special Agent John C. Dunn strove to preserve the tenuous peace until the Interior Department approved the reservation sites and Congress appropriated sufficient monies. This did not occur until March 1865. Shortly thereafter, Dunn reported from Prescott that settlers and the military had provoked a war with bands of Yavapais, Apache-Mohaves, and Walapais. Several whites had been killed, stock stolen, and all communications severed to and from Prescott.[56] The alienation of these peaceful peoples was a classic example of an expanding frontier's subversive effect on peaceful Indian relations.

Chronicling his extensive travels in California during the early 1860's, agriculturalist William H. Brewer remarked that intelligent men he knew unanimously agreed that whites caused most Indian troubles. His keen contemporary observer, J. Ross Browne, attributed the failure of the California reservation system to en-

53. CIA, 1862, pp. 187–88; Dole to Poston, July 16, 1863, OIA, FOR, Arizona Supty., Letter Book of Poston: 1863–1864, pp. 34–36.
54. George F. Hooper to General S. P. Heintzelman, September 21, 1863, enclosed in Lieutenant Colonel L. H. Lathrup to Dole, October 23, 1863, OIA, LR, Arizona Supty.
55. John C. Dunn to Dole, August 25, 1864, CIA, pp. 311–12.
56. Dunn to Dole, May 23, 1865, CIA, pp. 296–97.

croachments on Indian lands and the impracticality of guarding against them. By 1862 no place existed in the state where the Indian could safely live and work, according to the Indian commissioner.[57]

As early as December 1861, for example, Hanson noted the mounting number of whites in Round Valley. An unwise federal act which granted swamps and overflow lands to the states enabled some unruly settlers to purchase land within the agency grounds. After drinking sprees at a nearby establishment, they frequently abused agency employees, turned cattle into Indian fields, stole livestock, and provoked fights with peaceful red farmers. Following assassination attempts on the reservation supervisor and threats against all the Indians, Hanson appealed to General Wright at San Francisco for military protection. Neither troops nor a declaration of martial law stopped the skirmishes. In June 1862 whites killed twenty-five Wailakis, whom they accused of stealing cattle. One solution to the encroachment problem was to sell the Nome Lackee, Mendocino, and Klamath reservations and use the proceeds to pay for the improvements of settlers in Round Valley, who could then be removed.[58] Congress's refusal to endorse such a bill in 1863 meant the continuation of bloodshed. By the fall of 1865, whites occupied nearly half the arable land in Round Valley.[59]

Encroachment was not confined to the north. The principal Luiseño Indian village of Temecula, situated in Riverside County, flourished prior to the mid–1850s; tribesmen cultivated rich fields and marketed surpluses to neighboring emigrants. With the death of Chief Pablo-Apis the Golden Age terminated abruptly. Unprincipled whites infiltrated the settlement, cohabiting with Indian women and demoralizing braves with whiskey. Fields lay

57. Brewer, *Up and Down California in 1860–1864; The Journal of William H. Brewer, Professor of Agriculture in the Sheffield School from 1864 to 1903,* ed. by Francis P. Farquhar (New Haven, 1930), p. 301; Browne to Dole, December 27, 1863, OIA, LR, California Supty.; CIA, 1862, p. 191.

58. Hanson to Dole, December 31, 1861, CIA (1862), pp. 458–59; Hanson to Wright, May 20, 1862, OR, Ser. 1, 50, Pt. 1, p. 1084; Hanson to Dole, October 10, 1862, CIA, p. 455.

59. Maltby to Cooley, September 15, 1865, CIA, pp. 279–80.

fallow, fences went unrepaired, homes deteriorated. Many pov-
erty-stricken Indians drifted away from the hamlet or did white
men's work for whiskey money. The fate of the natives was not
unique; in California, crimes committed by Indians while under
the influence of alcohol caused the government to spend $200,000
each year for prosecutions.[60]

Kidnapping Indian children, the most vicious form of white
trespass, was widespread in the north and very lucrative, since
captured children sometimes sold for hundreds of dollars. California law encouraged the practice by permitting the indenture of
Indians; in return for room, board, and clothing, whites received
the earnings of their young wards. Minimal penalties for violations
of the law and lax enforcement led to widespread abuse as well
as virtual enslavement of children. Evidence suggests that such
outrages probably prompted Indian raids in Humboldt and Mendocino Counties during the summer of 1861. To combat kidnapping, Hanson dispatched special agents to intercept the abductors
and memorialized the legislature to revoke the indenture statute.[61]

A constant theme in Pacific Northwest agency reports was
white encroachment on Indian lands, particularly by miners. The
prospectors' frontier intruded onto the Umatilla reservation and
Flathead lands in the Bitterroot Valley, yet the most far reaching
difficulties for the Indian Office resulted from Elias Davidson
Pierce's gold discovery of February 1860 in the Nez Percé country. Nez Percé Agent Andrew J. Cain tried to prevent the inevitable rush of miners, but by December 2 a party of thirty,
evading a military force, reached Orofino Creek and erected
cabins on Indian land.[62]

To concerned officials, the intrusion was ominous. Though the
Nez Percés remained friendly, the Washington territorial legislature expected serious difficulties between red man and white
unless the federal government quickly secured this new mining

60. Special Agent J. Q. A. Stanley to Wiley, May 19, 1865, CIA, p. 293;
Lovett to Wiley, May or June, 1865, CIA, pp. 290–91.

61. CIA, 1861, pp. 640–41; Hanson to Dole, July 15, 1861, CIA, p. 759; Hanson
to Dole, December 31, 1861, CIA (1862), p. 459; Lippitt to Drum, January 12,
1862, OR, Ser. 1, 50, Pt. 1, pp. 803–4.

62. Greever, *The Bonanza West*, pp. 257–58.

district.[63] Superintendent Edward R. Geary believed it impossible, even with a military force, to keep the miners out. The gold fever raged out of control, and organized parties of miners reportedly planned to invade the Nez Percé lands in the spring. The inevitable Indian war that would result must be avoided at all cost, Geary wrote. The resourceful Nez Percés exerted great influence on surrounding tribes. Furthermore, because of the ruggedness of their country and the scattered locations of Washington's frontier settlements, an entire army would be needed to quell hostilities. Since most of the gold fields lay north of the Clearwater and its main southern tributary, Geary proposed that the government persuade the Nez Percés to sell this portion of their reservation.[64]

In the meantime Agent Cain assured the Indians that if necessary the military would be sent in the spring to evict the miners. The Nez Percés waited patiently in the mistaken belief that the prospectors would leave after digging gold from the river banks. Instead, their numbers increased daily, and in early April Cain proposed an emergency council between angry tribal leaders and government representatives. Superintendent Geary journeyed to the agency on Lapwai Creek with a small escort of dragoons, arriving on the ninth.[65]

One Nez Percé faction refused to negotiate because of the government's bad faith in previous treaties, but Geary finally convinced the Nez Percés to open up for the miners that portion of their reservation north of the Snake and Clearwater Rivers, the South Fork of the Clearwater and the trail from this waterway across the Bitterroot Mountains. The Indians did not cede the area. The agreement permitted only mining, and the prospectors were still subject to the intercourse laws of the United States. The southern section of the reservation remained closed to all but Indian Office officials and those with the permission of the

63. Memorial to the President of the United States, December 18, 1860, enclosed in Henry Marshall to James Buchanan, January 21, 1861, OIA, LR, Oregon Supty.

64. Geary to Greenwood, December 27, 1860, OIA, LR, Oregon Supty.

65. Geary to Dole, April 23, 1861, *ibid.*; Beal, *"I Will Fight No More Forever,"* p. 18.

Nez Percés. The United States promised to station sufficient troops on the reserve to protect Indian rights. Superintendent Geary considered the treaty the best possible one under the circumstances and recommended that Congress appropriate $50,000 to indemnify the Nez Percés.[66] Washington approved $40,000.[67]

Shortly after, whites invaded the forbidden portion of the reservation. In June, miners from Orofino discovered gold on the South Fork of the Clearwater and established Elk City. Another strike occurred the following month on the Salmon River, a hundred miles southeast of Lewiston. By November ten thousand miners organized a settlement at Florence.[68] "The excitement is more intense here at this time than I ever saw it anywhere in my life," wrote William Purvine to the editor of the Salem *Oregon Statesman* in September 1861. "It appears that Salmon river is the great El Dorado north of California." Superintendent Bion F. Kendall, unable to avert the influx of prospectors, simply instructed the Lapwai agent to tolerate them for the present.[69]

Additional strikes during 1862 in the eastern Nez Percé country loosed a flood of new miners. Simultaneously an economy developed to feed, transport, and entertain the gold seekers, estimated at fifteen thousand by June 1862. White squatters on agricultural and grazing lands greatly annoyed the Nez Percés,[70] yet they gave tacit approval to the construction of permanent buildings at the junction of the Clearwater and Snake. Lewiston, which sprang from this site, became the landing depot for steamboats ascending the Snake to supply miners in the hinterland.[71]

66. Geary to Dole, April 23, 1861, OIA, LR, Oregon Supty.; Articles of Agreement with the Nez Percés, April 10, 1861, enclosed in Geary to Dole, April 23, 1861, *ibid*.

67. Alvin M. Josephy, Jr., *The Nez Perce Indians and the Opening of the Northwest* (New Haven, 1965), p. 402.

68. Greever, *The Bonanza West*, pp. 258–60.

69. Purvine to Editor, September, 23, 1861, in *Oregon Statesman*, October 14, 1861; Kendall to Dole, January 2, 1862, CIA, pp. 447–48.

70. John W. Anderson to Hale, August 20, 1862, enclosed in Hale to Dole, September 4, 1862, OIA, LR, Washington Supty.; Hutchins to Hale, June 30, 1862, CIA, p. 566.

71. Francis Haines, *The Nez Percés: Tribesmen of the Columbia Plateau* (Norman, 1955), pp. 142–45.

Despite these rapid developments many Nez Percés remained cordial. They supplied the miners with livestock, guides, and laborers, and fraternized freely in the mining camps, imbibing the good and the bad which that society offered. Many Indians began to dress like whites, eat their food, drink their liquor, speak their language.[72] In return for their friendship the Nez Percés often reaped a harvest of "villany and insult." News of plundering and fraud soon reached Agent Charles Hutchins at Lapwai.[73]

Circumstances forced Hutchins to turn for assistance to the army, without whose support there would be nothing to prevent whites from plying Nez Percé rivers with ferries, squatting on all the arable land, destroying fences, debauching the Indians with liquor, stealing their horses and cattle, and ultimately annihilating the Indians themselves.[74] When eighty soldiers of the Oregon cavalry under Major Jacob L. Rinearson arrived early in August 1862 and encamped six miles from the agency, Hutchins asked the major to remove all whites found on the Indians' land and to destroy houses, fences, and grog shops in the vicinity of Indian villages or encampments. Rinearson refused to carry out this and other similar requests, claiming that he had no instructions to perform such duties and that his force and equipment were too meager. Such inaction distressed the Nez Percés, Hutchins warned, and threatened the maintenance of law and order in their country.[75]

Superintendent Hale informed Benjamin Alvord, commanding the military District of Oregon, of treaty violations in the Nez Percé country. Rinearson was then instructed to offer maximum assistance to the Indian Office. He could dislodge any whites settled on agricultural lands contrary to the wishes of the Indians and their agent, and, upon the request of Office officials, destroy saloons on reservation land which sold liquor to the Nez Percés. Houses, fences, and other illegal improvements should be re-

72. Josephy, *Nez Perce*, pp. 404–5.

73. Purvine to Editor, March 20, 1862, in *Oregon Statesman*, April 28, 1862; Hutchins to Dole, March 20, 1862, OIA, LR, Washington Supty.

74. Hutchins to Kendall, January 4, 1862, OIA, FOR, Washington Supty., LR (Nez Percé).

75. Hutchins to Hale, September 2, 1862, *ibid.*

moved as well.[76] To further reinforce the military's position Alvord visited the Nez Percé reservation in October 1862 and personally assured chiefs of the government's desire to protect their people. He also established a fort two and one-half miles upstream from the agency and assigned to the post a company of infantry and one of cavalry.[77]

John Anderson, Hutchins's replacement at Lapwai, requested early in December that Rinearson send a detachment of troops to Slate Creek, where whiskey dealers allegedly threatened the peace between whites and Nez Percés. When Anderson briefed Superintendent Hale about the incident three weeks later, Rinearson had not yet removed the hucksters.[78] Major Andrew W. Bowman succeeded Rinearson at Fort Lapwai in March 1863, with orders to use every reasonable effort to safeguard Indian rights, but because of the burgeoning mining communities even he could not provide the protection pledged to the Nez Percés in April 1861.[79]

John J. McGilvra, United States attorney in Washington Territory, believed a partial solution to the problem of unruly whites would be to keep all alcohol out of the Indian country. Since miners squatted on reservation land, the possession of spirituous liquors, whether for their own consumption or for trade, violated federal law, and the army's duty was to enforce this legislation. Yet Alvord refused to declare martial law and order the eviction of trespassers. The Nez Percé country was extremely large and he had only two or three companies to patrol the entire reservation. The Army of the Potomac could not stop the miners from obtaining whiskey.[80]

76. Hale to Dole, September 30, 1862, OIA, LR, Washington Supty.; Alvord to Rinearson, September 7, 1862, OR, Ser. 1, 50, Pt. 2, pp. 103–4.

77. Alvord to Hale, November 4, 1862, OIA, FOR, Washington Supty., LR (Misc.).

78. Anderson to Rinearson, December 10, 1862, USAC, Fort Lapwai, Idaho, LR; Anderson to Hale, January 2, 1862, enclosed in Hale to Dole, January 29, 1863, OIA, LR, Washington Supty.

79. Lieutenant Frederick Mears to Bowman, March 9, 1863, OR, Ser. 1, 50, Pt. 2, p. 344.

80. Alvord to Dole, September 8, 1863, OIA, LR, Washington Supty.; Tegeder, "The Territories and the Lincoln Administration," pp. 217–19.

If Alvord's troops were unable to defend the property rights of the Nez Percés and the miners could not be kept out of the Indian country, another reduction of the reservation seemed the only recourse.[81] Congress voted $40,000 in July 1862 for a new Nez Percé treaty, and Interior Secretary Caleb Smith appointed as commissioners superintendents Rector of Oregon and Hale of Washington and Agent Hutchins. Despite Congress's wish that they commence as soon as possible, Hale advised that the negotiations be delayed until the spring of 1863.[82]

At first the Nez Percés hesitated to enter into another agreement with the United States. Ratification of the treaty of 1855 consumed four years, and whites utterly ignored the covenant of 1861. Yet the Indians realized they must at least meet with the commissioners in order to preserve what remained of their homeland.[83]

Nez Percés who gathered at the Lapwai Agency for the May 1863 council suspected the government's intentions. Certain whites, to prevent the Indians from coming in for the meeting, had warned them that the United States would forcibly drive them from their lands, and before the red men would begin talks the commissioners had to assure them that such rumors were false. Whiskey smuggled into the Indian camp also disrupted the council, as did the continued encroachments of foolish miners at nearby Lewiston.[84]

The chiefs divided into three parties according to their reactions to the commission's proposal that they relinquish most of their reservation. One group led by Lawyer, an amiable head chief, favored the new treaty and its many proposed benefits for the Nez Percé people, including handsome salaries for Lawyer and his associates. A second faction controlled by Chief Big

81. By the spring of 1861 approximately seven hundred troops were left in the Pacific Northwest for policing the frontier. The rest had been withdrawn for duty elsewhere, Charles H. Carey, *A General History of Oregon, Prior to 1861* (2 vols., Portland, 1936) 2:626.

82. *United States Statutes at Large* 12:529; Josephy, *Nez Perce*, pp. 410–12.

83. Josephy, *Nez Perce*, p. 414.

84. Hale to Dole, May 22, 1863, OIA, LR, Washington Supty.; Hale to Steinberger, May 25 and 28, 1863, USAC, Fort Lapwai, Idaho, LR.

Thunder refused to bargain with the whites until the government removed all trespassing miners from Nez Percé lands. Chief Eagle-from-the-Light represented a third, openly hostile segment opposed to any agreement with the Indian Office, even one based on ъhe favorable treaty of 1855. As the council dragged on, the divisions became more pronounced. Finally a meeting of fifty-three headmen rejected Lawyer as head chief of their people. Thereby they severed all political bonds and returned to the pre-1842 state in which each chief functioned as the independent leader of his own band.[85]

Indian Office representatives at the Lapwai council sowed the seeds of future administrative woes when they accepted the signatures of Lawyer and the pro-treaty faction as binding on all Nez Percés.[86] In return for over $300,000 and numerous reservation improvements, the Nez Percés relinquished about nine-tenths of their reservation, retaining only ten thousand square miles east of Lewiston in the valleys of the Clearwater and its South Fork. By the terms of the treaty, all tribesmen had to move there one year after its ratification. As a precaution against encroachments within the new boundaries, Hale sent copies of the covenant to the press.[87] The Olympia *Washington Standard* exclaimed to its readers: "The satisfactory result of this council will be of incalculable benefit to the new Territory, and will give Lewiston, where mining operations must center, an impetus which will before many years rank it with the great interior emporiums of the West. . . . They [the commissioners] have succeeded, . . . and the eastern country is saved from the disastrous effects of an Indian war which was but lately so imminent."[88]

The condition of the Nez Percé people scarcely improved during the months following the agreement of June 1863. Miners overran the newly ceded tracts before ratification of the treaty; traders continued to sell whiskey to the natives; frequent clashes

85. Haines, *Nez Percés*, pp. 145–47.
86. Josephy, *Nez Perce*, pp. 430–31.
87. Hale to Dole, June 29, 1863, OIA, LR, Washington Supty.; Kappler, *Indian Affairs* 2:843.
88. *Washington Standard*, June 20, 1863.

occurred between whites and Indians over stock and grazing and farming lands. More than twenty-five Nez Percés were murdered during the ensuing years, while Indians reportedly slew only one or two whites.[89] On July 1, 1863, the Indian Office transferred the Flathead and Nez Percé agencies to Governor William H. Wallace of Idaho, ex officio superintendent of Indian affairs for the new territory.[90] Delay of the bond of James O'Neill, the new Nez Percé agent, held up operating funds.[91] During their tenure both O'Neill and Caleb Lyon, Wallace's successor in the governor's office, absconded with thousands of dollars appropriated for the Nez Percés. Lawyer's party, which surrendered so much to the government, had reason to be disillusioned. The nontreaty Nez Percés meanwhile followed their old ways outside the confines of the new reservation, and no one could force them upon it until ratification of the 1863 treaty, which came in 1867.[92] Still, another decade passed before whites drove the inscrutably patient Nez Percés to open warfare.

The steady advance of white frontiersmen as well as the need for closer Indian Office supervision of its charges necessitated reservation consolidation outside the Pacific Northwest. Commissioner Dole discovered that two superintending agents directing affairs in separate districts of California were unnecessary, and recommended the creation of a superintendent's office as equally efficient and more likely to promote administrative uniformity. Congress concurred, creating such a position in April 1864. It also called for the consolidation of the state's Indians on not more than four reservations, with an agent for each.[93] Lincoln's Indian Office officials had long favored such a change. Wentworth, for example, suggested in July 1861 that the Indians of southern California be gathered at Tulé River Farm and Tejon. Because of traditional hostility between the northern mountain Indians and the lower valley and coastal tribes, Hanson recom-

89. James O'Neill to Caleb Lyon, July 9, 1865, CIA, p. 421; Josephy, *Nez Perce*, pp. 431–32.
90. Hale to Dole, September 1, 1863, CIA, p. 555.
91. CIA, 1865, p. 197.
92. Josephy, *Nez Perce*, pp. 433–37.
93. CIA, 1862, pp. 192–93; *United States Statutes at Large* 13:39–41.

mended settlement of the latter at Smith River, with Round Valley becoming the new home for the interior mountain tribes. The Interior Department could purchase settlers' claims in each area with profits from the sale of the Nome Lackee, Mendocino, and Klamath reserves. The commissioner approved Hanson's plan and early in 1863 submitted a draft to Congress.[94]

The California legislature opposed the scheme. Citizens living near Smith River and Round Valley, it said, objected to the influx of more red men; besides, hostiles already infested nearby areas and if captured and taken to either valley they would easily escape and go back to their hunting grounds. Needed was a reservation sufficiently distant so captured Indians could not return.[95] As might be expected, Congress pleased neither California nor the Indian Office. In the spring of 1863 it defeated the bill for the sale of the reserves, yet offered no alternative to Hanson's proposal. The commissioner, who planned to apply again for permission to sell these tracts, meanwhile instructed Hanson to use his own judgment about preserving peace between the races and preventing further white encroachment on Indian lands.[96]

In December 1863 Special Agent J. Ross Browne, an able, witty, muckraking journalist, underscored the need for concentration. Past congressional funding was indeed deficient, yet with the present reservation system additional monies alone would not eradicate racial conflict. To succeed with the reservation policy in California the Indian Office must first isolate the Indian. But where? This was the rub. Since miners and farmers had seized the best lands, there seemed no alternative but removal from the state. Browne suggested colonization on one or more of the islands off Santa Barbara which possessed good range and farm land. Even then, the integrity of Indian Office officials and public cooperation could not be counted on. His own predisposition was

94. Wentworth to Dole, July 14, 1861, CIA, pp. 752–53; Hanson to Dole, September 1, 1862, CIA, pp. 466–67; Dole to Usher, January 28, 1863, OIA, Report Books, 13:54.

95. Resolutions of the Legislature of California, in Relation to Indian Affairs in that State, April 20, 1863, *House Misc. Doc.* 29, 38 Cong., 1 Sess., pp. 1–2 (Ser. 1200).

96. Dole to Hanson, May 25, 1863, OIA, LS, 70:481.

to turn the Indians over to the military, which at least could give them security.[97]

When Austin Wiley assumed office as superintendent of Indian affairs for California in 1864, he championed removal, but only for the northern tribes. Both army and Indian Office personnel erred in their belief that the people could be kept on reserves in their own country. Wiley estimated that not one Indian sent to Mendocino in 1858 or Smith River in 1860 stayed longer than two months before returning to his old haunts. The government had to spend over $200,000 to catch them again. As for the south, Wiley directed a special agent to collect the Tejon Indians at Tulé River Farm, the safest place for them and the only location with sufficient crops. By mid-July the job was done.[98] Yet for the state as a whole there persisted the need for further native concentration on isolated and protected reservations, where government wards could learn to support themselves.

Between 1862 and 1865, many of the same problems plagued the Minnesota Chippewas and prompted their brief outbreak: the whiskey trade, unscrupulous traders, disease, and unpaid annuities. In 1863 the Indian Office further concentrated the Chippewas in the northern part of the state in order to protect them and to appease Minnesotans. The Mississippi Chippewas ceded six scattered reservations in north central Minnesota in return for a larger one surrounding Cass, Leech, and Winnibigoshish Lakes. The Pillager and allied bands settled on their shores. A treaty with the Red Lake and Pembina bands gave the United States full rights to the American Valley of the Red River of the North.[99] Had the Chippewas not been so scattered across the northern Minnesota swamplands, they probably would have met the same fate as the Winnebagos.[100]

97. Browne to Dole, December 27, 1863, OIA, LR, California Supty.

98. Wiley to Mix, June 1, 1864, CIA, pp. 269–71; Wiley to Dole, July 11, 1864, OIA, LR, California Supty.

99. Kappler, *Indian Affairs* 2:839–42, 853–55; Folwell, *History of Minnesota* 4:193.

100. Richard A. Chute to Dole, September 26, 1862, OIA, LR, Chippewa Agency; Caleb Smith to Aldrich, December 16, 1862, *House Report* 13, 37 Cong., 3 Sess.

In Wisconsin the most serious difficulties arose from the Indian Office's inability to care for and to protect the scattered reservation tribes. Though the Indian Office battled disease, poverty, and the whiskey trade, its small staff could not cope with such difficulties. In his annual report for the 1862 Commissioner Dole called for the concentration of Wisconsin's Indians on one reservation and the assignment of land in severalty, but this recommendation was not adopted during the Civil War years.[101]

The forty-five hundred Chippewas of Lake Superior, who roamed the extreme northern portion of Wisconsin, came under the jurisdiction of Agent Luther E. Webb. His agency, which had its headquarters at Bayfield, Wisconsin, also included Chippewas on three reservations in northeastern Minnesota. Because these wards were so scattered, the Indian Office exerted little influence over them. Too, the shortness of the growing season, the cost of clearing heavily timbered lands and the difficulty of transporting surplus crops to market hindered agriculture. To bring the Indians under greater government contol and to separate them from trouble-making whites who provoked minor Indian depredations, Webb began to concentrate the Interior bands at the lake reserves in 1863. Here was ample land for the assignment of eighty acre severalty tracts; here the Indian could learn agricultural techniques from agency farmers. Yet most natives continued to live off products of the forests and lakes.[102]

On the eve of the Civil War, Michigan's eight thousand Indians resided on twenty reservations scattered throughout the state's northern reaches. About two thousand lived on the Upper Peninsula: the Chippewas and Ottawas on Sugar Island and at Sault Ste. Marie and Point Iroquois; the Chippewas of Lake Superior at Keweenaw Bay. Another quarter, mainly Chippewas, dwelt in the Saginaw Bay region and in Isabella County. The remaining Chippewas and Ottawas inhabited lands in Oceana and

101. CIA, 1862, p. 193.
102. Webb to Thompson, September 18, 1861, enclosed in Wycoff to Dole, September 30, 1861, OIA, LR, La Pointe Agency; Webb to Dole, February 6, 1862, enclosed in Wycoff to Dole, February 27, 1862, *ibid.*; Webb to Dole, June 26, 1863, *ibid.*

Mason counties, in west central Michigan, and near Grand Traverse and Little Traverse Bays. Several hundred roamed Garden Island, about thirty-five miles west of Mackinac Straits. Michigan Indians, especially those on the Great Lakes, derived their livelihood from fishing, hunting, and trapping. The inland bands farmed and made maple sugar.[103]

The scattered locations of Indians diminished the influence of the Indian Office and encouraged unscrupulous whites to exploit them. The Indian commissioner noted in 1862 that the tribes were so widespread that Agent DeWitt C. Leach, headquartered at Detroit, had to travel two thousand miles at annuity time. No missionaries, school teachers, or other government employees labored on the smaller reservations. In fact the Indians became little more than vagrants, falling prey to gamblers and white hucksters.[104]

To alleviate some of these problems Agent Leach took steps to concentrate his charges. In 1863 he recommended the negotiation of a treaty by which the bands living on five small reservations in northwestern Michigan would cede their lands and move to the Little Traverse reservation. Here, after its expansion, the government should concentrate all the Ottawas and Chippewas of the Lower Peninsula.[105] Dole approved Leach's report, and in September 1864 the Office of Indian Affairs appointed Dr. H. J. Alvord a special commissioner to negotiate with Agent Leach the treaties needed to gather the Chippewas of Saginaw, Swan Creek, and Black River onto the Isabella County reservation and the Ottawas and Chippewas presumably at Little Traverse Bay.[106] Perhaps because of the lateness of the season and the importance of dealing first with the southernmost bands who requested that the Indian Office treat with them, the commissioners met only with the Saginaw, Swan Creek, and Black River Chippewas. The parley

103. CIA, 1863, p. 154; DeWitt C. Leach to Dole, November 12, 1861, CIA, p. 800; Leach to Dole, October 26, 1862, CIA, pp. 486–88; CIA, 1861, p. 643.
104. CIA, 1862, pp. 154, 193.
105. Leach to Dole, October 17, 1863, CIA, pp. 497–98.
106. Dole to Usher, April 12, 1864, OIA, Report Books, 13:376; Dole to Alvord, September 3, 1864, OIA, LS, 75:181.

occurred on October 18 and by mid-November the treaty was in the hands of the commissioner of Indian affairs.[107] Not until after Appomattox did the Senate accept an amended version of the document. There are no other records for the war years about implementing the concentration policy in Michigan.

Poor morale in the Indian service sometimes affected the government's administration of Indian policy. The absence of esprit de corps was most notable in the Pacific Northwest superintendencies and resulted from delayed superintendency funds, the devaluation of paper currency, disenchantment with the annuity system and frequent personnel changes. Three different men served as superintendent of Indian affairs in Oregon between April 1861 and April 1865. The Territory of Washington had four. William H. Wallace remained in the territory for less than a year before winning election as delegate to Congress. Lincoln appointed Caleb Lyon, a minor New York politician, to fill the office and he lingered for a brief period, whereupon territorial secretary C. DeWitt Smith assumed his duties.[108] The widespread practice of absconding with agency and superintendency records magnified the disruptive effects of change, which were most serious on the agency level. When Hutchins assumed control of the Flathead Agency in 1862, his predecessor sold all the government stock and farm equipment, remarking to Hutchins that when he first came there was nothing at the reserve and Hutchins "might obtain them as he did."[109]

Bickering between agents and their superiors likewise contributed to an unfavorable atmosphere. In October 1862 Oregon superintendent Rector suspended Siletz agent Biddle for alleged fraudulent acts, speculation and failure to promote the welfare of Indians under his charge. Biddle accused Rector of acting without evidence. The latter stated his charges but Biddle rebutted

107. CIA, 1864, p. 188.

108. W. Turrentine Jackson, "Indian Affairs and Politics in Idaho Territory, 1863–1870," *Pacific Historical Review* 14 (September, 1945): 311–12.

109. Hutchins to Hale, December 2, 1862, enclosed in Hale to Dole, January 6, 1863, OIA, LR, Washington Supty.

each of them.[110] Rector then gave the quarrel an impersonal tone by noting the larger issue involved: an insubordinate agent could thwart his superintendent because the government gave the superintendent only supervisory powers. Rector suggested either abolishing the office of agent or permitting superintendents to appoint their own subordinates. Upon the advice of Oregon's senators the Indian Office viewed the matter as a personal feud. The impracticality of investigating Rector's accusations and the belief that the public service suffered from "the neglect, inefficiency or dereliction of one or both of them," resulted in their removal early in 1863.[111]

A more serious internal discord with political overtones occurred in Washington Territory. Bion F. Kendall, appointed superintendent of Indian affairs in July 1861 on the recommendation of Winfield Scott, did not find favor with disgruntled territorial Republicans, because they had wanted someone else for the job. The *Washington Standard* denounced him as a life-long Democrat who misrepresented himself to the president. Kendall's straightforwardness and apparent desire to reform the superintendency turned out to be even worse offenses. In October 1861 he removed the Reverend James H. Wilbur, a well-known Methodist missionary and superintendent of teaching at the Yakima Agency.[112] This not only brought upon him the wrath of Methodists and Republicans, but provoked a power struggle between himself and certain agents who believed, as had Biddle in Oregon, that their superintendent wanted the power to nominate subordinates.[113] The Indian Office received complaints about the arbitrary use of Kendall's appointive power at the agencies.

110. Rector to Dole, October 15, 1862, OIA, FOR, Oregon Supty., LS, H: 232–33; Biddle to Dole, October 23 and November 14, 1862, OIA, LR, Oregon Supty.

111. Rector to Dole, November 11, 1862, and January 23, 1863, OIA, LR, Oregon Supty.; B. F. Harding and Nesmith to Dole, December 24, 1862, *ibid.*

112. *Washington Standard*, August 24, 1861; Willis A. Katz, "Benjamin [*sic*] F. Kendall, Territorial Politician," *Pacific Northwest Quarterly*, 49 (January, 1958): 32–33.

113. Katz, "Benjamin F. Kendall, Territorial Politician," pp. 33–34; Anson G. Henry to Dole, October 28, 1861, Lincoln Papers.

Dole wrote that although the right to select an agent's employees legally rested with the superintendent, efficiency in the field depended upon harmony among agency personnel. The superintendent should therefore respect the agents' staff recommendations.[114]

The feuding continued. In January 1862 Puyallup agent Ezra Baker confided to Dole that Kendall had insulted Agent Henry A. Webster of Neah Bay. Baker considered Kendall the wrong man for superintendent. The *Washington Standard* censured Kendall for attempting to control all agency appointments and for waging open war with his agents. Before his removal in 1862, the result of political pressure on President Lincoln, the superintendent suspended Webster and Baker. The *Washington Standard* intimated it was because they were Republicans; Kendall insisted they were incompetents and drunkards. In any case, dissension temporarily crippled the Indian service in Washington.[115]

114. Dole to Kendall, November 7, 1861, OIA, FOR, Washington Supty., LR.
115. Baker to Dole, January 13, 1862, OIA, LR, Washington Supty.; *Washington Standard*, November 16, 1861, and March 29, 1862.

CHAPTER VIII

Conclusion

With the reservation people of the Pacific Northwest, California, Arizona, and east of the ninety-eighth meridian, the Indian Office encountered a legion of administrative difficulties. Most important among those which might be called internal agency problems was unpleasant living conditions. Scattered or isolated reservation sites often encompassed poor agricultural land subject to drought and grasshoppers. These climatic conditions plus inadequate diets sapped the Indians' strength as well as their incentive to scratch out a livelihood by farming. Inappropriate or delayed annuities and a few dishonest agents worsened their plight. The resultant Indian restlessness and uncooperativeness manifested itself in several ways: dissension between "farmer" and "blanket" factions of the Santees and Potawatomis; intertribal feuding amongst the uprooted Santees and Winnebagos at Crow Creek; and the propensity of hapless Indians such as the Stockbridges and Munsees to leave their reservation and wander back to former hunting grounds or search for sustenance elsewhere.

To these must be added several administrative troubles, external in origin, for which Indian hostiles were partly to blame. Shoshoni, Apache, Cheyenne, and Teton Sioux nomads terrorized the Pawnees, Poncas, the confederated tribes of central Oregon at Warm Springs, and the Apache-Mohaves, Yumas, Pimas, and Papagos of southern and western Arizona. The direct impact of the white man's Civil War likewise brought panic and dispersion to several tribes of the Central and Southern Superintendencies. Throughout the West whites bent on private profit nibbled at the boundaries of fertile Indian lands and at least once launched a wholesale invasion of a mineral-rich tract. In violation of federal statutes, whiskey hucksters peddled their wares indiscriminately, with little to fear from sympathetic frontier juries or impotent Indian agents with no police force to defend Indian property rights. Nor could the cavalry be summoned quickly enough to apprehend wily liquor merchants or the hit-and-run Indian marauders. At the Lapwai Agency and at Fort Gibson, frustrated civil and military authorities ended up bickering with each other. Serious fiscal problems in the Pacific Northwest and Kansas and at Crow Creek completed the rather dismal picture.

The uprising of 1862 not only led to the expulsion of the Sissetons, Wahpetons, Mdewakantons, and Wapekutes from Minnesota, thus destroying their geographic unity, but to a federal assault on their cultural identity. In the spring of 1866 the Indian Office transferred the Lower Sioux at Crow Creek to a new reserve at the mouth of the Niobrara River in northern Nebraska, which contained more land suitable for farming and which could be more easily provisioned. Despite the early success of an allotment program in the 1870s, the Santees' acculturation progress disappointed Office officials by the close of the decade. True, missionaries and school teachers won some young converts and an elective council partially replaced the headmen in directing tribal affairs, but the 736 Santees still depended upon federal economic support. A smallpox epidemic in 1873 whittled away at Indian morale and their sense of security, as did frequent droughts, grasshopper plagues, and constant alterations of agency policies and personnel. By the close of the century the Santee population showed an increase for the first time since the calamity in 1862. The number of school children also rose. However, the Santees had slipped economically. The decade of drought which began in the mid-1880s was partly to blame, together with the Interior Department's unwillingness to admit that the grazing land of the Santee Agency could not support the 1,019 Lower Sioux. Too hasty an acceptance of the Dawes Severalty Act by the Indian Office induced many of the Santees to lease valuable new allotments to whites at a low rate and retire from farming. This set back the "civilization" program and put even more Santees on the government dole.[1]

Strikingly similar was the fate of the Upper Sioux, located since 1867 in Dakota Territory on the triangular Sisseton reservation between Lakes Traverse and Kampeska and on the Devils Lake reserve. The hurried allotment of their land after 1887 regrettably reversed the gradual movement toward acculturation and economic self-sufficiency. The once-mighty Santees thus passed into the twentieth century in an impoverished state, ill-prepared to seize control of their own destiny. The high hopes once held for them by white friends were shattered by the agonies of war and removal to a drought-stricken land, by frontier hatreds, and by a sheer lack of understanding.[2]

That the Indian Office at times faced divergent management problems with the nomadic people and the reservation people was due to basic differences between the two. The former, for the most part still economically and politically independent in the early 1860s, continued with but minor modifications their traditional ways of life and repeatedly frustrated federal negotiators who tried to restrict their wanderings. Often rent with factionalism, the relatively docile reservation tribes depended to a greater degree on government economic support and protection from whiskey dealers and other trespassers.

More pronounced was the similarity of problems in dealing with the nomadic and reservation people. The Civil War directly affected tribes in both groups, as did the rapid influx of white miners and farmers. When Indian resentment of such infringement erupted into open hostilities in California, Colorado, Minnesota, and elsewhere, public opinion demanded their chastisement and expulsion. Persistent trespassing on Indian soil also necessitated a stricter separation of the races, which left the Indians with less and less land. Neither the plains and desert vagabonds nor the first generation reservation dwellers delighted in the prospect or

1. Meyer, *Santee Sioux*, pp. 156ff.
2. *Ibid.*, pp. 198ff.

the experience of confinement on limited tracts of land. And, try as it might, the Indian Office failed to make these supposed sanctuaries either safe or inviting.

What made the Office of Indian Affairs so impotent during the Civil War years, unable either to round up the nomadic tribes or adequately care for those under its protection? Granted the inevitability of the white man's seizure of most Indian land, were the bloodshed, unfulfilled promises, dishonor, and lasting ill will also unavoidable? A close look at the nation and the Indian Office provides some answers.

Crises and rapid change characterized the United States—East and West—in the sixties. The accelerated movement of pioneers to towns and mines and farms beyond the Mississippi taxed the entire federal bureaucracy, and neither red men nor white had enough patience, flexibility, tolerance, trust, and cooperativeness for the Office of Indian Affairs to effect a humane racial adjustment. Other general factors noted in the Introduction worked at cross purposes with the reservation scheme: racism, rivalry between the Interior and War Departments, the patronage system, Congress's susceptibility to public opinion—particularly in regard to unpopular minorities—and the understandable preoccupation of Washington with the North-South struggle.

That the Office of Indian Affairs could not reverse the Indians' seemingly inevitable fate was due in part to its dual role. During most of the nineteenth century its management of Indian affairs aimed at facilitating the expansion of America's white population. Promoting the natives' welfare and "civilization" ranked a clear second. Sometimes the office protected its wards from aggressive frontiersmen or redirected the advancing white tide, but when miners rushed into Montana, Colorado, Idaho, and Nevada, it could only ratify the loss of Indian land. Perhaps the peace might be preserved, but always at the expense of Indian rights and acculturation.

Still other reasons for Indian Office impotence should be noted. The need for an agency police force was most obvious among the reservation people, the victims of both white and native criminals. Too, sufficient cavalry detachments should have been at the

Office's call for rounding up reservation runaways and some of the wanderers of the deserts and plains. The absurd treaty system created a host of administrative ills and broken promises. With nomadic hostiles such as the Apaches and Navajos, treaties had no binding force whatsoever; nor could these documents restrain white miners if they smelled gold on Indian lands. To obtain the approval of reluctant headmen to such agreements, federal negotiators often had to promise more than Washington would ever deliver. Even when Indian Office intentions were honorable, the Senate pigeonholed or refused ratification of many such covenants—for reasons not always clear. By the time the President proclaimed a ratified treaty, layers of bureaucracy still delayed the fulfillment of government obligations, while cash annuities provided for by treaty drew scoundrels to the reservations like bears to honey.

Though Lincoln had neither the time nor the inclination to reform the Indian system, some assistance to beleaguered agents and superintendents was offered by Commissioner Dole, whose rhetoric and actions demonstrated a commitment to protect Indian property rights and to preserve peace on the frontier. Dole campaigned for a presidential pardon for the condemned Minnesota Sioux, directed much of Superintendent Thompson's work in removing the Sioux and Winnebagos from Minnesota, and tried to expedite the return of the Kansas refugees. If the field troubles were fiscal, as they were to some degree at Crow Creek, in Kansas, at Bosque Redondo, and in Utah, the commissioner sought special appropriations from Congress. When reports reached Washington about the misdirected efforts of Agent Balcombe and Governor Evans or the imbroglios in which Superintendents Coffin, Steck, and Kendall became involved, Dole offered words of censure and caution and advice.

Dole had the skillful administrator's concern for facts. Upon assuming office he dispatched a flurry of circulars to field personnel requesting information about agency employees, schools, and farms, and asking for administrative suggestions. When the hurried replies were too sketchy to be of much use, the commissioner became more insistent and exacting, asking for detailed pen and ink maps of each reservation and a full statement on agency employees: what they turned out and the uses made of the products. Hereafter superintendents and agents were also to submit to the central office quarterly financial statements and estimated expenses for the coming three months.[3]

Since Dole's innovativeness extended no further than his desire for a detailed knowledge of field conditions, he did little to modify the reservation policy he inherited with its goal of the acculturated and self-supporting farmer Indian. Governor Evans's encouragement of stock raising among the Cheyennes got no support from Washington. When the House asked about the propriety of appointing special investigators to inquire into the condition of the Indian tribes, Dole dismissed the resolution as unnecessary. Why should such investigators be more trustworthy or efficient than the Indian Office's own employees?[4] Reinforcing this conservatism was the commissioner's political sensitivity and determination, as in the case of Superintendent Albin, that the Indian service not embarrass the administration.

Though this study treats but a brief time period and focuses mainly on Indian Office field problems, it has considerable value for students of nineteenth century America. To affirm that the Indian was wronged is easy enough. To probe the past for the reasons why is a far more challenging and important task. That the answers to this question must come from an understanding of Indian Office activities in the West is the premise on which my study is based. This particularly holds true for the Civil War years, when the greater share of the Office's administrative difficulties pertained to the implementation of the reservation policy adopted by the government for the trans-Mississippi West in the 1850s. The overwhelming complexity of the "Indian problem" also becomes apparent when analyzing administration in the field.

3. Dole to Fielding Johnson, January 11, 1862 (circular), Delaware Agency Papers, John Gill Pratt Collection, Kansas State Historical Society, Topeka; Mix to Johnson, June 18, 1862 (circular), *ibid.*

4. Dole to Usher, January 9, 1863, OIA, Report Books, 13:22. For a brief and rather general discussion of Dole's career as Indian Commissioner, see Harry Kelsey, "William P. Dole and Mr. Lincoln's Indian Policy," *Journal of the West* 10 (July, 1971): 484–92.

When historians possess more in-depth studies as well as topical ones on treaty making and the Indian agent (his background, political and business activities, and tenure in office), we can generalize more authoritatively about the significance of Indian Office bureaucrats on the frontier.[5]

Events in the 1840s and 1850s predetermined many Civil War Indian troubles. The Mexican cession and the Kansas-Nebraska Act threw open millions of acres of lush farm and grazing land, while California gold lured those in quest of quicker profits. Washington's institution of the reservation policy to protect as well as to "civilize" the embattled red man seemed logical enough, but developments in the West continually outran the understaffed and unreformed Indian Office. By 1861, the Union faced a crisis in the West as well as in the South.

The fate of both the nomadic people and the reservation people in the Civil War years also underscored the truth of one of Alexis de Tocqueville's most penetrating insights about nineteenth century America:

> From whichever side we consider the destinies of the aborigines of North America, their calamities appear to be irremediable: if they continue barbarous, they are forced to retire: if they attempt to civilize their manners, the contact of a more civilized community subjects them to oppression and destitution. They perish if they continue to wander from waste to waste, and if they attempt to settle, they still must perish; the assistance of Europeans is necessary to instruct them, but the approach of Europeans corrupts and repels them into savage life. . . .[6]

The story of the uprooted tribes at Crow Creek and Bosque Redondo and in southern Kansas illustrates the type of physical

5. Two such studies of high quality are already available for the nineteenth century. Francis Paul Prucha's *American Indian Policy in the Formative Years: The Indian Trade and Intercourse Acts, 1790–1834* deals with the persistent problems of white encroachment, trade regulations, and crimes in the Indian country. Alban W. Hoopes's *Indian Affairs and Their Administration, with Special Reference to the Far West, 1849–1860* is a narrative of regional Indian-white relations.

6. Alexis de Tocqueville, *Democracy in America*, trans. Henry Reeve (2 vols., 4th ed., New York, 1841), 1: 384–85.

and emotional stress that Indians so frequently endured at the white man's hands. Torn from the land of their ancestors, herded together like cattle, their political and social fabrics rent assunder, fed condemned flour and beef; why wonder that they died by the score? That their spirits were broken? That they became a permanent problem for white Americans?[7]

The early 1860s presented still another truism: the Indian problem was primarily a white problem. To be sure, the historian must not become so overly sentimental about the aborigine that he overlooks the bitter intertribal wars that bloodied the continent long before the white man's coming and the Indians' own inability to get along with the European. Yet who can deny that white expansion prompted most hostile forays of plains and desert tribes and necessitated their confinement on barren reserves where they succumbed to disease, reservation traders, and the whiskey jug?

The Civil War was probably the most frustrating and difficult period the Indian Office experienced in the trans-Mississippi West. At no other time were field problems more numerous or varied. The Lincoln administration's preoccupation with the Confederacy and the unavailability of troops for the frontier reduced Washington's support for the Indian service just when it was most needed for gathering the recalcitrant nomadic people on isolated reserves. Simultaneously the Indian Office grappled with fitful first-generation reservation Indians in Minnesota, Kansas, Nebraska, Dakota, the Pacific Northwest, and California.

Although the events of the sixties and its own bureaucratic weaknesses prevented the Indian Office from safeguarding and "civilizing" its charges, it still played a major role in the development of the West. Because it fostered peaceful relations with a majority of the Indian tribes, at a minimum cost in troops and greenbacks, the Union could tap the human and material resources of the West and by so doing deny them to the Confederacy. Po-

7. For a brief discussion about the effects of such stress on Indian societies, see Peter Farb, *Man's Rise to Civilization as Shown by the Indians of North America from Primeval Times to the Coming of the Industrial State* (New York, 1968).

tential European interventionists surely noted the strength which a united East and West gave the Union cause.[8] On the state and territorial levels, Indian Office bureaucrats helped to open up Indian lands for pioneer exploitation and created jobs for white artisans at their agencies. Some provided nearby towns with surplus products from Indian farms and forests and ranges. Usually involved in party politics, Indian agents and superintendents also served as important links between local settlers and the national government.

Deplorable as the Indians' plight was during the early sixties it would have been far worse without the special protection of the Indian Office. The office alone stood between them and utter degradation and annihilation. More than a century later the Indians still realized that, despite its faults, only the office stood "between the Indian and total, unilateral renunciation of all federal treaty obligations."[9] Most humanitarians distressed by the Indians' lot during the Civil War therefore tried to ameliorate it by championing reforms in Indian Office procedure and personnel. Perhaps in their view the most notable impact of the Civil War years on federal Indian relations was public disgust with the Sand Creek incident, which caught the attention of Congress and led to a major inquiry into the condition of the Indian tribes.

8. Riegel and Athearn, *America Moves West*, p. 468.
9. Edgar S. Cahn, ed., *Our Brother's Keeper: The Indian in White America* (Washington, D.C., 1969), p. 14.

Postscript

The history of white-Indian relations east of the Mississippi demonstrated that when aggressive Europeans sought new homes and natural resources beyond their frontier line, the weaker, "primitive" owners of the region had to retreat before them. Cultural differences and headlong white expansion ruled out a peaceful settlement of differences. Driving the red man westward to one big area beyond the Mississippi solved the incompatibility problem until the mid-nineteenth century; by then the Indian had his back to the mountains and deserts, game was fast disappearing, and white settlers converged upon him from east and west.

Most altruistic observers believed that under the circumstances a program of smaller reservations would be the best substitution. Ethnologist Lewis Henry Morgan remarked in 1859 that the wild Indians must either perish or abandon their traditional ways and become farmers. The Reverend L. H. Wheeler at the Odanah mission in Wisconsin and Minnesota Bishop Henry Whipple championed concentration so that "civilizing" forces could exert maximum impact upon the aborigines.[1] Perhaps the most cogent argument for separation of the races was furnished by events

1. Morgan, "Journal of a Visit to Kansas and Nebraska in May and June, 1859," *Indian Journals*, p. 36; Wheeler to G. E. H. Day, December 5, 1861, American Board of Commissioners for Foreign Missions Papers, Houghton Library, Harvard University, Cambridge, Mass.

during the Civil War years, particularly the rush of white miners into Indian territory and the resultant hostilities. That the Indians ultimately lost the bulk of their land and had to be shielded from belligerent whites was lamentable. Nevertheless, as historian Alban W. Hoopes astutely notes, the paternalistic reservation system at least prevented genocide.[2] Recognizing this, reformers questioned which executive department could best administer the policy.

Morgan advocated returning control over Indian affairs to the War Department; its honest officers commanded the Indians' respect and could best determine when to utilize force.[3] General Pope warned that the Indian problem would persist as long as the government divided responsibility between seasoned military men and inexperienced civil officials. Dole scoffed at such a prediction. If the Interior Department handed over peaceable Indians to the military, the tribesmen would surely rebel; moreover, how could army camp followers and avaricious military contractors possibly improve reservation conditions?[4] No decision was reached on the transfer issue during the Civil War years, and Congress's Joint Special Committee on the Condition of the Indian Tribes recommended in January 1867 that the Office of Indian Affairs remain where it was. The Interior Department had no monopoly on bureaucratic corruption and inefficiency, the committee observed; untested army officers had more than once blundered into Indian wars, and treaty-making plus the sale of former Indian territory were too closely tied to the department's General Land Office.[5] The January report sparked a heated congressional debate on the transfer question which continued throughout the 1870s and only diminished because of Indian Office administrative reforms and President Hayes's appointment of Carl Schurz as Secretary of the Interior. In retrospect, friction between the War and Interior Departments served some purpose; it kept before

2. Hoopes, *Indian Affairs*, pp. 236–38.
3. Morgan to Lincoln, December 3, 1863, ID, LR Miscellaneous.
4. Dole to Usher, April 6, 1864, CIA, pp. 573ff; Pope to Doolittle, 1865, JSC, p. 426.
5. JSC, pp. 6–7.

the public the pressing Indian question, while each department acted as a check on the other.[6] Yet for Bishop Whipple the transfer controversy seemed pointless. "A bad bank book is not made good by changing pockets." What needed revising was the bad system.[7]

The 1863 treaty with the Mississippi Chippewas required the government to appoint a board to investigate annually agency improvements and Indian complaints. After its initial visitation in November 1863, the board recommended extending the protection of law to the Chippewa people, the lack of which "has been one of the greatest obstacles to the progress of civilization and Christianity among this people.... His tribal relations are weakened by the new circumstances which surround him. His chief often becomes the creature of the trader or government employé, and is powerful for mischief but powerless for good. The Indian has no protection in person, property, or life."[8] A decade later the commissioner of Indian affairs emphasized the importance of legal safeguards for all tribes and proposed that reservations be made subject to United States statutes, with violators tried in federal courts. Outside Indian territory, state laws should have jurisdiction over criminal cases involving Indians. Eventually he hoped that the president would extend state laws over Indian land. In the meantime, Indian protection depended on effective enforcement of federal trade and intercourse legislation which, according to Congress's Indian Peace Commission, needed thorough revision by the late 1860s. To administer these laws efficiently, in view of the declining control of chiefs over their people, the commissioner asked for more deputy marshals and for the authority to establish elective native governments.[9]

6. For a thorough discussion of the transfer issue, see Donald J. D'Elia, "The Argument Over Civilian or Military Indian Control, 1865–1880," *The Historian* 24 (February, 1962): 207–25.

7. Whipple to Editors, Saint Paul *Pioneer-Press and Tribune*, July 17, 1876, in *Faribault* (Minnesota) *Democrat*, July 28, 1876.

8. Whipple, Thomas L. Grace, and T. S. Williamson to Dole, n.d., CIA, 1863, pp. 461–65.

9. CIA, 1874, pp. 14–16; Report of the Peace Commission, *House Exec. Doc.* 97, 40 Cong., 2 Sess., 11:20.

The trading and annuity systems also required revision. Lewis Henry Morgan urged Lincoln to abrogate the licensed trading system, since grasping merchants so frequently collaborated with agents in bilking the red man. Yet the Indians must trade their surpluses somewhere in order to buy supplies; thus Bishop Whipple preferred a closely controlled trade with no credit purchases.[10] Reformers were in more accord on the evils of the annuity system, which fostered Indian indolence and economic dependence. The Chippewa Board of Visitors, of which Whipple was a member, advised using trade goods rather than cash payments. Control over so much money, an irresistible temptation for agents, Morgan observed, could be avoided by quarterly payments in kind or by having government paymasters distribute tribal funds.[11] In its January 1868 report the Indian Peace Commission specifically advocated annuities of clothing, cattle, farm machinery, and other items necessary to encourage economic self-sufficiency. To assure a more equitable distribution, Congress ordered the following year that agents and superintendents witness the disbursement of government merchandise by chiefs.[12]

If trustworthy agents were so vital to oversee the economic practices of chiefs and traders, Washington would have to improve upon the quality of Indian Office field personnel. Whipple believed that neither departmental directives nor Treasury audits could restrain an unscrupulous agent; the solution lay in appointing only God-fearing men of high character to such offices. Navajo Agent John Ward argued in 1865 that job insecurity prompted Office officials to meddle in politics and other non-agency matters. Their administrations would be far more honest and enlightened when they retained office during good behavior rather than at the president's whim or for just a four-year term.[13]

10. Morgan to Lincoln, December 3, 1862, and Whipple to Caleb Smith, April 10, 1862, ID, LR Misc.

11. Whipple, Grace and Williamson to Dole, n.d., CIA, 1863, pp. 461–65; Morgan to Lincoln, December 3, 1862, ID, LR Misc.

12. Report of the Peace Commission, *House Exec. Doc.* 97, 40 Cong., 2 Sess., 11:18; *United States Statutes at Large* 16:39.

13. Whipple to the Secretary of the Interior, February 23, 1861, Whipple Papers; Ward to Doolittle, August 24, 1865, JSC, pp. 459–60.

During the late sixties President Grant appointed church nominees to Indian Office field positions, and in 1873 Congress required that federal inspectors periodically examine agency and superintendency accounts as well as the condition of reservation tribes.[14] Even so, the continued failures of Grant's agents to improve markedly the red man's lot indicated that the root of the "Indian problem" went deeper than bureaucratic ineptitude and dishonesty.[15]

Reformers discussed still another peripheral problem: the treaty system. According to General Pope, Indian headmen regarded treaty presents and later annuities as little more than bribes. Shrewd chiefs also realized that when they wanted more government goods, they need only murder a few whites and then open negotiations with the Indian Office. In the eyes of Samuel Bowles, Washington was equally faithless. Besides Senate delays and treaty amendments, Interior Department officials at all levels whittled away at government promises.[16] The continued expansion of the white frontier necessitated new treaties—and more infidelity. The fiction of Indian autonomy persisted until March 1871, when Congress refused any longer to recognize Indian tribes as independent nations, to be dealt with by treaty.[17] Yet a change in status by no means alleviated the red man's plight.

Besides analyzing the problems of the past, it behooves the historian to offer a solution or two when he can. How might federal administrative aims and procedures be modified so as to strike at the root of the "Indian problem" without repeating the mistakes of the Civil War years? Outlined below is one program that Washington might have implemented during the last half of the nineteenth century.

To assemble the elusive Indians on reservations was the government's first task. Not all could be rounded up at once, of course; there were too many intractable bands roaming the trans-Missis-

14. *United States Statutes at Large* 17:463–64.
15. Priest, *Uncle Sam's Stepchildren*, p. 28.
16. Pope to Halleck, November 3, 1864, OR, Ser. 1, 41, Pt. 1, p. 139; Samuel Bowles, *Our New West; Records of Travel Between the Mississippi River and the Pacific Ocean* . . . (Hartford, Conn., 1869), pp. 157–58.
17. *United States Statutes at Large* 16:566.

sippi West and too few army regulars, particularly during the Civil War years. When villages finally surrendered to superior white technology and numbers, the War Department shipped them off to tribal reserves, where there awaited an even more challenging phase of the Indian problem which could best be handled by a civilian Indian bureau.

Granted the necessity of a reservation system, its goal should have been to achieve economic self-sufficiency and self-determination for the Indians, so that they did not become a perpetual financial and psychic burden for white Americans. Roy Meyer writes in his history of the Santees that the federal government together with sundry humanitarian reformers dissipated too much energy, time, and money in foolishly forcing unnecessary cultural changes on the Eastern Sioux. The same holds true for other reservation tribes. Had economic independence been the government's sole aim, there would be no reason to assail Indian religion, language, dress, family structure and tribal collectivism; no struggle to transform red men into middle class whites.[18] To be sure, the aborigine had to adjust, as did rural Anglo-Saxon farmers, to a growing urban industrial society.[19] Yet demanding that he forsake only intertribal warfare and his hunting-fishing-gathering economy was eminently more accomplishable than complete metamorphosis.

How might such people have been motivated to take up an agricultural, pastoral, or commercial life? First the government should have learned about the red man's heritage: the forces which shaped him and the strength of his beliefs. The firsthand knowledge of missionaries, trappers, traders, squaw men, army officers, and civil bureaucrats would have revealed an enormous number of cultural differences, requiring the Indian Office to tailor its program whenever possible to each tribe's reservation resources, its own propensity to wander or to till the soil, its attitudes toward whites as well as fellow Indians, and its proximity to both.

It was essential as well that each tribe be consolidated on a res-

18. Meyer, *Santee Sioux*, pp. 359–60.
19. William T. Hagan, *Indian Police and Judges: Experiments in Acculturation and Control* (New Haven, 1966), p. 168.

ervation selected to make the best use of human and natural resources: where its people could become self-supporting and
integrated into a regional economy. Oil rights, uranium deposits,
the attractiveness of such locations to white tourists—all twentieth century sources of Indian income—obviously could not be
considered.

Once the tribes came together on reservations, detrimental outside forces such as white encroachers, whiskey dealers, and unlicensed traders should have been barred; tribal funds, held in trust
by the government, invested wisely and vigorously; the outflow
of Indian money as well as natural resources checked through a
vigilant control of trading posts, with their easy credit and over-
priced consumer goods, and the breaking up of "Indian rings."[20]
If one admits that the Anglo-Saxon value system need not have
been imposed on the red man, then the federal government was
also free to encourage cooperative Indian agriculture and ranch-
ing. For decades the Interior Department employed white artisans
to train natives in needed skills, but without the proper supervision and the application of stimuli that would induce tribesmen
to take advantage of new abilities.

Another crucial phase of the program could have been the
development of localized Indian leadership, without which the
paternalistic hand of the Indian Office would forever hang heavy.
Tribal leaders ought to have been delegated increasingly greater
authority, and Indian Office personnel made partially accountable
to them. Indians might have been trained for federal jobs on the
reservation, thereby avoiding the task of finding suitable white
officials willing to live in isolated country among an alien people.[21]
William T. Hagan's volume on the development and use of Indian
police and judges during the 1870s and 1880s illustrates how
native leaders could be used for active and vigorous roles in their
own affairs.[22]

To be sure, this program has been painted in broad strokes;

20. Some of these ideas are adapted from a critique of present-day Indian affairs in Cahn, *Our Brother's Keeper*, pp. 93–99.
21. *Ibid.*, pp. 142–44, 150.
22. Hagan, *Indian Police and Judges.*

much detail remains to be added. But why carry on? Though the plan would have solved several Indian Office administrative problems in the early 1860s, its acceptance and successful implementation in the milieu of the mid-nineteenth century was dubious at best. Neither moral suasion nor the threat of interminable economic support could have convinced short-sighted frontiersmen and congressmen to preserve valuable land for the red man. In fact, after the Indian ceased to be a military threat, Congress had scant interest in and even less money for Indian matters. To advance the notion of cultural relativity would only have brought derisive hoots from the floor. Precipitant events beyond the Mississippi also worked against a proposal that required research and insights into Stone Age cultures in conjunction with the slow forging of policies for individual tribes. And what of the doubtfulness of sufficient Indian cooperation in the entire program?

The unlikelihood of a radical change in the reservation policy, based on this plan or any other, meant that the Indian Office would fumble on toward the goal of acculturation. Consequently, Indian Office records reveal the persistence of Civil War administrative troubles well into the 1870s, as Uncle Sam doctored with half-measures the symptoms of the "Indian problem."

The plight of American Indians today, a century later, is rooted in the seizure of the red man's land in the mid-1800s and the initiation of a senseless assault on Indian culture.

Bibliography

I. Primary Sources

A. Private Papers and State Documents

American Board of Commissioners for Foreign Missions. Papers. Houghton Library, Harvard University, Cambridge, Mass.
———. Selected Typed Copies of Correspondence Concerning Minnesota. Minnesota Historical Society, Saint Paul.
Bent, George. Papers. Yale University Library, Western Americana Collection, New Haven, Conn.
Evans, John. Autobiographical Statement of [1888?]. Hubert Howe Bancroft Collection, Bancroft Library, University of California, Berkeley.
———. Interview with H. H. Bancroft, 1884. Bancroft Library, University of California, Berkeley.
Furnas, Robert W. Papers. Nebraska State Historical Society, Lincoln.
Indian Affairs Letterpress Book, 1863–1864. Colorado State Archives and Records Service, Denver.
Legislative Committee on Indian Affairs. Indian War Files, California State Archives, Sacramento.
Lincoln, Abraham. Papers. Library of Congress, Washington, D.C.
Pratt, John Gill. Collection. Kansas State Historical Society, Topeka.
Riggs, Stephen R. Papers. Minnesota Historical Society, St. Paul.
Sibley, Henry H. Papers. Minnesota Historical Society, St. Paul.
Steck, Michael. Papers. Zimmerman Library, University of New Mexico, Albuquerque.

Thompson, Clark W. Papers. Minnesota Historical Society, St. Paul.
Usher, John P. Papers. Kansas State Historical Society, Topeka.
Wallace, William H. Papers. University of Washington Library, Seattle.
Whipple, Henry B. Papers. Minnesota Historical Society, St. Paul.
Williamson, Thomas Smith. Family Papers. Minnesota Historical Society, St. Paul.
Young, Brigham. Papers. Yale University Library, Western Americana Collection, New Haven, Conn.

B. FEDERAL DOCUMENTS (UNPUBLISHED) IN THE NATIONAL ARCHIVES

Records of the Bureau of Indian Affairs.
  Documents Relating to the Negotiation of Ratified and Unratified Treaties with Various Tribes of Indians.
  Letters received. From superintendencies: Arizona, California, Central, Colorado, Dakota, Nevada, New Mexico, Northern, Oregon, Southern, Washington. From agencies: Cherokee, Chippewa, Creek, Delaware, Great Nemaha, Green Bay, Kansa, La Pointe, Oto, Pawnee, Ponca, Potawatomi, Saint Peter's, Seminole, Shawnee, Upper Arkansas, Upper Platte, Wichita, Winnebago.
  Letters sent.
  Records of the Arizona Superintendency. Letters sent.
  Records of the Civilization Division.
  Records of the Dakota Superintendency.
  Records of the New Mexico Superintendency. Letters received.
  Records of the Northern Superintendency. Letters received.
  Records of the Oregon Superintendency. Letters received and sent.
  Records of the Washington Superintendency. Letters received and sent.
  Report Books, 12–14.
  Special Files, Numbers 201, 235.
Records of the Department of State, Nevada Territorial Papers.
Records of the Department of the Interior, Office of the Secretary of the Interior, Indian Division. Letters received and sent.
Records of the Legislative Branch, House Committee on Indian Affairs. Wartime Records, 37th and 38th Cong.
Records of the War Department.
  Adjutant General's Office. Letters received.

United States Army Commands.
  Army of the Frontier. Letters sent.
  Department of New Mexico. Letters sent.
  Department of Kansas. Letters sent.
  District of Kansas. Letters sent.
  Fort Lapwai, Idaho. Letters sent.

C. FEDERAL DOCUMENTS (PUBLISHED)

1. GENERAL

Congressional Globe, 38th Cong.

Kappler, Charles J., ed. *Indian Affairs: Laws and Treaties.* 2 vols., 2nd ed., Washington, D.C.: United States Government Printing Office, 1904.

Royce, Charles C. "Indian Land Cessions in the United States," *Eighteenth Annual Report of the Bureau of American Ethnology.* Washington, D.C., 1896–97.

Scott, R. N., et al., eds. *The War of the Rebellion: A Compilation of the Official Records of the Union and Confederate Armies,* 70 volumes in 128, Washington, D.C.: United States Government Printing Office, 1880–1901.

United States Statutes at Large, vols. 4, 12, 13, 16, 17.

United States Superintendent of the Census. *Population of the United States in 1860; Compiled from the Original Returns, Under the Direction of the Secretary of the Interior.* Washington, D.C.: United States Government Printing Office, 1864.

2. SPECIAL

House Executive Documents
  No. 1, 37th Cong., 3rd Sess., 2 (Serial 1157).
  No. 1, 38th Cong., 1st Sess., 3 (Serial 1182).
  No. 58, 38th Cong., 1st Sess., 9 (Serial 1189).
  No. 1, 38th Cong., 2nd Sess., 5 (Serial 1220).
  No. 1, 39th Cong., 1st Sess., 2 (Serial 1248).
  No. 97, 40th Cong., 2nd Sess., 11 (Serial 1337).
House Miscellaneous Documents
  No. 29, 38th Cong., 1st Sess. (Serial 1200).
House Reports
  No. 13, 37th Cong., 3rd Sess. (Serial 1173).

Senate Executive Documents
  No. 1, 34th Cong., 1st Sess., 1 (Serial 810).
  No. 5, 34th Cong., 3rd Sess., 2 (Serial 875).
  No. 2, 36th Cong., 1st Sess., 1 (Serial 1023).
  No. 1, 36th Cong., 2nd Sess., 1 (Serial 1078).
  No. 1, 37th Cong., 2nd Sess., 1 (Serial 1117).
  No. 7, 37th Cong., 3rd Sess., 1 (Serial 1149).
  No. 26, 39th Cong., 2nd Sess., 2 (Serial 1277).
Senate Miscellaneous Documents
  No. 97, 38th Cong., 1st Sess., 1 (Serial 1177).
Senate Reports
  No. 379, 33rd Cong., 1st Sess., 2 (Serial 707).
  No. 142, Pt. 3, 38th Cong., 2nd Sess. (Serial 1214).
  No. 156, 39th Cong., 2nd Sess. (Serial 1279).

D. NEWSPAPERS AND MAGAZINES

Colorado Republican and Rocky Mountain Herald (Denver).
Commonwealth and Republican (Denver).
Daily Alta California (San Francisco).
Daily News (Gold Hill, Nevada).
Daily Oregonian (Portland).
Daily Times (Leavenworth, Kansas).
Daily Union (Sacramento).
Faribault (Minnesota) *Democrat*.
Missionary Herald of the American Board.
Montana Post (Virginia City).
New York Times.
Oregon Statesman (Salem).
Pioneer and Democrat (St. Paul *Pioneer* after September, 1862).
Press (St. Paul).
Washington Standard (Olympia).
Weekly Gazette (Santa Fe).

E. BOOKS

Bensell, Royal A. *All Quiet on the Yamhill: The Civil War in Oregon; The Journal of Corporal Royal A. Bensell, Company D, Fourth California Infantry*. Edited by Gunther Barth. Eugene: University of Oregon Books, 1959.

Bowles, Samuel. *Across the Continent: A Summer's Journey to the Rocky Mountains, the Mormons, and the Pacific States, with Speaker Colfax.* Springfield, Mass.: Samuel Bowles & Co., 1865.

————. *Our New West; Records of Travel Between the Mississippi River and the Pacific Ocean* . . . Hartford, Conn.: Hartford Publishing Co., 1869.

Brewer, William H. *Up and Down California in 1860–1864. The Journal of William H. Brewer, Professor of Agriculture in the Sheffield Scientific School from 1864 to 1903.* Edited by Francis P. Farquhar. New Haven: Yale University Press, 1930.

Bryant, Charles S. *A History of the Great Massacre by the Sioux Indians in Minnesota, Including the Personal Narratives of Many Who Escaped.* Cincinnati: Rickey and Carroll, 1864.

Chase, Salmon P. *Inside Lincoln's Cabinet: The Civil War Diaries of Salmon P. Chase.* Edited by David Donald. New York: Longmans, Green and Co., 1954.

Dale, Edward Everett, and Litton, Gaston, eds. *Cherokee Cavaliers: Forty Years of Cherokee History as Told in the Correspondence of the Ridge-Watie-Boudinot Family.* Norman: University of Oklahoma Press, 1939.

Lincoln, Abraham. *The Collected Works of Abraham Lincoln.* Edited by Roy P. Basler et al. 9 vols. New Brunswick, N.J.: Rutgers University Press, 1953.

Melville, Herman. *The Confidence-man: His Masquerade.* New York: Russell & Russell, Inc., 1963.

Minnesota, State of. *Executive Documents for the Year 1862.* St. Paul: William R. Marshall, State Printer, 1863.

Morgan, Lewis Henry. *The Indian Journals, 1859–62.* Edited by Leslie A. White. Ann Arbor: University of Michigan Press, 1959.

Nicolay, John G. *Lincoln's Secretary Goes West; Two Reports by John G. Nicolay on Frontier Indian Troubles, 1862.* Edited by Theodore C. Blegen. LaCrosse, Wisc.: Sumac Press, 1965.

Riggs, Stephen R. *Mary and I: Forty Years with the Sioux.* Chicago: W. G. Holmes, 1880.

————. *Tah-koo Wah-kan; or the Gospel Among the Dakotas.* Boston: Congregational Publishing Co., 1869.

Stuart, Granville. *Forty Years on the Frontier as Seen in the Journals and Reminiscences of Granville Stuart.* . . . Edited by Paul C. Phillips. Glendale, Calif.: Arthur H. Clark Co., 1957.

Swisshelm, Jane Grey. *Crusader and Feminist: Letters of Jane Grey*

Swisshelm, 1858–65. Edited by Arthur J. Larson. St. Paul: Minnesota Historical Society, 1934.

Tocqueville, Alexis de. *Democracy in America.* Translated by Henry Reeve. Vol. I. 4th ed. New York: J. & H. G. Langley, 1841.

Welles, Gideon. *Diary of Gideon Welles; Secretary of the Navy Under Lincoln and Johnson.* Edited by Howard K. Beal, assisted by Alan W. Brownsword. 3 vols. New York: W. W. Norton Co., 1960.

Whipple, Henry Benjamin. *Lights and Shadows of a Long Episcopate; Being Reminiscences and Recollections of the Right Reverend Henry Benjamin Whipple, Bishop of Minnesota.* New York: Macmillan Co., 1912.

F. ARTICLES

Browne, J. Ross. "A Peep at Washoe." *Harper's New Monthly Magazine* 22 (January, 1861): 145–62.

Cremony, John C. "The Apache Race," *The Overland Monthly* 1 (September, 1868): 201–9.

Daniels, Asa W. "Reminiscences of Little Crow." *Collections of the Minnesota Historical Society* 12 (St. Paul, 1908): 514–30.

Davenport, T. W. "Recollections of an Indian Agent." *The Quarterly of the Oregon Historical Society* 8 (March, 1907): 1–41.

Gwyther, George. "An Indian Reservation." *The Overland Monthly* 10 (February, 1873): 123–34.

Holcombe, Robert I., ed. "Chief Big Eagle's Story of the Sioux Outbreak of 1862." *Collections of the Minnesota Historical Society* 6 (St. Paul, 1894): 382–400.

Johnson, Charles W. "Narrative of the Sixth Regiment." *Minnesota in the Civil and Indian Wars, 1861–65,* 2 vols., 1 (St. Paul, 1890–93): 300–328.

Nicolay, John G. "The Sioux War." *Continental Monthly,* 3 (February, 1863): 195–204.

"Official Correspondence Pertaining to the War of the Outbreak, 1862–65." *South Dakota Historical Collections* 8 (Pierre, South Dakota, 1916): 100–588.

"Our Indian Policy." *The Nation* 2 (January 25, 1866): 102–3.

Triplett, Joe F. "The Diary of Joe F. Triplett." Transcribed by Edna B. Patterson. *Nevada Historical Society Quarterly* 2 (January–March, 1959): 3–14.

White, Mrs. N. D. "Captivity Among the Sioux, August 18 to September 26, 1862." *Collections of the Minnesota Historical Society* 9 (St. Paul, 1894): 395–426.

II. SECONDARY WORKS

A. BOOKS

Able, Annie Heloise. *The American Indian as Slaveholder and Secessionist: An Omitted Chapter in the Diplomatic History of the Southern Confederacy.* Cleveland: Arthur H. Clark Co., 1915.

Angel, Myron, ed. *History of Nevada.* . . . Oakland, Calif.: Thompson and West, 1881. Reproduced, Berkeley, Calif.: Howell-North Company, 1958.

Bailey, L. R. *The Long Walk: A History of the Navajo Wars, 1846–68.* Los Angeles: Westernlore Press, 1964.

Bancroft, Hubert Howe. *History of Arizona and New Mexico, 1530–1888.* Vol. 17 of *The Works of Hubert Howe Bancroft.* San Francisco: History Co., 1889.

——. *History of Nevada, Colorado, and Wyoming, 1540–1888.* Vol. 25 of *The Works of Hubert Howe Bancroft.* San Francisco: History Co., 1890.

——. *History of Utah, 1540–1886.* Vol. 26 of *The Works of Hubert Howe Bancroft.* San Francisco: History Co., 1889.

Barton, Winifred W. *John P. Williamson, A Brother to the Sioux.* New York: Fleming H. Revell Co., 1919.

Beal, Merrill D. *"I Will Fight No More Forever": Chief Joseph and the Nez Perce War.* Seattle: University of Washington Press, 1963.

Beck, Warren A. *New Mexico: A History of Four Centuries.* Norman: University of Oklahoma Press, 1962.

Berthrong, Donald J. *The Southern Cheyennes.* Norman: University of Oklahoma Press, 1963.

Billington, Ray Allen. *Westward Expansion: A History of the American Frontier,* 3d ed. New York: Macmillan Co., 1967.

Blegen, Theodore C. *Minnesota: A History of the State.* Minneapolis: University of Minnesota Press, 1963.

Burlingame, Merrill G., and Toole, K. Ross. *A History of Montana.* 3 vols. New York: Lewis Historical Publishing Co., 1957.

Cahn, Edgar S., ed. *Our Brother's Keeper: The Indian in White America.* Washington, D.C.: New Community Press, 1969.

Carey, Charles H. *A General History of Oregon, Prior to 1861.* 2 vols. Portland: Metropolitan Press, 1936.

Carley, Kenneth. *The Sioux Uprising of 1862.* St. Paul: Minnesota Historical Society, 1961.

Castel, Albert E. *A Frontier State at War: Kansas, 1861–65.* Ithaca, New York: Published for the American Historical Association by Cornell University Press, 1958.

Chittenden, Hiram M., and Richardson, Alfred T. *Life, Letters, and Travels of Father Pierre-Jean de Smet, S.J., 1801–1873, . . .* 4 vols. New York: Francis Harper, 1905.

Colton, Ray C. *The Civil War in the Western Territories: Arizona, Colorado, New Mexico, and Utah.* Norman: University of Oklahoma Press, 1959.

Dale, Edward Everett. *The Indians of the Southwest: A Century of Development under the United States.* Norman: University of Oklahoma Press and the Henry E. Huntington Library, 1949.

DeVoto, Bernard. *The Year of Decision: 1846.* Boston: Little, Brown and Co., 1943.

Ewers, John C. *The Blackfeet: Raiders on the Northwestern Plains.* Norman: University of Oklahoma Press, 1958.

Farb, Peter. *Man's Rise to Civilization as Shown by the Indians of North America from Primeval Times to the Coming of the Industrial State.* New York: E. P. Dutton & Co., 1968.

Farish, Thomas Edwin. *History of Arizona.* 4 vols. Phoenix: Filmer Brothers Electrotype Co., 1915–16.

Fisher, Margaret M., comp. and ed. *Utah and the Civil War. . . .* Salt Lake City: Deseret Book Co., 1929.

Folwell, William Watts. *A History of Minnesota.* Vol. 2. St. Paul: Minnesota State Historical Society, 1924.

Forbes, Jack D., ed. *The Indian in America's Past.* Englewood Cliffs, N.J.: Prentice-Hall, 1964.

Foreman, Grant. *History of Oklahoma.* Norman: University of Oklahoma Press, 1942.

Fritz, Henry E. *The Movement for Indian Assimilation, 1860–1890.* Philadelphia: University of Pennsylvania Press, 1963.

Gibson, A. M. *The Kickapoos: Lords of the Middle Border.* Norman: University of Oklahoma Press, 1963.

Greever, William S. *The Bonanza West: The Story of the Western*

Mining Rushes, 1848–1900. Norman: University of Oklahoma Press, 1963.

Grinnell, George Bird. *The Fighting Cheyennes.* Norman: University of Oklahoma Press, 1956.

Hafen, LeRoy Reuben, and Hafen, Ann W. *Colorado, a Story of the State and Its People.* Denver: Old West Publishing Co., 1945.

Hagan, William T. *American Indians.* Chicago: University of Chicago Press, 1961.

――――. *Indian Police and Judges: Experiments in Acculturation and Control.* New Haven: Yale University Press, 1966.

Haines, Francis. *The Nez Percés: Tribesmen of the Columbia Plateau.* Norman: University of Oklahoma Press, 1955.

Hart, Herbert M. *Old Forts of the Northwest.* Seattle: Superior Publishing Co., 1963.

Hill, Edward E., comp. *Preliminary Inventory of the Records of the Bureau of Indian Affairs.* 2 vols. Washington, D.C.: National Archives, 1965.

Hodge, Frederick Webb, ed. *Handbook of American Indians North of Mexico.* 2 vols. Washington, D.C.: Government Printing Office, 1907–10.

Hoebel, Edward Adamson. *The Cheyennes: Indians of the Great Plains.* New York: Holt, Rinehart, and Winston, 1960.

Hoig, Stan. *The Sand Creek Massacre.* Norman: University of Oklahoma Press, 1961.

Holcombe, Return I., and Hubbard, Lucius F. *Minnesota in Three Centuries* Vol. 3. New York: Publishing Society of Minnesota, 1908.

Hoopes, Alban W. *Indian Affairs and Their Administration, with Special Reference to the Far West, 1849–1860.* Philadelphia: University of Pennsylvania Press, 1932.

Hunt, Aurora. *The Army of the Pacific: Its Operation in California, Texas, Arizona, New Mexico, Utah, Nevada, Oregon, Washington, Plains Region, Mexico, etc. 1860–1866.* Glendale, Calif.: Arthur H. Clark Co., 1958.

Hyde, George E. *Life of George Bent, Written from His Letters.* Edited by Savoie Lottinville. Norman: University of Oklahoma Press, 1968.

――――. *Rangers and Regulars.* Columbus, Ohio: Long's College Book Co., 1952.

————. *Red Cloud's Folk: A History of the Oglala Sioux Indians.* Norman: University of Oklahoma Press, 1937.

————. *Spotted Tail's Folk: A History of the Brulé Sioux.* Norman: University of Oklahoma Press, 1961.

Jackson, Helen Hunt. *A Century of Dishonor: A Sketch of the United States Government's Dealings with Some of the Indian Tribes.* New York: Harper and Brothers, 1881.

Jones, Robert Huhn. *The Civil War in the Northwest: Nebraska, Wisconsin, Iowa, Minnesota and the Dakotas.* Norman: University of Oklahoma Press, 1960.

Josephy, Alvin M., Jr. *The Nez Perce Indians and the Opening of the Northwest.* New Haven: Yale University Press, 1965.

————. *The Indian Heritage of America.* New York: Alfred A. Knopf, 1968.

Keleher, William Aloysius. *Turmoil in New Mexico, 1846–68.* Santa Fe: Rydal Press, 1952.

Kelsey, Harry E., Jr. *Frontier Capitalist: The Life of John Evans.* Denver: State Historical Society of Colorado and the Pruett Publishing Co., 1969.

Kluckhohn, Clyde, and Leighton, Dorothea. *The Navaho.* Rev. ed. Garden City, N.Y.: Doubleday and Co., 1962.

Lamar, Howard Roberts. *Dakota Territory, 1861–1889; A Study of Frontier Politics.* New Haven: Yale University Press, 1956.

————. *The Far Southwest, 1849–1912: A Territorial History.* New Haven: Yale University Press, 1966.

Lavender, David Sievert. *Bent's Fort.* Garden City, N.Y.: Doubleday and Co., 1954.

Leckie, William H. *The Military Conquest of the Southern Plains.* Norman: University of Oklahoma Press, 1963.

McMechen, Edgar C. *Life of Governor Evans, Second Territorial Governor of Colorado.* Denver: Wahlgreen Publishing Co., 1924.

McReynolds, Edwin C. *The Seminoles.* Norman: University of Oklahoma Press, 1957.

Meyer, Roy W. *History of the Santee Sioux: United States Indian Policy on Trial.* Lincoln: University of Nebraska Press, 1967.

Munden, Kenneth W., and Beers, Henry Putney. *Guide to Federal Archives Relating to the Civil War.* Washington, D.C.: National Archives, 1962.

Oehler, C. M. *The Great Sioux Uprising.* New York: Oxford University Press, 1959.

Olson, James C. *History of Nebraska.* Lincoln: University of Nebraska Press, 1955.

Paul, Rodman Wilson. *Mining Frontiers of the Far West: 1848–1880.* New York: Holt, Rinehart, and Winston, 1963.

Pomeroy, Earl S. *The Territories and the United States, 1861–1890: Studies in Colonial Administration.* Philadelphia: University of Pennsylvania Press, 1947.

Priest, Loring Benson. *Uncle Sam's Stepchildren: The Reformation of United States Indian Policy, 1865–1887.* New Brunswick, N.J.: Rutgers University Press, 1942.

Prucha, Francis Paul. *American Indian Policy in the Formative Years; The Indian Trade and Intercourse Acts, 1790–1834.* Cambridge, Mass.: Harvard University Press, 1962.

Raney, William Francis. *Wisconsin: A Story of Progress.* New York: Prentice-Hall, 1940.

Richardson, Elmo R., and Farley, Alan W. *John Palmer Usher: Lincoln's Secretary of the Interior.* Lawrence: University of Kansas Press, 1960.

Richardson, Rupert N., and Rister, Carl C. *The Greater Southwest: The Economic, Social, and Cultural Development of Kansas, Oklahoma, Texas, Utah, Colorado, Nevada, New Mexico, Arizona, and California from the Spanish Conquest to the Twentieth Century.* Glendale, Calif.: Arthur H. Clark Co., 1935.

Riegel, Robert E., and Athearn, Robert G. *America Moves West.* 4th ed. New York: Holt, Rinehart, and Winston, 1964.

Roddis, Louis H. *The Indian Wars of Minnesota.* Cedar Rapids, Iowa: The Torch Press, 1956.

Rogers, Fred B. *Soldiers of the Overland: Being Some Account of the Services of General Patrick Edward Connor and His Volunteers in the Old West.* San Francisco: Grabhorn Press, 1938.

Roske, Ralph J. *Everyman's Eden: A History of California.* New York: Macmillan Co., 1968.

Sale, Randall D., and Karn, Edwin D. *American Expansion: A Book of Maps.* Homewood, Ill.: Dorsey Press, 1962.

Schmeckiebier, Laurence F. *The Office of Indian Affairs: Its History, Activities, and Organization.* Baltimore, Md.: Johns Hopkins Press, 1927.

Toole, Kenneth Ross. *Montana: An Uncommon Land.* Norman: University of Oklahoma Press, 1959.

Trenholm, Virginia Cole. *The Arapahoes, Our People.* Norman: University of Oklahoma Press, 1970.

Trenholm, Virginia Cole, and Carley, Maurine. *The Shoshonis: Sentinels of the Rockies*. Norman: University of Oklahoma Press, 1964.

Tyler, S. Lyman. *Indian Affairs. A Study of the Changes in Policy of the United States toward Indians*. Provo, Utah: Brigham Young University, 1964.

Underhill, Ruth M. *The Navajos*. Norman: University of Oklahoma Press, 1956.

Utley, Robert M. *Frontiersmen in Blue: The United States Army and the Indian, 1848–1865*. New York: Macmillan Co., 1967.

Wallace, Ernest, and Hoebel, E. Adamson. *The Comanches, Lords of the South Plains*. Norman: University of Oklahoma Press, 1952.

Webb, Walter Prescott. *The Great Plains*. Boston: Ginn and Co., 1931.

Woodward, Grace Steele. *The Cherokees*. Norman: University of Oklahoma Press, 1963.

B. Articles

Able, Annie Heloise. "The Indians in the Civil War." *American Historical Review* 15 (October, 1909): 281–96.

Babcock, Willoughby M. "Minnesota's Indian War." *Minnesota History* 38 (September, 1962): 93–98.

Bender, A. B. "Frontier Defense in the Territory of New Mexico." *New Mexico Historical Review* 9 (October, 1934): 345–73.

Carey, Raymond G. "Colonel Chivington, Brigadier General Connor, and Sand Creek." *The 1960 Brand Book: Being Volume Sixteen of the Denver Posse of The Westerners*, pp. 103–36.

———. "The Puzzle of Sand Creek." *Colorado Magazine* 41 (Fall, 1964): 279–98.

Dale, Edward Everett. "The Cherokees in the Confederacy." *Journal of Southern History* 13 (May, 1947): 159–85.

D'Elia, Donald J. "The Argument Over Civilian or Military Indian Control, 1865–1880." *The Historian* 24 (February, 1962): 207–25.

Ellison, Joseph. "The Currency Question on the Pacific Coast During the Civil War." *Mississippi Valley Historical Review* 16 (June, 1929): 50–66.

Farb, Robert C. "Robert W. Furnas as Omaha Indian Agent, 1864–1866." *Nebraska History* 32 (September, 1951): 186–203, and (December, 1951): 268–83.

Garfield, Marvin H. "Defense of the Kansas Frontier, 1864-'65." *Kansas Historical Quarterly* 1 (February, 1932): pp. 140–52.

Gibson, A. M. "Confederates on the Plains: The Pike Mission to Wichita Agency." *Great Plains Journal* 4 (Fall, 1964): 7–16.

Gluek, Alvin C., Jr., "The Sioux Uprising: A Problem in International Relations." *Minnesota History* 34 (Winter, 1955): 317–24.

Hoffman, Walter James. "The Menomini Indians." *Fourteenth Annual Report of the Bureau of Ethnology*, Pt. I (Washington, 1896), pp. 1–328.

Jackson, W. Turrentine. "Indian Affairs and Politics in Idaho Territory, 1863–1870." *Pacific Historical Review* 14 (September, 1945): 311–25.

Katz, Willis A. "Benjamin F. Kendall, Territorial Politician." *Pacific Northwest Quarterly* 49 (January, 1958): 29–39.

Kelsey, Harry. "Background to Sand Creek." *Colorado Magazine* 45 (Fall, 1968): 279–300.

———. "William P. Dole and Mr. Lincoln's Indian Policy." *Journal of the West* 10 (July, 1971): 484–92.

Lass, William E. "The 'Moscow Expedition.'" *Minnesota History*, 39 (Summer, 1965): 227–40.

———. "The Removal from Minnesota of the Sioux and Winnebago Indians." *Minnesota History* 38 (December, 1963): 353–64.

Lecompte, Janet. "Charles Autobees." *Colorado Magazine* 35 (July, 1958): 219–25.

———. "Sand Creek." *Colorado Magazine* 41 (Fall, 1964): 315–35.

Masterson, James R. "The Records of the Washington Superintendency of Indian Affairs, 1853–1874." *Pacific Northwest Quarterly* 37 (January, 1946): 31–57.

Mead, James R. "The Wichita Indians in Kansas." *Transactions of the Kansas State Historical Society* ... 8 (Topeka, 1904): 171–77.

Mellor, William J. "The Military Investigation of Colonel John M. Chivington Following the Sand Creek Massacre." *Chronicles of Oklahoma* 16 (December, 1938): 444–64.

Meserve, John Bartlett. "Chief Opothleyahola." *Chronicles of Oklahoma* 9 (December, 1931): 439–53.

Mooney, James. "The Cheyenne Indians." *Memoirs of the American Anthropological Association* 1 (Lancaster, Pa., 1905–07): 361–442.

Morton, Ohland. "Confederate Government Relations With the Five Civilized Tribes." *Chronicles of Oklahoma* 31 (Summer, 1953): 189–204, and (Autumn, 1953): 299–322.

Murphy, Lawrence R. "William F. M. Arny, Secretary of New Mexico Territory, 1862–1867." *Arizona and the West* 8 (Winter, 1966): 323–38.

Porter, Kenneth W. "Billy Bowlegs (Holata Micco) In the Civil War (Part II)." *Florida Historical Quarterly* 45 (April, 1967): 391–401.

Quaife, Milo M. "The Panic of 1862 in Wisconsin." *Wisconsin Magazine of History* 4 (1920–21): 166–95.

Reeve, Frank D. "The Federal Indian Policy in New Mexico, 1858–1880." *New Mexico Historical Review* 13 (January, 1938): 14–49 and (April, 1938): 146–91.

Relf, Francis H. "Removal of the Sioux Indians from Minnesota." *Minnesota History* 2 (May, 1918): 420–25.

Renaud, E. B. "The Indians of Colorado." *Colorado: Short Studies of its Past and Present.* Edited by Junius Henderson et al. Boulder: University of Colorado Press, 1927.

Scott, Leslie M. "Indian Diseases as Aids to Pacific Northwest Settlement," *Oregon Historical Quarterly* 29 (June, 1928): 144–61.

Sievers, Michael A. "Sands of Sand Creek Historiography." *Colorado Magazine* 49 (Spring, 1972): 116–42.

"Taoyateduta is Not a Coward," *Minnesota History* 38 (September, 1962): 115.

Tegeder, Vincent G. "Lincoln and the Territorial Patronage: The Ascendency of the Radicals in the West." *Mississippi Valley Historical Review* 35 (June, 1948): 77–90.

Trimble, W. J. "American and British Treatment of the Indians in the Pacific Northwest." *Washington Historical Quarterly* 5 (January, 1914): 32–54.

Unrau, William E. "A Prelude to War." *Colorado Magazine* 41 (Fall, 1964): 299–313.

Utley, Robert M. "Kit Carson and the Adobe Walls Campaign." *The American West* 2 (Winter, 1965): 4–11, 73–75.

Walker, Charles S. "Causes of the Confederate Invasion of New Mexico." *New Mexico Historical Review* 8 (April, 1933): 76–97.

Wissler, Clark. "The North American Indians of the Plains." *Popular Science Monthly* 82 (January–June, 1913): 436–44.

C. Unpublished Studies

Albright, Robert Edwin. "The Relations of Montana with the Federal Government: 1864–1889." Doctoral dissertation, Stanford University, Palo Alto, 1933.

Burlingame, Merrill G. "The Military-Indian Frontier in Montana, 1860–1890." Doctoral dissertation, University of Iowa, Iowa City, 1936.

Coan, Charles Florus. "The Federal Indian Policy in the Pacific Northwest, 1849–1879." Doctoral dissertation, University of California, Berkeley, 1920.

Tegeder, Vincent G. "The Territories and the Lincoln Administration: Northern Ascendency and Radical Experiments in the West." Doctoral dissertation, University of Wisconsin, Madison, 1949.

Unrau, William Errol. "The Role of the Indian Agent in the Settlement of the South-Central Plains, 1861–1868." Doctoral dissertation, University of Colorado, Boulder, 1963.

Waltman, Henry George. "The Interior Department, War Department and Indian Policy, 1865–1887." Doctoral dissertation, University of Nebraska, Lincoln, 1962.

Index

Abbott, George H., 160
Abiquiu Agency, 54
Acton, Minnesota: murders at, 8, 103, 104
Adams, Chester, 116, 119–20
Adobe Walls, Battle of, 82
Albin, William, 164
Aldrich, Cyrus, 108, 110, 117
Alseas, 142
Alvord, General Benjamin, 186, 187
Alvord, Dr. H. J., 194
Anderson, John, 187
Annuities: and profiteering, 6–7; for Blackfeet, 68; and whiskey problem, 101, 139; for Santees, 102–3; for Pacific Northwest, 150, 161–62; for Minnesota Chippewas, 159; for Five Civilized Tribes, 169; policy reform of, 210; mentioned, 3, 4, 198
Apache-Mohaves, 180, 181, 198
Apacheria, 56
Apaches: hostility of, 56, 75; futility of treaties with, 67; jurisdiction over, 180; terrorize reservation Indians, 198; mentioned, 13
Arapahos, 13, 24, 25, 159. *See also* Cheyennes; Northern Arapahos; Northern Cheyennes; Southern Cheyennes
Arikaras, 49, 147, 158

Arivaipas, 56
Arny, William F. N., 55, 65, 85
Assiniboins, 49, 147, 158

Baker, Ezra, 197
Baker, William B., 80
Balcombe, St. André Durand: arranges Winnebago removal, 117; and Winnebago flight from Crow Creek, 119–22
Bald Hill Indians, 150
Bancroft, Ashley, 162
Bannack, Montana, 50
Bannocks: raids of, 52, 60; defeated at Battle of Bear River, 60
Barnhart, William H., 142, 149, 162–63
Bear Hunter, 60
Bear River, Battle of, 60
Bear River Indians, 150
Benedict, Judge Kirby, 85
Bennet, Hiram Pitt, 29
Bensel, Corporal Royal A., 162
Bent, Charles, 24
Bent, George, 24–25, 31, 92
Bent, William, 24, 29, 36
Bent's Fort, 22
Biddle, Benjamin R., 150, 195–96
Big Thunder, 188–89
Black Bob's Shawnee band, 165

Blackfeet: disease among, 48–49, 51; raids and wars by, 57–58, 64, 74; treaty talks with, 64; annuity complaints of, 68

Blackfoot Agency: farming, financial, and whiskey problems at, 73–74; transfer of, 148

Black Kettle, 42–43, 44

Blake and Carruthers Company, 102

Bloods, 48–49

Blunt, General James: and return of Kansas refugee Indians, 171, 175; feud with Coffin, 172–74

Boone, Albert G., 41

Bosque Redondo: military complex at, 77; administrative problems at, 77–78; Steck-Carleton feud over, 79, 82–86; issue in New Mexican politics, 84–85; investigated by Washington, 85–86; Navajos and Mescaleros leave, 86; impact on Navajos, 90

Bowlegs, Billy, 170

Bowles, Samuel, 58, 211

Bowman, Major Andrew W., 187

Bozeman, John, 50

Bozeman Trail, 46

Brewer, William H., 181

Brown, Joseph R., 98

Brown, Sam E., 28–30

Browne, J. Ross, 181–82, 191

Brulé Sioux, 159

Buck, 61

Bull Bear, 31

Burche, John C., 53

Burleigh, Walter A., 118–19, 163–64

Cain, Andrew J., 183, 184

Calhoun, James S., 56

California, State Legislature of, 191

California Superintendency, 190

California Volunteers, 59, 60

Cameron, Simon, 166

Camp Douglas, 60, 76

Camp McClellan, 111

Camp Porter, 118

Camp Release, 106

Camp Weld Conference (1864), 42–43

Canby, Colonel Edward R. S., 75

Capote Utes, 54, 69

Carleton, Colonel James H.: sends cattle to Fort Union, 55; approves of reservation policy, 65; and Bosque Redondo problems, 77–78, 80, 81; feud with Steck, 79, 81–87, 90

Carruth, Edwin H., 135, 170

Carson, Colonel Kit, 36, 77, 82

Carson Valley Agency, 52

Caruanas, 151

Cass Lake Reservation, 137

Castakes, 151

Cattle rustling, 178–79

Cayuses, 140

Central Superintendency: and refugee problem, 137; jurisdiction of, 145; "Indian Rings" of, 163; Civil War impact on, 199

Chavez, Colonel J. Francisco, 85

Cherokees: as refugees in Kansas, 134, 172; alliance with Confederacy, 165–66, 167, 169; return to Indian Territory, 174, 175

Cheyennes: complain about agents, 8; as representative Indian group, 17; driven from Minnesota, 21, 96; plains culture of, 21–24; divisions of, 22, 29; alliance with Arapahos, 24; lands assigned by Fort Laramie treaty, 25; and Sand Creek Reservation, 26, 27, 32; resentment of Overland Stage, 32–33; raids by, 32–33, 35, 36, 39, 158, 159, 198; at Camp Weld Conference, 42–43; mentioned, 13. *See also* Northern Cheyennes; Southern Cheyennes

Chickasaws, 134, 167

Chippewa Board of Visitors, 210

Chippewas: wars with Sioux, 96, 99–100, 103–4; land cession of, 137; of Minnesota, 137–38, 159, 192, 209; of Wisconsin, 139; of Lake Superior, 193; of Saginaw, Swan Creek, and Black River, 194–95

Chippewas and Munsees, 145

Chippewas and Ottawas of Michigan, 193–94

Chiricahuas, 56

Chivington, Colonel John M.: and killings near Fort Larned, 37; and Colorado militia, 42; at Camp Weld Conference, 42–43; and Sand Creek, 44–45

Choctaws, 167

Chouteau, Pierre, Jr., and Company, 110

Chupco, John, 170

Coeur d'Alênes, 142

Coffin, Dr. Archibald V., 136

Coffin, William G.: and refugee Indians in Kansas, 132, 133, 134, 135–36, 137, 172; becomes superintendent, 168; and return of refugees to Indian Territory, 170, 173, 176–77; has feud with military, 172–73, 175–78; and cattle rustling, 179

Cogswell, John B., 127

Coleman, Isaac, 135

Colley, Dexter, 36

Colley, Samuel G.: as Cheyenne Indian agent, 30–31, 34, 37–38; accused of fraud, 36

Collins, James L.: as Indian superintendent, 54, 55, 65, 67, 74; supports Carleton, 84–85

Colorado, Territory of: described, 24–25; established, 26; isolation of, 39, 40; opinions of public and the press on, 40, 41–42; hundred-day militia, 42

Colvilles, 142

Comanches: and federal government, 25, 33; raids on Santa Fe Trail, 32, 159; and Confederacy, 41; removed from Colorado, 46–47; loss at Battle of Adobe Walls, 81–82; mentioned, 13

Confederacy: and plains tribes, 41; invasion of Southwest, 74, 180; and Santees, 104; relations with Indian Territory, 131–32, 165–66, 167; guerrillas attack eastern Kansas, 165

Congress. *See* United States Congress

Connelly, Governor Henry, 65, 77, 84

Connor, General Patrick E., 60, 61, 76

Cooper, Colonel Douglas H., 169

Corn Creek Indian Farm, 72

Cowskin Prairie, Missouri, 172

Creeks: as refugees in Kansas, 132, 134, 170; alliance with Confederacy, 167, 169

Cremony, John, 56, 67

Crooked River, Battle of, 157

Crow Creek Reservation: Santees' removal to, 110–13; subsistence problems at, 113–14, 115; financial problems at, 114–15; prostitution at, 114; disease at, 115–16; Indians flee from, 115, 118–19; threatened by hostiles, 116–17; Santee-Winnebago feud at, 118; administrative problems summarized, 123–24

Crows, 49, 147

Curtis, General Samuel: and Governor Evans, 35, 40; and Indian Territory, 175, 179

Curtis, W. M., 37

Cutler, George A., 135, 173–74

Daily News (Gold Hill, Nevada), 89

Dakota Superintendency, 123, 147

Davenport, 95, 111

Davenport, Timothy W., 162–63

Davies, Benjamin, 59

Davis, Moses M., 139, 140, 144

Dawson, John W., 76

Deep Creek Reservation, 71–72

Delaware Reservation, 146, 148

Denver, Colorado, 25, 35, 39, 40

Deseret News (Salt Lake City), 76

De Smet, Father Pierre, 107, 118

Devil's Lake Reservation, 126, 200

"Digger" Indians, 13, 59

Disease: among Indians of Colorado, 33, 36; among Indians of Montana, 49, 51, 58; among Santees, 111, 115–16, 199; among refugees of Five Civilized Tribes, 135–36, 174, 176; on Pacific Northwest reservations, 143–44; on Wisconsin reservations, 144

Dole, William P.: relied on by
  Lincoln, 15; and Colorado Indian
  affairs, 29–30, 36, 38, 43, 44, 54–55,
  65; and Nevada Indian affairs, 63,
  73; and New Mexico Indian affairs,
  82, 83; and Santee and Winnebago
  affairs, 108, 110, 117, 120, 122, 127;
  and refugees of Five Civilized
  Tribes, 131, 132, 168–69, 175, 176–77;
  and Stockbridge and Munsee
  dissatisfaction, 145; and fear of
  embarrassing Lincoln administration, 164; has Poston select reserves,
  181; recommends consolidation in
  California, 190; recommends reservation for Wisconsin's Indians, 193;
  appraisal of as Commissioner of
  Indian Affairs, 202–3; disagrees
  with Morgan over control of
  Indian affairs, 208; mentioned,
  194, 197
Donnelly, Lieutenant Governor
  Ignatius, 105–6, 109
Doolittle, James R., 175
Doty, James Duane, 62, 72–73, 76
Dull Knife, 92
Dunn, John C., 181

Eagle-from-the-Light, 189
Elbert, Samuel H., 46
Encroachment by whites on Indian
  lands: Indian Office policy on, 1,
  5–6, 16, 199, 204; in Colorado, 16,
  25–26, 54–55; on Nez Percé
  Reservation, 16, 183–88, 189; in
  Montana, 50; in Nevada, 51, 53; in
  California, 155, 182–83; in Arizona,
  181
Evans, Colonel George S., 60
Evans, Governor John: Indian policy
  of, 27, 35–36; councils with
  Cheyennes and Arapahos, 28, 30–31,
  32; protests Fort Wise cession line
  ruling, 29; fears plains Indian
  conspiracy, 34, 35; attempts to
  separate friendly Indians from
  hostiles, 37; wars on hostiles, 38;
  political position of, 39–40, 42; at

Camp Weld Conference, 42–43; and
  Utes, 65, 68–69; mentioned, 71
"Expedition to Moscow," 114

Factionalism: among Cherokees, 169;
  among Creeks, 169; among Nez
  Percés, 188–89, 190
Farming on reservations: advocated
  by Nye, 63; in Montana, 73; by
  Navajos, 78; by Santees, 98–99, 104,
  113, 115, 199–200; in Central and
  Dakota Superintendencies, 145,
  148–49, 158; problems with, 149–50,
  152–53, 198
Financial problems of Indian Office,
  72, 73, 78, 114–15, 160, 199
Fish, James L., 50
Five Civilized Tribes: location of,
  13; composition of, 166; alliances
  with the Confederacy, 167, 168.
  See also Cherokees; Chickasaws;
  Choctaws; Creeks; Seminoles
Flathead Agency, 74, 190, 195
Flathead Reservation, 141
Flatheads, 141
Florence, 111
Fort Arbuckle, 166
Fort Berthold Agency, 147
Fort Bridger Agency, 71
Fort Cobb, 166
Fort Gibson, 174
Fort Larned, 25
Fort Lyon, 44
Fort Randall, 115, 119
Fort Ridgely, 105
Fort Snelling, 95, 111
Fort Sumter, 13
Fort Washita, 166
Fraud at Indian agencies, 8, 36,
  162–64, 190, 198
Furnas, Robert W., 121–22, 177

Galbraith, Thomas, 100–101, 103, 107,
  119n
Geary, Edward R., 184–85
Gerry, Eldridge, 31
Gila Apaches, 56
Gilpin, Governor William, 27, 41

Gold rushes. *See* Encroachment by whites on Indian lands
Grande Ronde Reservation, 141
Grant, President Ulysses S., 211
Graves, Julius K., 86
Great Nemaha Agency, 7
Great Nemaha Reservation, 146, 148
Gros Ventres, 49, 74, 147, 158
Grouse Creek Indians, 155
Gull Lake Reservation, 137
Gwyther, Dr. George, 80–81

Hagan, William T., 213
Hale, Calvin H., 143, 150, 186, 188
Hamburg Indians, 155
Hanson, George M., 151–52, 153, 154, 182, 183, 190–91
Harding, Stephen S., 76
Harlan, Senator James, 85
Harlan, Justin, 173, 175
Hatch, Frederick W., 71
Hayes, President Rutherford B., 208
Haynes, S. C., 114
Hazelwood Republic, 98–99, 100
Head, Lafayette, 54
Hinman, Samuel, 95
Hole-in-the-Day, 159–60
Holladay, Ben, 50
Hoopas, 155
Hoopa Valley Reservation, 155
Hooper, W. H., 75
Hoopes, Alban W., 208
Humboldt Indians, 150
Hungate family, 35, 41–42
Hunter, General David, 131, 132, 170
Huntington, J. W. Perit, 161
Hutchins, Charles, 74, 186, 188, 195
Hyde, George E., 30–31

Indian Peace Commission, 11, 90, 209, 210
"Indian Ring," 7, 163, 213
Indian Territory, 178–79
Inkpaduta, 99
Intertribal warfare, 49, 52, 74, 78, 99–100, 156–57, 158
Iowas, 7, 146
Irish, Orasmus H., 69, 89

Jackson, Helen Hunt, 11
Jicarilla Apaches, 54, 55, 56
John Day Indians, 141
Joint Special Committee on the Condition of the Indian Tribes, 14, 208

Kansa Agency, 146
Kansa Reservation, 148, 165
Kansas, Territory of, 6
Kawia Indians, 151
Keith, Charles B., 163
Kendall, Bion F., 185, 196, 197
Kibe's Band, 71
Kickapoo Allotment Treaty (1863), 163
Kickapoo Reservation, 146, 163, 165
Kidnapping of Indian children, 57, 183
Kile, Dr. William, 132, 133
Kings River Farm, 151
Kiowa-Apaches, 25
Kiowas, 13, 25, 81–82, 159
Klamaths, 142, 153–55
Klamath River Reservation, 150, 152, 155
Klikitats, 140–41
Knapp, Judge Joseph, 85
Kusas, 142
Kutenais, 141

Labadi, Lorenzo, 78, 79, 80
Lake Winnibigoshish Reservation, 137
Lapwai Agency, 188
Latta, Samuel N., 158
Lawyer (Chief), 188, 189
Leach, DeWitt C., 194
Leavenworth, Jesse H., 33, 80
Leech Lake Reservation, 137
Lincoln, Abraham: has minor role in Indian affairs, 14–16, 202; meets with plains chiefs, 33; sets aside Uintah Valley for Indians, 62; and Santee prisoners, 107–8; and Kansas Indian refugees, 170, 171–72, 177
Lippitt, Colonel Francis J., 153–54
Little Crow, 95, 104, 105, 116–17, 126
Lockhart, Jacob, 61
Logan, William, 156–57

Loree, John, 30, 31–32
Lower Pend d'Oreilles, 142
Lower Santee Agency, 99
Lower Santees, 104
Lyon, Caleb, 190, 195

McCulloch, General Benjamin, 167
McDonald and Fuller Company, 177–78
McGilvra, John J., 187
McIndoe, Walter D., 128
McIntosh faction of Creeks, 169
McKee, Henry, 177
Mandans, 49, 147, 158
Manderfield, William H., 85
Mankato, Minnesota, 108–9
Mann, Luther, 71
Maricopas, 181
Martin, Henry W., 170
Mausinares, José Antonio, 54
Mdewakanton Sioux, 96, 99. *See also* Santees
Melville, Herman, 10–11
Mendocino Reservation, 150
Menominee Reservation, 138
Menominees, 139, 144
Mescalero Apaches, 56, 77, 78, 86
Meyer, Roy, 212
Mik-ko-hut-kay, 178
Mille Lacs Reservation, 137
Miller, Judge Andrew G., 139–40
Miller, William W., 143
Mimbreños, 56
Minnesota, State of: and Chippewas, 96; and Santees, 96, 98, 104, 106, 108, 109; and Winnebagos, 117
Moache Utes, 54, 55, 69
Modocs, 142, 153–55
Mogollons, 56
Mohaves, 151
Monos, 155
Monroe, Eugene, 53, 63-64
Montana, Territory of, 74
Montana Post (Virginia City), 89
Mooney, James, 48
Moonlight, Colonel Thomas, 46
Morgan, Lewis Henry, 8, 207, 208, 210

Mormons, 58, 60, 75, 76
Mullan Road, 50

Navajos: inhabit Southwest, 55–56; wars with, 57, 68, 75; at Bosque Redondo, 77, 78, 86, 90; mentioned, 13
Nesmith, Senator James W., 157, 161–62
Nevada, Territory of, 51
Nevada Superintendency, 52, 73, 89
New Mexican (Santa Fe), 85
New Mexico Superintendency, 68
New Ulm, 105, 107
Nez Percé Reservation, 140, 183, 190
Nez Percés: dispossessed, 10; as horseman, traders, and hunters, 13; and gold miners, 184, 185, 190; treaties with, 184–85, 188–89; factionalism among, 190
Niobrara Reservation, 123, 199–200
Nome Lackee Reservation, 151
North, Robert, 34
Northern Arapahos, 147. *See also* Arapahos
Northern Cheyennes, 28, 46, 91, 92, 147. *See also* Cheyennes; Southern Cheyennes
Northerner, 95, 111
Northern Superintendency, 101, 123
Northern Utes, 58
Nye, Governor James Warren, 52, 61, 63, 73

Office of Indian Affairs: development by 1861, 2, 3, 6, 13–14, 15–16; poor pay for staff of, *6n*, 15–16; and War Department, 9, 78, 208; and development of the West, 12, 201, 205–6; impotence during Civil War, 14, 67, 68, 91, 158, 201–2; and removal of Santees, 112; fears embarrassing Lincoln, 164; urges return of refugees, 170; poor morale in, 195; as protector of Indians, 206
Oliver, A. J., and Company, 50
Olney, Lieutenant Colonel James R., 154

Omaha Reservation, 120, 121–22, 146–47
Oneida Reservation, 138
Oneidas, 130, 139, 140
O'Neill, James, 190
Opothle Yahola, 131, 134, 169
Osage Reservation, 165
Osage River Agency, 145
Osages, 132
Otis, Elmer, 41
Oto and Missouri Reservation, 146, 163
Ottawa Agency, 146
Ottawa Reservation, 132, 165
Ottawas, 145
Ottawas of Michigan, 193–94
Overland Stage, 32–33
Overland Trail, 12–13, 39
Owens River Indians, 151, 155–56
Owens River War, 61, 155–56

Pablo-Apis, 182
Pacific Northwest Reservations, 142–44, 149–50, 162–63
Paiutes, 52, 53, 61, 155
Paloos, 140–41
Papagos, 180–81, 198
Pash-e-co, 60
Pawnee Reservation, 146, 158
Pawnees, 198
Perea, Francisco, 84
Phillips, Colonel William A.: returns Cherokees to Indian Territory, 173–74; feud with Indian Office, 175–78
Piegans, 48–49
Pierce, Elias Davidson, 183
Pike, Captain Albert, 41, 167, 169
Pillager Chippewas, 137
Pimas, 180–81, 198
Pitt River Indians, 150
Pocatello (Chief), 60
Pokegama Lake Reservation, 137
Ponca Reservation, 147, 148, 158
Poncas, 198
Pope, General John, 106, 127, 128–30, 208, 211
Poston, Governor Charles D., 6n, 180, 181

Potawatomi Reservation, 146, 148
Potawatomis, 127–28, 198
Press (St. Paul), 108
Proctor, A. G., 175
Prostituton, 114, 143, 149
Purvine, William, 185
Pyramid Lake Reservation, 64

Quantrill's raiders, 165
Quapaw Reservation, 131–32
Quapaws, 132, 134, 176

Rabbit Lake Reservation, 137
Ramsey, Governor Alexander, 108, 109
Rector, Elias, 168
Rector, Henry M., 165–66
Rector, William H., 157, 188, 195–96
Red Cloud's War, 46
Redwood Agency, 99
Redwood Indians, 155
Reed, Amos, 72
Refugee Indians in Kansas, 131–36, 170–76
Rice, Senator Henry M., 107
Rice Lake Reservation, 137
Ridge party, 169
Riggs, Stephen R., 98, 102, 107, 123n
Rinearson, Major Jacob L., 186, 187
Rogue River Indians, 141
Ross, D. H., and Company, 178
Ross, John, 165–66, 169, 171
Ross party, 169
Round Valley Reservation, 150, 182
Ruby Valley Reservation, 63

Sac and Fox, 134, 137
Sac and Fox of Missouri, 146
Sac and Fox Reservation, 136, 145–46
Sacramento Valley Indians, 150
Sagwitch, 60
Salomon, Colonel Frederick, 171
Sand Creek "Massacre," 11, 14, 44–45, 46, 206
Sand Creek Reservation, 26, 35–36
Sandy Lake Reservation, 137
San Pete Indian Farm, 72
Santa Fe Trail, 32, 36, 81, 159

Santee Reservation, 101–2
Santees: take up farming, 13; as
  representative reservation people,
  17; removal from Minnesota, 95–96,
  109, 111–12, 199; composition of, 96;
  prairie culture of, 96–98; acculturation of, 98, 100–101, 104, 198, 199–
  200; attitude toward government
  agencies, 99, 103; and Chippewas,
  99–100, 103–4; and Winnebagos,
  100, 118, 198; annuities of, 101,
  102–3; 1862 uprising of, 103, 104–6;
  as military prisoners, 106–9, 123; at
  Crow Creek Reservation, 113–14,
  115; friendlies not at Crow Creek,
  125, 126
Schurz, Carl, 208
Scotts Valley Indians, 155
Seminoles, 134, 136, 167, 170, 176
Seneca and Shawnee Reservation,
  131–32
Seneca Reservation, 131–32
Senecas, 132, 134, 176
Senecas and Shawnees, 132, 134, 176
Shastas, 155
Shawnee Reservation, 146, 165
Shokup, 61
Shoshonis, 52, 58–59, 60, 198. *See also*
  Snakes
Sibley, Colonel Henry Hastings, 106,
  107, 125–26, 129
Sibley, General Henry Hopkins, 74
Simpson, Benjamin, 162
Siletz Reservation, 141–42, 149–50, 162
Sioux, 96, 158. *See also* Santees; Teton
  Sioux; Yanktons
Sisseton Reservation, 126, 200
Sissetons, 96, 99. *See also* Santees
Smith, Caleb B., 108, 110, 117, 133,
  169, 188
Smith, C. DeWitt, 195
Smith, John, 34, 36
Smith River Reservation, 150
Snakes, 142, 156–57. *See also* Shoshonis
Southern Cheyennes, 35–36, 46–47, 91.
  See also Cheyennes; Northern
  Cheyennes

Southern Superintendency, 132, 133,
  199
South Fork Indians, 155
Spanish Fork Canyon, Battle of, 60
Spanish Fork Reservation, 71
Spokan Indians, 142
Stanton, Edwin M., 11, 34, 79
Starvation of Indians, 33, 36, 59,
  61, 68–69
Steck, Michael, 78–87, 89, 90
Steele, Elijah, 155
Stockbridge and Munsee Reservation,
  138–39
Stockbridges and Munsees, 139,
  144–45, 198
Suislaw Indians, 142
Sully, General Alfred, 128–29
Swisshelm, Jane, 106–7, 109

Tabeguache Utes, 54, 65, 69
Tahlequah, 174
Taopi, 125
Tataguas, 151
Tejon Reservation, 151
Tejons, 155
Temecula, 182–83
Teninos, 141
Teton Sioux, 13, 46, 96, 147, 198.
  See also Sioux
Thompson, Benjamin, 111
Thompson, Clark W., 101, 110, 113–15,
  116, 119, 120, 121
Tocqueville, Alexis de, 204
Traders, 4, 7, 32, 210
Treaties with Indians:
—Cheyennes, 25 (1851); 26, 28–30
  (1861); 46–47, 91 (1865); 91 (1868)
—Chippewas, 192 (1863); 194–95
  (1864)
—Comanches, Kiowas, and Kiowa-
  Apaches, 25 (1853); 46 (1865)
—Nez Percés, 184–85 (1861); 188–89
  (1863)
—Navajos, 86 (1868)
—Kickapoos, 163 (1863)
—Santees, 98 (1851); 99 (1858)
—Shoshonis, 63 (1863)
—Snakes, 157 (1864); 157 (1865)

—Utes, 65 (1863); 69–70 (1868); 70 (1880)
Treaty of Fort Laramie, 25, 49
Treaty system, 2, 3, 4, 32, 67–68, 211
Triplett, Joe, 51
Tulareños, 155
Tulé River Farm, 151
Tulé River Indians, 151
Two Moons, 92
Tyighs, 141

Uintah Valley Reservation, 62, 69–70
Uintahs, 58
Umatilla Reservation, 140, 142, 149, 160, 162–63
Umatillas, 140
Umpqua Subagency, 142
Umpquas, 142
Uncompahgres. *See* Tabeguache Utes
Union Vedette (Camp Douglas), 76
United States Congress: neglect of Indian affairs, 1–2, 11, 14, 214; laws affecting Indian affairs, 7, 14, 40, 179, 211; investigates Indian affairs, 14, 206; rejects Comanche treaty, 33; appropriates funds for Indian affairs, 60, 64, 72–73, 181, 185, 188; and Unitah Valley reserve, 62–63; members investigate Bosque Redondo, 85–86; and Santee removal, 109, 110; and Winnebagos, 117, 119, 128; and Indian refugees in Kansas, 132–33, 175–76; creates superintendent's office in California, 190
Upper Arkansas Agency, 26
Upper Missouri Agency, 26, 147
Upper Pend d'Oreilles, 141
Upper Platte Agency, 26, 147
Upper Santee Agency, 103. *See also* Yellow Medicine Agency
Upper Santees, 105. *See also* Santees
Upson, Gad E., 50, 51, 64, 66, 68, 73–74
Usher, John P., 110, 128, 177
Utah, Territory of, 58, 89
Utah Superintendency, 72
Ute Agency, 26–27, 54
Utes, 13, 27, 54, 55, 58, 59, 60, 65, 69

Wabasha, 106
Wahpekutes, 96, 99. *See also* Santees
Wahpetons, 96, 99. *See also* Santees
Wailakis, 150, 182
Wakefield, Dr. John S., 116
Walapais, 151, 181
Walker, Lucius C., 159–60
Walker River Reservation, 52–53, 63–64
Wallace, William H., 195
Walla Walla Council of 1855, 140
Wallawallas, 140
Walpapis, 157
Ward, John, 210
War Department, 9, 40, 57, 66, 68
Warm Springs Reservation, 141, 156–57, 162, 198
Wascos, 141
Washakie, 60
Washington Standard (Olympia), 189, 196–97
Washos, 52–53
Wasson, Warren, 61
Watie, General Stand, 169, 174, 177, 179
Webb, Luther E., 193
Webb, Walter Prescott, 21
Webster, Henry A., 197
Weekly Gazette (Santa Fe), 85
Weer, Colonel William, 171
Wentworth, John P. H., 151, 156, 190
Western Apaches, 56. *See also* Apaches
Wheeler, L. H., 207
Whipple, Bishop Henry B., 11–12, 101, 108, 125, 207, 209, 210
Whiskey problem, 7–8, 32, 36, 73–74, 101–2, 127, 136, 137–38, 140, 142–43, 149, 182–83, 188, 199
Whitely, Simeon, 37
White River Utes, 58
Wichitas and affiliated bands, 132
Wilbur, James A., 162, 196
Wiley, Austin, 192
Wilkinson, Morton S., 108
Williamson, John P., 95, 107, 112, 113, 116
Williamson, Thomas S., 123*n*

Wilson's Creek, Battle of, 169
Wiminuche Utes, 54, 69. *See also* Utes
Windom, William, 108
Winnebagos: in Minnesota, 99–100; removed from Minnesota, 117, 118; at Crow Creek, 118, 198; flee from Crow Creek, 118–19; on Omaha Reservation, 120–23; in Wisconsin, 127–28
Winnibigoshish Chippewas, 137
Woolson, T. W., 85
Wood Lake, Battle of, 105–6
Wright, General George, 59, 61, 153–55, 156
Wyandots, 146

Wynkoop, Major Edward, 42–43, 44

Yahuskin Snakes, 157
Yakima Reservation, 140–41, 160, 162
Yakimas, 140–41
Yanktonais, 96
Yankton Reservation, 119, 147, 163–64
Yanktons, 96
Yavapais, 181
Yellow Medicine Agency, 99. *See also* Upper Santee Agency
Young, Brigham, 69, 75
Yukis, 150
Yumas, 151, 180, 198